Digital Creatives and the Rethinking of Religious Authority

Much speculation was raised in the 1990s, during the first decade of internet research, about the extent to which online platforms and digital culture might challenge traditional understandings of authority, especially in religious contexts. *Digital Creatives and the Rethinking of Religious Authority* explores the ways in which religiously-inspired digital media experts and influencers online challenge established religious leaders and those who seek to maintain institutional structures in a world where online and offline religious spaces are increasingly intertwined. In the twenty-first century, the question of how digital culture may be reshaping notions of whom or what constitutes authority is incredibly important. Questions asked include:

- Who truly holds religious authority and influence in an age of digital media? Is it recognized religious leaders and institutions? Or religious digital innovators? Or digital media users?
- What sources, processes and/or structures can and should be considered authoritative, online and offline?
- Who or what is really in control of religious technological innovation?

This book reflects on how digital media simultaneously challenges and empowers new and traditional forms of religious authority. It is a gripping read for those with an interest in Communication, Culture Studies, Media Studies, Religion/Religious Studies, Sociology of Religion, Computer-Mediated Communication, and Internet/Digital Culture Studies.

Heidi A. Campbell is a professor at the Department of Communication and an affiliate faculty in the Religious Studies Interdisciplinary Program at Texas A&M University, USA.

Media, Religion and Culture

Series Editors

Stewart Hoover, *University of Colorado, Boulder, USA*
Jolyon Mitchell, *University of Edinburgh, UK*
Jenna Supp-Montgomerie, *University of Iowa, USA*

For more information about this series, please visit: www.routledge.com/Media-Religion-and-Culture/book-series/MRC

Digital Creatives and the Rethinking of Religious Authority

Heidi A. Campbell

Routledge
Taylor & Francis Group

LONDON AND NEW YORK

First published 2021
by Routledge
2 Park Square, Milton Park, Abingdon, Oxon OX14 4RN

and by Routledge
52 Vanderbilt Avenue, New York, NY 10017

Routledge is an imprint of the Taylor & Francis Group, an informa business

© 2021 Heidi A. Campbell

British Library Cataloguing-in-Publication Data
A catalogue record for this book is available from the British Library

Library of Congress Cataloging-in-Publication Data
Names: Campbell, Heidi, 1970– author.
Title: Digital creatives and the rethinking of religious
authority / Heidi A. Campbell.
Description: Abingdon, Oxon; New York, NY: Routledge, 2020. |
Series: Media, religion and culture |
Includes bibliographical references and index. |
Identifiers: LCCN 2020004556 | Subjects: LCSH: Mass media in religion. |
Digital media–Religious aspects–Christianity. |
Social media–Religious aspects–Christianity. |
Authority–Religious aspects–Christianity. | Christianity and culture.
Classification: LCC BV652.95.C34 2020 | DDC 206/.5–dc23
LC record available at https://lccn.loc.gov/2020004556

ISBN: 978-1-138-37092-0 (hbk)
ISBN: 978-1-138-37097-5 (pbk)
ISBN: 978-1-003-04562-5 (ebk)

Typeset in Bembo
by Newgen Publishing UK

For My Troy

Contents

Acknowledgments

This book project has involved a nine-year journey exploring how religious digital creatives around the world engage in digital work, which is inspired by their deep religious convictions and a spirit of innovation. I am grateful for all the individuals who took the time to meet with me and answer my questions so that I could uncover how their work inspires new opportunities and challenges to religious communities.

First I am grateful to the many digital creatives from around the world that I had the opportunity to learn from over the course of this research journey. Thank you for taking the time from your busy work schedule to meet with me and share your experience and honest reflection on how technology is and will continue to shape contemporary church ministry. I especially want to thank Professors Larry Hurtado and Tim Bulkley who are no longer with us here on this earth, but whose stories were key in shaping my thinking on theoblogians and the relationship between traditional religious institutions and digital media.

Next, I would like to acknowledge the support of St. Johns College and the Institute for Advanced Studies at the University of Durham that facilitated my initial research and interviews with digital creatives in the UK during my time there as a Cofund Senior Scholar in Fall 2012. I would especially like to thank the input of Bex Lewis, Pete Philips and David Wilkinson on the early stages of my research. My early writing was also supported through a visiting fellow position at New College in the Faculty of Divinity at the University of Edinburgh in Spring 2013 where I received helpful advice from Jolyon Mitchell and Elizabeth Koepping.

The substance of the initial theoretical and methodological chapters of this book took shape during Spring 2016, when I held an internal faculty fellowship at the Melbourne G Glasscock Center for Humanities Research at Texas A&M University. I am especially grateful to the support and help offered by Glasscock staff members Joe Golson, Sarah Meissner and Amanda Dusek, who created a wonderful intellectual climate and writing environment.

Arguments related to this work were also further refined during workshop and visiting lectures given in 2017 and 2018 at the Bruno Kesler Institute at the University of Trento (Italy), the University of Milan (Italy), Villanova University (USA) and the Center for Religious Studies (CERES) at Ruhr Universität Bochum

(Germany). I am especially grateful for the critical feedback and recommendations offered by Tim Hutchings, Giulia Evolvi, Mia Lovheim and Carlo Nardela, which helped further refine my arguments in this book.

In addition, I would like to thank William Cowen, Zachary Sheldon, Knut Lundby, Pauline Hope Cheong and Charles Ess for offering input on my writings and discussion of authority in digital culture, which I have explored in this book, as well as their willingness to review and offer insights on portions of chapters in the book.

This book would not have come to fruition without the hard work of copy editor extraordinaire Kathy DiSanto and the Media, Religion and Culture Book Series editors Jolyon Mitchell, Stewart Hoover and Jenna Supp-Montgomerie who provided valuable feedback on the final version of this manuscript. I am also thankful for Routledge editor Rebecca Shillabeer for her oversight of this project.

Also, this book would not have been possible without my family and friends who offered me much encouragement, cups of tea, chocolate and words of inspiration along the way, that kept me writing on hard days. I am especially grateful for the support of John & Sally Stuart, Heather & Robb Elmatti, John Campbell, Sabrina Springer, Robin Jones, Iris Villareal and Brad & Judy Shepherd.

Finally, and most of all, I want to thank my ever-positive and supportive husband Troy Shepherd, to whom this book is dedicated. He has been the best cheerleader an academic could hope for in their writing journey. I have also learned from him much about the thinking behind integrating technology into worship environments and spiritual entrepreneurship in contemporary church ministry in our journey together. You would have made a great case study for this book, but I am glad you became my partner instead!

Introduction

In February 2011, Little i Apps, a small American software company that seeks to develop "mobile applications with a Catholic twist," launched "Confession: A Roman Catholic App." Released just in time for Lent, an important religious season focused on repentance and self-denial within the Anglo-Catholic Christian religious calendar, the Confession app was designed to help users prepare for the sacrament of confession, which is normally administered by a priest. According to its creators, "to be used in the confessional, this app is the perfect aid for every penitent" (http://littleiapps.com/confession), taking users through a set of questions designed around the Ten Commandments in order to help them examine their conscience and identify their sins. This close personal reflection is considered a prerequisite before undergoing formal confession with a priest. After the user has responded to the app questions, they are provided with a list of relevant sins, and directions concerning appropriate acts of contrition appear on the screen. Then users are guided through a text, similar to the one found in any Catholic prayer book, regarding the steps of confession.

Little i Apps developed this app in consultation with several American Catholic leaders, including the Executive Director of the Secretariat for Doctrine and Pastoral Practices of the United States Conference of Catholic Bishops and a local priest from Queen of Peace Catholic Church in Indiana. Though it was not designed to be a substitute for face-to-face confession, the app caused quite a stir among many Catholics and Church officials around the world, including the Vatican. A significant part of the controversy was caused by the fact that the Bishop of Fort Wayne–South Bend–Indiana, who was consulted by the app designers, gave the app an imprimatur or official approval, thus confirming the Catholic Church's support and licensing use of the app. This act gave the app unique status; this appeal to church authority granted it an official religious sanctioning, affirming the app's function was not in conflict with Catholic teachings or sacramental practices. According to the Little i App's site, this is the "first known imprimatur to be given for an iPhone/iPad application" (http://littleiapps.com/confession).

This act, and the resulting attention the app received by new media internationally, forced the Vatican to respond. This was the second instance where the issue of authority was raised, as Vatican sources asserted their authoritativeness, verifying to the press and public that the app was acceptable as a preparatory guide, but strongly stressing it could in no way substitute for the embodied act of confession, which can only be heard and forgiveness granted via a priest. As Rev. Federico Lombardi, a Vatican spokesperson, stated, "It is essential to understand well that the Sacrament of Penance requires necessarily the rapport of personal dialogue between penitent and confessor and absolution by the present confessor," (Holdren, 2011). Thus, the Vatican stressed that a computer application cannot substitute for this embodied act. Rev. Lombardi further stated, "One cannot speak in any way of 'confession by iPhone' …. But a believer could use a digital instrument, such as an iPhone, to prepare for confession in the same way people once did with a pen and paper" (Gilgoff & Messia, 2011).

It is important to note that this is not the first time a technology or digital service has been created to facilitate the process of confession. In 2003, Virgin Mobile (UK) stirred similar controversy by introducing a "Sin to Win" service that encouraged people to use the service to confess their sins—with the best confessions receiving prizes ("Virgin Mobile Users Confess," AP, 2004). This led the Catholic Bishops Conference of the Philippines to publicly denounce the service and affirm that making confessions or offering absolution by SMS is "unacceptable." It also came on the heels of the Vatican issuing a strong warning against priests using the internet to hear "online confession" (Owen, 2003). The Pontifical Council for Social Communications (PCSC) had also previously spoken out on other online confession services, highlighting the facts that confession is one liturgical sacrament that should be kept offline, and confessions facilitated via email, web or phones would never be sanctioned by the Vatican (Gilgoff & Messia, 2011). In the past two decades, the PCSC has played an important role in offering Church leaders and members guidance on the positive and negative uses of the internet for religious purposes. In addition, while in this case they voiced concern about how digital innovations that significantly modify church and/or theological practice would be viewed problematically, the PCSC strongly advocated Catholic engagement with the internet. For example, as early as 2001, the then PCSC president Archbishop John Foley is quoted saying:

> Internet offers the church the opportunity to make the saving message of Christ accessible throughout the world [...] In societies that don't allow the presence of priests, nuns, religious or lay missionaries, internet can offer people undertaking a spiritual quest, or even just the curious, a chance to obtain information or find an inspiration that would otherwise be impossible.
>
> (Wilian, 2001)

At its heart, the controversy over the perceived broad and official sanctioning of the Confession app by the Church was not because the app was a digital innovation, but the notion that it could be seen as transforming Catholic tradition, and thus, its institutional authority in relation to media.

The Catholic Church has a long record of monitoring and reflecting on the social implications various forms of media have for its members. Since the late

1940s, the PCSC has played an important role in issuing theological and ethical statements that support the papal office's views on the impact of media—or what it refers to as modern processes of social communication—on society. Over the last four decades, the PCSC has released a number of noteworthy public statements and papal speeches that address Catholic theological thinking on computer-mediated and digital technologies. As early as 1990, the Vatican released a statement regarding how computers should be ethically used by Catholics for the service and work of the Church, via the Pope's World Communications Day message (PCSC, 1990). Then, in 2002, the PCSC issued two official statements, *The Church and the Internet* (PCSC, 2002a) providing guidelines on how the internet should be employed for Church ministry, and *Ethics in Internet* (PCSC, 2002b), outlining Catholic views on proper and improper social and religious uses of the internet.

Even though the Catholic Church has been quite directive in how it perceives digital media, it has not been shy about embracing these technologies for its own ends. It is also noteworthy that in 1996 the Catholic Church became the first religious denomination to launch an official internet site (www.vatican.va). In 2003, Pope John Paul II began offering a service of daily inspirational SMS messages and prayers via a texting service run by the Vatican ("Pope Spreads the Word by SMS," 2003). This service was also used to inform subscribers of John Paul II's death, funeral details and the new pope's election. Pope Benedict XVI has carried on the same "thought for the day" text service, sending out his first SMS just days after his induction stating, "Let us go forth in the joy of the risen Lord and trusting in his permanent help" ("Let us go forth," SMS message, 2005). Further innovations have included the Pope App launched in 2013 to allow the faithful to easily follow the pope's daily activities and sayings, and in 2016, Pope Francis took to Instagram, establishing the first papal account on the platform.

The Catholic Church's embrace of the internet has been strongly informed by attempts to culture or shape the technology, not only in line with the Church's theological convictions, but its institutional structures and prescribed roles. For instance, the Vatican launched a special YouTube channel in early 2009 (www.youtube.com/user/vatican), providing daily news coverage of the pope's activities and other Vatican events. However, unlike most other YouTube channels, the Vatican asked YouTube to disable the ranking function and comment mode for clips, thus preventing users from ranking or discussing the content provided. Seeking to manage the interactivity of the platform and block negative comments from appearing next to their videos was a clear attempt to moderate and control the Church's identity presentation online. Similarly, when the Catholic Church launched its own online news portal (www.news.va) in 2011, it was presented as a way to centralize and aggregate Vatican updates and information from multiple sources such as Twitter, Facebook and the Church's own website. Yet in other respects it could be seen as an attempt to solidify and create a coherent and "official" online presence.

The case of the Confession app, alongside the Catholic Church's history with the internet and digital media as briefly described here, not only reveal an interesting tension between the Catholic Church leaders and technology designers but also point to a broader tension experience by many religious organizations that are required to interact with emerging technologies and religious users of them. Protestant as well as Catholic churches in contemporary culture are increasingly required to engage with digital media. Yet there are often invisible boundaries to what religious leaders considered acceptable use and innovation. In my previous work, I have shown that religious leaders often play an important role in monitoring church members' technology use and guiding their engagement with the internet. Members are expected to monitor and restrain their online religious activities in light of religious values, which are seen as restrained by unspoken community expectations established by the church structures and leaders offline over time. This points to unique challenges that can emerge between religious digital media users, innovators and the offline religious communities they identify with. At the heart of this study is the question of the relationship between religion, technology and authority in a digital age. The case of the Confession app shows the increasing incorporation of new digital media technologies into the contemporary life and work of religious organizations, and these actions may have broader consequences than often recognized. In the past decade, we have begun to see how integration of digital media into religious organizations by church members and religious innovators can alter the established influence of traditional religious structures and their leaders. Those who seek to bring digital media tools into the church for both official and experimental purposes often unwittingly create new challenges to the way these institutions function. It is this emerging context that the book explores.

Digital creatives as new actors of religious authority: An idea for exploration

At the heart of this book is the question, "What does religious authority look like in an age of digital media, and, is it still held and defined by recognized religious leaders and the structures they work within? Or, are digital media experts employed by Christian organizations and religious innovators who seek to use their technology skills to modernize the work of the church the new power brokers within religious communities?" By focusing attention on these new types of religious workers and influencers who are armed with the latest digital tools, I seek to investigate the roles they play in informing how religious authority is conceived of and enacted within digital culture. To focus this investigation, attention is placed on the rise of a new class of Christian workers that I call religious digital creatives (RDCs). The term "digital creative" is often used in digital marketing and public relations (PR) to describe web and software designers or social media innovators whose work focuses on creating digital content and tools. Owing to their specialized skills in technology and information management, digital creatives are able to leverage their expertise not only for professional purposes but also to advance their personal passions or agendas through digital networks or platforms. RDCs are individuals whose digital media work and skills grant them unique status and influence within their religious communities. In the opening example in this chapter, the Little i Apps team can be considered as Catholic digital creatives. Their goal was to design mobile applications to serve the mission of Catholic organizations and the religious practices of the Catholic Church. While these Catholic digital creatives work outside the traditional religious structure of the Catholic Church, their goal was to create and provide digital tools to serve Catholics. Thus, their digital work put them in close association and in relationship with the wider mission of the Church, an institution which historically has embraced the dominant media of the day to serve the mission and purposes of the Church.

However, RDCs are not only those found working outside religious institutions. Christian organizations are increasingly employing digital creatives to help them build and manage their online presence and facilitate public conversation about faith through social media. RDCs may work as communication or press officers for a specific church, diocese or religious leader. Since they are employed by a religious denomination, they are meant to serve the needs of that institution. Yet their use of digital media may be seen to undermine the very structures they serve. This study will show that still other RDCs hold recognized roles within a Christian community (i.e., pastors, priests, deacon/deaconess, etc.), where their main job is to oversee aspects of religious education, spiritual development or institutional leadership. However, increasingly, some of these individuals find taking on the role of an RDC is crucial to this work. By embracing digital tools and strategies, they are able to further expand their ministry opportunities in ways that can transform accepted religious practices. In all of these cases, the work and presence of RDCs within Christian communities create unique tensions and opportunities between digital media workers or users and the offline or traditional religious authorities with which they affiliate. This book documents and analyzes the work of Christian RDCs, highlighting examples of RDCs at work within Catholic and Protestant churches and organizations in America and Europe.

The aim of this book is to unpack the complex issues surrounding the performance, presentation and negotiation of religious authority between RDCs and religious organizations. I argue that the pervasiveness of the internet shaping contemporary work and religious culture has created a space allowing RDCs to arise. These RDCs are not simply digital workers with a religious goal in mind. They are individuals who intentionally and unintentionally exert influence within religious institutions due to their digital work. Their digital work and the positions this creates mean RDCs often simultaneously challenge and support traditional notions and structures of authority. This duality and complexity of how digital media empower and undermine both RDCs and religious leaders is explored in more detail in Chapter 2. For now, it is simply important to note that this book will tease out the implications of this duality and the extent to which established religious organizations and hierarchies resist, welcome or partner with RDCs for the sake of their communities' advancement and adaptation to digital culture. Through presenting and analyzing a series of in-depth case studies, I spotlight the different types of RDCs at work in a range of Christian communities and their relationship with these affiliations. Overall, this book offers theoretical reflection on the strategies engaged by these individuals who often act as new forms of religious authorities both online and offline.

Innate challenges to studying authority and the character of new/digital media

In the initial waves of Internet Studies, discussion within Sociology of Religion and Media Studies often assumed that the appearance of new forms of authority online would displace traditional authorities and lead to struggles over membership, official interpretations and personal religious identities (i.e., Hennerby & Dawson, 1999). Yet this study will show that while friction over issues of authority does emerge online, it is not simply a war of the new versus the old, in which traditional sources of influence are diminishing. This book uncovers the hidden dynamics and subtexts used by newer expressions of religious authority online to present and justify their work and its perceived impact on their communities and institutions. These subtexts are described as a technological apologetic, a unique pattern of discourse used by RDCs to justify and explain their digital work, which also presents how they see their relationship to religious institutions and structures they must navigate. The idea of the technological apologetic is further defined in Chapter 3. For now, it is simply important to note that careful attention is given in this study to the narratives offered by RDCs and to consideration of how this discourse frames digital media and promotes technology use within their respective religious contexts.

Scholars have argued that some of the innate features of the internet and attributes of digital media set them in opposition to older forms of media and social structures. Scholars in Media Studies have often referred to network- and computer-based technologies such as the internet as "new media" based on a digital binary code that is translated by a computer. This is in contrast to mass media, now often referred to as "old media," which is based on light, sound and text that is stored and engaged in a linear and analog format. New media by their nature are highly flexible, dynamic and changeable, while old media are static and limited by their composite and assembled features. New media is a term used to describe a range of different digital and mobile technologies including computers, the internet, cell and smart phones, social networking software and digital recording devices. The term "new media" represents a category that many scholars argue is distinctly different from traditional forms of mass media. Yet the question is often asked, what is "new" in new media? Lev Manovich (2001), in the *Language of New Media*, identified five principles of new media technology that he argued represent its unique character: New media have distinct facets of numerical representation, modularity, automation, variability and transcoding.

First, new media are digitally coded and based on numerical representations, where information is stored and transferred via binary code instead of via light or sound wave. This means the DNA of new media is encoded to be read and interacted with via computer technology. Second, new media are modular in that elements maintain separate identities so that they can be stored together but manipulated separately. As a result, new media products and information are highly flexible and can be transferred into new forms quickly and simultaneously. Third, new media are easily automated, as operations can be programmed into the media system, removing in part the human element. This means new media offer new opportunities for engagement, but are computer dependent. Fourth, new media technologies are variable because they allow multiple versions and interface possibilities from the same data. Finally, new media involve transcoding, the translation of data and products into other or additional formats.

Together these technological features mean new media are dynamic, malleable, programmable and able to be personalized in ways that were not possible with older forms of media. It is important to note that new media also encourage production processes that are highly interactive, audience generated and dynamic. The dynamic environment facilitated by new media technologies is often framed as a space of freedom, potential and creativity. Yet as Manovich asserted, this is freedom under a set of conditions, shaped by the structure or authority of digital culture, as it were. Nevertheless, the narrative of the open and fluid nature of digital society, that digital culture and its technologies are transformative, has become a dominant narrative and the one often cited and critiqued as being highly problematic for religious groups bound by theological ideologies and convictions based on set codes, practices and traditions. Therefore, the very logic and nature of new media may be seen as a threat to theological structures.

The situation is further complicated by the fact that new media can be seen as encouraging a cultural shift that runs counter to traditionally based understandings of ecclesiology. Manovich argued that the ontology of the computer gives rise to a set of cultural interfaces encouraging certain beliefs. First, he stated, new media encourage a "meta-realism" in which the user is the master with the power to discern, deconstruct and control the reality or "illusion" with which he or she is presented. This is in contrast to the modern, "old-style realism" of traditional media in which the user can simply accept or reject the illusion or reality presented (Manovich, 2001, pp. 208–209). Meta-realism is based on autocritique; people are taught not to take what they are given at face value but are exhorted to investigate, experiment and change it. This infers that traditional hierarchies are meant to be questioned and dismantled.

This leads to a second cultural interface: New media highlight a shift from a set, prescribed narrative to an interactive, changeable configuration. New media empower people to manipulate structures and meanings. This, some claim, teaches that nothing is ever final or complete; there is always room for improvement. Whereas traditional media products were story driven, new media products are information or data driven. This means that fixed practices are meant to be constantly revised and questioned, a mindset undermining the vetted patterns of liturgical process.

Finally, Manovich argued that these traits create a unique logic that is built into new media. That is, while old media were based on a linear view of the world where technology was dependent on a fixed, sequential logic and hierarchy, new media are based on the logic of the database. While the cultural format of narrative or story "creates a cause and effect trajectory out of which seemingly unordered items and events find order," the database represents the "world as a list of items that it refused to put in a set order" (Manovich, 2001, p. 230). In a database, each individual unit and its combination hold privilege over the overarching narrative structure they represent. Therefore, connections are primary and the complete entity is secondary. Database logic means individuals have the ability to easily change the content and the system or structures; they are not bound by one predetermined path. So while old media provide a "window on the world," or one person's view of reality, new media offer users a "control panel" of multiple possibilities to create new versions of the world.

Thus, the nature of new media technology provides media creators and users new opportunities to construct and present information, as well as share media content with a network of individuals that may be outside the traditional boundaries of their established communities and institutions. These unique technological features give users and innovators the chance to present their particular views and convictions online in a public, uncensored way that enables them to be shared and go viral beyond their initial or intended audience. Other authors have elaborated on this metaphor and approach. Similarly, Baym, Zhang and Lin (2004) and other authors have written persuasively about self-fashioning online and sources of personal identity derived from interacting online. The porous boundaries of new media and network-based communities can obviously challenge traditional sources and systems of authority established over time with designated gatekeepers and static or controlled boundaries.

Much speculation is raised in scholarly work about the extent to which the internet and digital culture have transformed and will transform accepted understandings and patterns of authority within digital and broader contexts (i.e., Anderson, 1999; Turner, 2007). The fluidity and transience of online environments suggest a multitude of challenges to established authority roles and structures. Some of the most noted tensions between traditional authority and authority forms encouraged within new media culture can be summed up in this way: Traditional authority structures are overseen or governed by a specific leader or group. Such roles are often granted to actors who have been sanctioned by the broader community, with these official authorities successfully completing a recognized training program or credentialing system. This sanction comes from structural or organizationally established hierarchies that bestow select members with positions of influence through recognized initiation rites, proving the individual has achieved a certain level of skill, institutional expertise or power (Campbell, 2012).

Yet scholars have argued authority within digital culture is established in a very different way. Instead of coming from external sources and protocols, authority is cultivated by and comes from within the media system itself. This is referred to as "algorithmic authority," where values are extracted from diverse information sources sorted and determined by nonhuman, computer-driven entities such as search engines (Shirky, 2009). This means what is considered authoritative is based on programmed ranking and reputation systems found online, such as where one's content falls in a Google search or the number of followers one's blog has or "likes" achieved via a Facebook post. Algorithmic authority is often measured by one's visibility online and the search-engine or Google-ranking prominence of the content produced. This authority is confirmed in numerical terms by an "unbiased" computer ranking or the number of links or endorsements received from others online. Thus, authority online is based primarily on visibility within media culture and on digital expertise that helps one build their own prominence in the media system, rather than being conferred from external mediated or monitored sources (Campbell, 2012). These are just some of the issues in need of serious exploration in relation to how authority is being reconfigured online; hence, the role played by algorithmic authority and other expressions of power online are considered carefully in this study. Overall, new media technologies and culture create novel challenges for the building and bestowing of authority among established religious systems. These unique challenges to religious authorities have been the focus of much scholarly reflection in Digital Religion Studies and are the focus of this book.

Early investigations of authority in Internet Studies and Religion online

The influence of the internet on issues of authority has long been a topic for discussion in studies of religion and the internet. Over a decade ago, a small international gathering of scholars assembled at the University of Copenhagen for the first official international conference on religion and the internet. The Religious Encounters with Digital Networks 2001 Conference brought together a group of senior scholars and PhD students exploring a variety of projects considering the rise of religious communication online. At the time, the internet was seen by many scholars, as well as the public at large, as a transformative space providing an exciting new context for social engagement for a variety of groups and individuals in modern society. Organizers hoped this event would help document and identify trends in relation to how religious encounters can now take place in digital settings that apparently transcend a number of conventional boundaries such as organizational structures, time zones, geographic borders, religious traditions, cultural divisions and ethnic identities (www.staff.hum.ku.dk/hojs/encounters/ purpose.html). Interdisciplinary conversations from the event gave rise to two important volumes interrogating emerging questions regarding the extent to which the internet was altering or enhancing religion and religiosity online (Dawson & Cowan, 2004; Hojsgaard & Warburg, 2005).

I was privileged to be part of this landmark event, having just completed a PhD based on an ethnographic study of how the formation and practices of Christian email-based communities informed religious individuals' perceptions and involvement in their offline faith groups. After a five-year, mostly solitary journey of conducting research online, it was exciting to be part of a conversation where scholars shared insights about how internet users were engaging in multireligious contexts online. We heard about the formation of Islamic internet sites and early debates over online fatwas in Europe (Bunt, 2004), challenges faced by Korean Buddhist monks using bulletin board systems (BBSs) to recreate traditional discourses online, how Buddhists were able to bypass traditional initiation rites (Kim, 2005) and how Nordic young people were experimenting with new religious identities in Christian and neo-pagan communities online (Lövheim & Linderman, 2005).

One question that frequently arose during the three-day event concerned how the internet might potentially reshape traditional practices and conceptions of religious life. At the heart of these discussions was a common concern over issues concerning who, if anyone, had control within these online religious contexts, and the extent to which individuals outside traditional religious power structures were being empowered by nonhierarchal or flattening features of the internet. Many presenters reported that online spaces offered practitioners new ways to present and practice their beliefs, enabling them to bypass traditional religious hierarchies. This was especially evident in studies of ex-cult members using websites to present alternatives or critiquing narratives of official groups online (Introvingne, 2000; Barker, 2005). Other studies highlighted the fact that the internet offered opportunities to create online communities or resources outside standard religious structures, thus offering a platform that gave rise to new groups, such as fundamentalists advocating specific forms of millennialism and "end of days" rhetoric and related practices (MacWilliams, 2004).

A concern that kept surfacing in various keynotes and conversations between participants was the potential impact the internet would have on religious authority. Scholars present noted religious website design and online community experimentation were often spearheaded by individual religious internet users, rather than initiated by specific denominations or organizations. In my mind, this raised a number of crucial questions such as: Were webmasters becoming a new form of religious authority? To what extent did moderators of religious discussion forums serve as religious leaders or mentors for their members? How are webmasters who create religious resources online perceived by offline religious institutions? Are religious internet innovators seen as competitors or allies by official groups?

After the conference, conversations about these issues continued online via email among a number of the participants. At one point, we discussed a collaborative project designed to explore how the role of the web moderator in early online communities and forums—e.g., email lists and newsgroups—might serve as a new type of religious authority by both providing leadership and establishing and enforcing protocols for these groups. While the project never got past the idea and planning stage, this struck me as a fascinating and important area of inquiry, an acknowledgment that the internet may be spawning new categories of religious authorities. Over the past two decades, I have studied how religious authority is conceived of and practiced online. This exploration has included studies of how members of Christian email communities often let their online experiences guide the evaluation and expectations of their offline faith communities (Campbell, 2005) and the ways religious bloggers use their blogs to affirm different forms of religious authority online (Campbell, 2010). I have studied debates emerging within the Anglican Communion over the legitimacy of online worship in Second Life, branded as an official online extension of the offline church (Campbell, 2010b). Authority also emerged as a theme while studying Israeli ultra-Orthodox rabbis who sought to establish control over the online world by banning internet use by community members at various times during the 2000s and advocating the use of filtering technologies (Campbell, 2011). These attempts, especially those aimed at controlling free speech and use of the internet via censorship, demonstrate how the internet is seen by some as a threat to their power, requiring them to exert authority over its use to reassert their power positions within the community.

The emergence of religion online has been lauded for its flexibility, empowering members to reform ritual, bypass traditional boundaries and transcend normal limits of time, space and geography. Attention is often given to how online religious communities pose potential threats, as well as opportunities, to offline religious groups. Thus, scholars have highlighted the notion of religious authority as an important area of inquiry online. The internet enables users to transcend or create new forms of hierarchy, meaning it can offer religious practitioners the opportunity to challenge traditional systems of legitimation or bypass recognized gatekeepers by creating new forums for community gathering (Herring, 2005). Gatekeeping as a theory within Media Studies highlights the people and processes by which information is filtered for dissemination; in the case of the internet, digital technologies allow people to bypass traditional gatekeepers and find alternate and unfiltered ways to share information outside official channels. This is why certain offline religious organizations have expressed concerns, especially about the effect of bringing normally closed private policy or theological discussions of religious leaders into public forums (Piff & Warburg, 2005). Yet scholars have also noted the internet provides offline religious organizations with unique opportunities to monitor members' activities online and control information, thereby reasserting their offline control online (Barker, 2005; Barzilai-Nahon & Barzilai, 2005). Here the online and offline contexts are often framed as separate and competing spaces seeking to offer new, or solidify old, forms of religious authority through different avenues of the internet.

Thus, the innate technological affordances of new media such as increased mobility, interactivity and individualized control often force recognized religious leaders to rethink the extent of their influence in a digital age, frequently leading some groups to innovate technologies in order to reassert their positional influence online as well as offline. These contexts and characteristics raise many interesting questions about who serves as the official or legitimate voice for a particular religious tradition or community in an age of internet. It is this crux—between recognized offline religious systems and roles created by established religious communities and emerging religious leaders, and spheres of influence created and facilitated by digital culture—this book seeks to explore and interrogate.

Rise of digital religion studies and attention to the question of authority

In the volume coming out of the Religious Encounters with Digital Networks Conference, Hojsgaard and Warburg (2005) outlined what they saw as the different phases, or "waves," of research on religion online. The initial wave of research presented the internet within either a utopian or a dystopian context (p. 5). The second wave sought to offer a more balanced approach by categorizing and analyzing in detail how the internet can be used for religious purposes and suggested the emerging third wave focused on the critical interpretation of the influence of the internet on religious culture (2005, p. 9). Consequently, the waves reflect a process, and this process will continue to evolve. Within this collection, the themes of authority, community and identity were prominently addressed by a number of scholars in relation to different religions. The narrative of the three waves has been important for scholars seeking to frame and map developments of studies of religion and the internet. Specifically, each wave sought to identify the key questions and approaches taken by scholars investigating the intersection between new media, religion and digital culture and to identify how different eras of scholarship connect and contribute to one another (i.e., Campbell & Virtullo, 2016). Wave one has been called the descriptive era, during which researchers sought to closely document new forms of religious practice emerging on the internet. This led to wave two, which focused on categorizing key trends within religious internet practice, as scholars attempted to provide concrete typologies. Wave three is often referred to as the theoretical turn, as attention turned to identifying common methods and the most robust theoretical frameworks for analyzing religion, online as well as offline, and religious communities' strategies related to new media use. Scholars have also suggested current work can be described as a fourth wave (Campbell & Lövheim, 2011; Campbell & Virtullo, 2016) focused on religious actors' negotiations between their online and offline lives and activities and considering how such intersections can create new, hybrid places for religiosity to be performed. This, in turn, can be seen as illuminating broader changes and understanding of the religiosity in contemporary society.

Scholars have noted a key area of interest within fourth-wave studies is close attention to "ways religious authority is negotiated between new actors and structures online and their offline counterparts" (Lövheim & Campbell, 2017, p. 1086). Here scholars note how religious actors must negotiate between multiple spheres of religious practice and meaning found online, offline and within newly created digital "third spaces" of religion (i.e., Hoover & Echchaibi, 2014). Within this fourth wave, increased scholarly attention is being given to how authority is being changed and reconceived as the online and offline contexts become blurred and more interconnected; this is where our exploration of RDCs and their relationships with affiliate religious communities situates itself.

With over 20 years of documented scholarly research on religion and the internet, this area is now commonly referred to as Digital Religion Studies (Campbell, 2013). It encompasses the investigation of how "digital media are used by religious groups and users to translate religious practices and beliefs into new contexts, as well as the reimagining of religion offered by unique affordances within these new mediums and spaces" (Campbell, 2017, p. 17). Within this area of inquiry, questions are still being raised about the ways internet technology allows people to bypass traditional gatekeepers or seek out alternative religious authorities that support their position or beliefs outside of established patterns of accountability and oversight. Many creators of digital environments, from websites to virtual worlds, have emerged and become unintentional authorities by creating new spaces for religious engagement. This is seen in this chapter's opening example, wherein a tool created by Catholic app developers was seen to challenge the accepted religious practices and rituals of the Catholic Church. In that case, the work of Catholic RDCs was granted authority by a church leader, only to subsequently be seen to undermine the ultimate or established authority of the Church's ecclesial body of oversight, the Vatican. This draws us back to the need to consider the complexity involved in trying to approach and study authority in such case studies.

Studying religious digital creatives' negotiation with authority

This book suggests one fruitful field of investigation for Digital Religion Studies regarding the question of authority lies in studying the work and practices of RDCs. Because digital professionals who work as denominational webmasters, institutional media officers, religious bloggers and social media thought leaders increasingly perform technology-focused roles that elevate the visibility of their work and position, I argue these RDCs have become both intentional and unintentional religious authorities for the organizations they work for and the faith communities they belong to.

In 2010–2012, while interviewing theologians and religious workers for a book exploring how networks could be seen as a theological model for understanding emerging patterns of religious communication and practices (see Campbell & Garner, 2016), I began to see an interesting trend. Those theologians and Christian thinkers that were often most cited on blogs were not those with the most publications or academic credentials, but those with the most visible and prominent online presence. At the same time, I began receiving a number of invitations from academic and religious institutions around the world to visit and present my research. At my public talks, it was not uncommon for different digital creatives to attend, drawn to the event after learning about my research on religious groups' use of technology online. During Q&A times and informal discussions after these meetings, I heard many stories, such as diocesan press officers in the UK experimenting with Facebook as a new news outlet, German bloggers dedicating their time online to discussing the policies and dogmas of their denominations, and American digital media experts voicing their frustration when trying to convince their church leaders about the benefits of going online.

These interactions led me to this project, where I conducted over 120 interviews over a five-year period with a variety of different digital creatives from around the USA and Europe. This began with interviews of former RCDs I met in my academic travels and connections I made with these types of individuals during various keynotes and lectures I was invited to give on my research. This work details these encounters and the analysis of their digital work and interview narratives collected over the course of this project.

Overview of book

A core argument of this book is that the nature of internet technologies and digital culture facilitates and empowers the rise of new religious actors and enhances the position of traditional religious systems and leaders, especially within Christian contexts. This study also considers the extent to which the performance of authority online may create unique hybrid structures and roles that represent shifts in both online and offline religious cultures. The book unpacks the role played by RDCs in current church and media culture. Through a series of interviews and case studies, this project provides an overview of these distinctive forms of religious authority and their relationships/negotiations with traditional religious leaders and communities.

Chapter 1 offers a theoretical overview of the concept of authority and how it is approached in this book. I provide a detailed review about how digital media use can both challenge and empower religious authority, while reflecting on what digital religion research has shown about complexity of the performance of authority online between established and emerging religious voices. Here we see how scholars have observed ways the internet gives voice to the voiceless and elevates the ideas and reputation of new religious actors. Yet at the same time, we find offline leaders empowered to further establish or shore up their influence online. The chapter provides an overview of the four most common approaches to authority applied within current Media and Internet Studies: Authority as role, power, relational or algorithmic based. This provides an essential overview of key conceptions of authority and the discussion partners who will help us discuss the very different ways each category of RDCs sees or even reimages the concept of authority in a digital age.

Chapter 2 introduces the key focus of this study, the study of RDCs and how their presence and work within various religious communities and institutions raise important questions about what constitutes authority in a digitally driven culture. I draw on the work of Anderson (1999) and his predictions based on early forms of Muslim alternative interpreters emerging online that he felt would challenge traditional forms of Islamic authority. Identifying these different types of religious interpreters or authorities emerging on the internet became a basis for developing a typology that helps define three distinct categories of RDCs identified in this research. Identifying each unique group of RDCs enables us to explore the multiple ways religious authority is emerging in new roles created through digital engagement within many Christian communities and institutions.

Chapter 3 presents the methodological approach to studying RDCs' performances of authority in institutional and digitally mediated contexts. I argue Goffman's work on authority provides a helpful metaphorical framing of authority as a performance. This is seen as what he called the dramaturgical approach, where actors are shaped both by the interpretations of the roles they take and the constraints of the structures of the theater. Goffman stressed that authority is something that is see-able and can be identified by paying attention to both what actors do and say. Using this model, I outline how we can map the media-making narrative of RDCs by outlining their work identity and understanding of authority as it is shaped by online and offline contexts. I also argue we must pay attention to a particular type of RDC-created discourse, the technological apologetic. This discourse frames RDCs' work in terms of certain motivations and assumptions about technology and their religious affiliation, both of which shape how they perform and perceive authority in multiple contexts.

In Chapter 4, the first of three unique RDC categories identified in this study is discussed, i.e., the emergence of "digital entrepreneurs." As highly trained technology workers with digital design and coding skills, these digital professionals see their work-based skills as potential tools that can be used to serve the church and the Christian organizations with which they affiliate. Because of their technical expertise, they often tithe their time and develop religious-based digital resources (websites, apps, etc.), which they see as serving the goals of their faith communities. However, since this work is performed outside of the oversight and established structures of these groups, and their digital resources can emerge as having as great or greater influence than the official digital presences of an institution, their position as unintentional religious authorities can frame them as competitors to the very groups they seek to serve. Thus, their specialized position and influence within digital culture, along with the gifts and tensions these digital professional creatives offer their religious communities and traditional religious leaders, are explored in depth.

In Chapter 5, the work of RDC "digital spokespersons" is explored. Digital spokespersons are media workers and officers whose job is to represent and support their specific religious organization or community through media content and production. In other words, they are employed to produce both digital and mass media content about their institutions and serve as liaisons between media outlets and their groups vis-à-vis the group's mission, and are thus committed to comment on institutional news and public events. One of the challenges that occur as this work becomes increasingly digital in nature, especially through representing their community via social media, is that what was once a utilitarian service role for their organizations has progressively become a role of identity presentation and management of the institution. Also, because digital content can easily go viral and institutional information placed online is no longer controlled by the message producer, religious institutions are increasingly leery of using digital media for institutional communication. Thus, digital spokespersons must carefully navigate and negotiate between the bounded structural authority and expectations of the organizations they serve and the flexible and dynamic character of digital culture.

Chapter 6 explores the unique roles performed by "digital strategists" and their implications for the religious communities with which they affiliate. Digital strategists hold a unique position located between that of digital entrepreneurs, who often operate outside institutional structures, and digital spokespersons, who serve as an extension or official representative of these structures. Digital strategists represent their community by holding recognized service and ministry positions for their institutions—e.g., priest/pastor or religious educator—while being involved in or taking on digital work that may extend or alter their position and influence within the community in some way. They may be, for example, an ordained religious leader who develops a social app to serve their church, which then extends their congregation beyond traditional local or denominational boundaries of their service remit. Or, we might see a religious trainee who is able through blogging to gain a following and lead a virtual parish before they are officially sanctioned to do so offline. As a unique form of hybrid authority, they move between online and offline spaces in their work and ministry, a situation that may offer them new religious service opportunities but may also stretch, even reshape, institutional boundaries related to sanctioned activities connected to certain traditional roles. They may even be able to transgress structural protocols of accountability. The digital strategist recognizes this space of tension as they seek to bring creativity and new technological tools or opportunities to their work and navigate how this process may challenge traditional authority structures and protocols.

Chapter 7 looks at the media-making narratives of all three categories of RDCs. Identifying these narratives and mapping how these professionals frame their work help reveal a range of perspectives that exist on what a religious authority looks like and how it functions within digital culture. Chapter 8 focuses on exploring the technological apologetic digital entrepreneurs, spokespersons and strategists construct to justify their work within their religious context and affiliations. Exploring their motivation, how this presents the way they see technology and religion intersect, and the ideological tensions this can create help reveal the nuanced difference in their rhetorical strategies. Taken together, these final two chapters not only highlight the key points of tension between new and traditional religious authority roles and expression but also enable us to consider how this speaks to new conceptual models about how authority is perceived and displayed in digital culture. Finally, in the conclusion, the key findings of this study and their implications for future conversations about religious authority in digital culture are presented.

In summary, by exploring three types of Christian digital creatives at work in multiple denominational and non-denominational contexts in the USA and Europe, this book raises important discussions about what constitutes religious authority in an age of digital media. I suggest the work of RDCs and the ways they negotiate their relationship with traditional Christian institutions point to important features of how religious authority is being lived out and conceived of in a digital society. This work and the findings discussed in the chapters that follow also have implications for our understanding of how we define and describe what authority is in contemporary culture. It is also important to note that while the focus of this book is on Christian digital creatives, the research presented will show readers how these descriptions of RDCs and the strategies they engage while they negotiate their role as new forms of religious authority have a potential broader resonance. On the basis of this work and my observation of digital creativity within other religious communities, especially within Jewish and Muslim groups, I suggest the classifications and strategies described in the pages that follow can be applied to many digital media actors in other such religious traditions as well.

Chapter 1

Investigating approaches to the study of authority

As stressed in the introduction, the concept of authority is at the center of discussions about how religious groups are shaped by within digital culture, as well as digital creatives influence or interact with traditional religious leader. Authority becomes a frame by which to consider the abilities of certain individuals or structure to gain or maintain influence over a certain group of people within digital spaces. However, the essential characteristics of authority are often not well defined. The term religious authority suffers from the same lack of clarity when used in studies of digital religion; it is used as an overarching term rather than a clearly defined category. At the heart of this book is the assertion that more detailed attention needs to be given not just to who can be seen as a religious authority but to what actually constitutes an "authority." Before we can study how certain individuals establish themselves as an authority, or function in a way that garners them authority within a respective religious or media context, we need to further interrogate how authority is understood.

The aim of Chapter 1 is to investigate how the concept of authority is employed in current literature and research. This is done in order to map out where, when and how religious digital creatives (RDCs) can be seen as a new form of religious authority in an age of internet. Exploring in more detail the different ways authority is enacted in digital and religious cultures prepares us to discuss in more detail how RDCs gain public sway and affect the religious groups they are affiliated with in specific ways. We begin with an overview of the way the concepts of authority and religious authority have been approached in Religious Studies and Sociology of Religion. I argue this has strongly influenced the ways digital religion scholars have talked about the nature of authority.

This leads us to consider discussions of authority within the field of Media Studies, which has primarily taken one of three approaches, seeing authority in terms of roles, power or relationality. Each of these framings of authority helps us identify the dominant framings and aspects of authority different categories of RDCs draw on when describing their digital work and relationship to their offline faith communities.

However, these discussions are grounded in how authority has traditionally been conceived in the offline context and do not present the whole picture of how authority is negotiated in digital culture. This requires us to approach authority as it surfaces in the subfields of Internet and Digital Media Studies, which look at authority as an algorithm. Algorithmic authority follows a very different logic and shows the influence technological structures have had on understanding human relations and structures. Discussions of algorithmic authority also point to new classifications of what some suggest authority looks like within digital platforms and organizations. Discussing the emergence of media influencers, thought leaders and digital leaders as different manifestations of authority in algorithmic culture provides us with further insights into how technology creates new spaces of influence and the strategies used by different digital actors to leverage those opportunities. Considering how both traditional and digital logics inform different framings of authority is essential, because, as will be shown in the chapters ahead, RDCs engage in multiple forms of authority positioning, depending on their work and goals. We will see that RDCs draw simultaneously on established or traditional understandings of authority, as well as newer conceptions related to digital culture, in order to frame their work as having community influence or be seen as authoritative.

What is the root of authority?

As discussed in the introduction, authority is a complex term, often not well defined in studies of religion and the internet. It can be used to refer to a number of different contexts, from positions of influence to specific individuals' or groups' rights to hold power, or to those structures having control over a certain sphere of society. A key focus of this study is to interrogate and outline a specific understanding of the concept of authority and so provide a concrete framework for investigating and discussing the challenges and opportunities digital technologies present religious communities in relation to such notions of authority. Such a task must begin with interrogating the meaning of the concept of authority when the term is used.

At its most basic level, authority evokes ideas of dominance and control, involving who or what does or does not possess these traits. Discourse related to authority can involve discussion of issues such as boundary making and maintenance for specific groups, training and specialized knowledge that bestows on an individual recognized expertise or the extent to which certain individuals or groups have the ability to make choices. In other situations, authority represents voluntary submission or giving up autonomy in order to live within the rules and benefits of a certain system or situation. Choosing a particular group or association can mean accepting certain moral constraints and can come with certain behavioral expectations, yet this affiliation may also offer advantages. In yet other contexts, authority is set by external or previously established constraints, and individuals do not have the choice of whether to opt in or out—e.g., the way being born as a citizen of a specific country determines one's nationality.

While authority is a characteristic often discussed in relation to how the internet affects relationships and structures within contemporary society, as I argue in previous works (Campbell, 2007, 2010), the way authority is defined in scholarly works is often not clearly contextualized. This is because what constitutes authority in new media or digital culture can be varied and context specific (Campbell, 2007; 2010). Within Internet Studies, the notion of authority has been approached in a variety of ways. These include discussing it in terms of: Organizational or community structures, systems or hierarchies, referencing leadership roles or positions of influence, an ideological notion such as moral or higher authority relative to issues of governance; as a general term synonymous with the term power and even to refer to nonhuman sources of authority such as documents, texts or historical events (Campbell, 2007). So when evoked, authority can mean different things to different researchers, and "there appears to be no unified understanding about what is meant when the concept of 'authority' is taken up in studies of the internet" (Campbell, 2007). This presents researchers of the internet and digital religion with a conundrum about how to frame such discussions. One approach is to turn to discussions within Religious Studies and Sociology of Religion to see how the term authority is approached.

Understanding authority in the context of religious authority

While authority is a complex term, it is often further complicated within studies of religion and digital media in trying to define or mark out what constitutes specifically "religious authority." Use of the term religious authority often invokes a set of assumptions about how religious communities and structures function, assumptions that are often not clearly articulated or interrogated.

Scholars have tried to define religious authority in a way to distinguish it from the general conception of authority and make its meaning or the focus of study more precise. In Sociology of Religion, religious authority is often described as drawing on a particular form of legitimation, often linked to a unique or divine source. As Chavez (1994) stated, "The distinguishing feature of religious authority is that its authority is made legitimate by calling on some supernatural referent" whether that be a specific actor (i.e., god or spirit) or designated structure (p. 756). This understanding of religious authority seeks to distinguish itself by noting it is divinely inspired and given to specific sources within a specific religious context. In this way, religious authority depends on the community recognizing and supporting this spiritual sanctioning of designated religious authorities. This means the legitimation of authority for specific religions or groups, such as Christianity, may rely at least partially on recognizing the fact that a particular divine source plays a role in offering external validation. Whom or what is considered an authority is not solely a human designation. While this understanding of religious authority is helpful in understanding the rationale behind many established religious structures of legitimation, it does not truly help us unpack what is meant by religious authority and its full defining features.

The term religious authority, in general, has been used as a broad concept in much as the same way the term authority has been used in much scholarship. What is actually being referenced (an individual, structure or hierarchy) as authoritative may vary greatly when the term is evoked. Use of the term has varied from seeing religious authority as divine authority granted to religious structures (De Pillis, 1966) or appointed gatekeepers or representing the sentiments and decision-making of God on earth (Wiles, 1971). Religious authority has also been conceived as a trust-based relationship given to institutional professionals (Chavez, 2003) or self-appointed leaders (Barnes, 1978) by their followers, or authority representing systems of knowledge able to define what constitutes religious authenticity, especially in relation to religious identity and membership (Jensen, 2006). Furthermore, religious authority can be used to refer to different religious systems, beliefs, structures, appointed positions and even ideological positions, which may or may not be clearly distinguished by those studying such issues. Similar to what has been argued in the introduction, the concept of religious authority, especially as it is typically used in Religious Studies as an amorphous concept, brings us no closer to a clear understanding of what authority is or does.

This fluidity of the use of the term is mirrored in discussions of religious authority and digital media and the internet. Turner, a sociologist of religion, argued, "Multimedia entertainment and communication systems challenge both the print-based authority of secular governments and the traditional authority of the world religions," especially in relation to who or what is recognized as qualified to validate communal "contents and meanings of knowledge and information" (Turner, 2007, p. 117). Scholars of Digital Religion Studies have used Turner's notion of religious authority as tied to the structures of established religious traditions and groups as a way to discuss the variety of ways religious groups' community boundaries are challenged by the internet. Baker similarly took a community or institutional approach when she discussed how the internet allows religious community members to make private institutional and theological discussions public (i.e., Barker, 2005). Others discuss the challenge the internet poses to religious authority in terms of the creation and privilege of alternative voices (inferred to be new forms of religious authority in established communities), as individuals seeking advice bypass official religious hierarchies (i.e., Herring, 2005; Piff & Warburg, 2005). From this brief review, we see references to religious authority typically indicate established religious structures or groups and how they respond to the new freedoms of communication offered by digital media, which allow members to bypass traditional gatekeepers or monitoring structures. So while evoking the term religious authority helps us focus attention on the specific concerns religious groups and structures may have about the internet, it does not help us further concretely clarify the features of what defines something or someone as authoritative in this digital context. Therefore, simply using the term religious authority as a way to define what authority is may in fact further obscure rather than clarify our understanding. This points to additional levels of complexity in relation to identifying the specific systems, power relations or sources the concept of authority potentially references. I argue for this study, which focuses on what constitutes religious authority in digital contexts and cultures; a more concrete approach is needed, especially in relation to how authority is performed in digital contexts.

Traditional approaches to authority in Media Studies: Authority as role, power or relational

It can be argued that within Communication and Media Studies, authority is typically approached in one of two ways—either seeing authority in terms of Max Weber's three categories of leadership roles or in conversation with Michel Foucault's discussion of power. Weber saw authority as role based, focused on leadership style and the ability to garner followers. Foucault saw authority as power based, focused on a structures' ability to control others. These have also become the primary lenses used by scholars within Internet Studies to discuss individuals' relationship to media technologies and the cultures they create.

Authority as relationship-based focuses on how actors situate themselves within specific social and media settings, as well as how they present themselves as having expertise and legitimacy. Unlike role- and power-based approaches to authority closely associated with the work of a specific scholar, authority as relational comes out of conceptual conversations about how authority is enacted. Both Weber and Foucault touched on notions of relationality in their approaches to authority. Weber made note of the relationship between different types of leaders and their followers, and Foucault highlighted the relationship individuals have to power structures. However, the relational model of authority differs from their approaches in that it places emphasis on the social negotiations between different actors, who enact a bonded relationship based on discourse.

In the sections that follow, I provide a brief overview of these two dominant and two more recent approaches to highlight how they each study authority, showing the specific factors each approach emphasizes when defining something or someone as authoritative. These lenses are engaged briefly in Chapters 4 through 6, and in detail in Chapter 7, as the basis of narrative frameworks each category of RDCs creates to define their understanding of authority, which, as we will see, engage one or more of these approaches.

Authority as role based

Arguably, the most common approach used to discuss authority within Media Studies and Digital Religion Studies is based on the work of Max Weber. As a sociologist, Weber paid close attention to how individual actions as well as large-scale social structures point to or affirm certain authority actors at work in society. In his work, Weber identified three types of authority that he saw as establishing certain actors as recognized sources of authority in society.

Scholars often highlight Weber's three forms of "pure legitimate authority"—legal, traditional and charismatic—which he used to "classify the types of authority according to the kind of claim to legitimacy typically made by each" (Weber, 1947, pp. 325, 328). He defined legal authority as authority based on a belief in the "legality" of patterns and normative rule, where loyalty is given to a legally established impersonal order. Traditional authority is seen as established by a belief in the "sanctity of immemorial traditions" (Weber, 1947, p. 328), where obedience is given to the person who occupies this traditionally sanctioned position of authority. Charismatic authority is described as based on devotion to an individual who shows a particular characteristic, ideal or exemplary quality that motivates others to adhere to the normative patterns sanctioned by that individual. He identified individuals or groups utilizing these different leadership styles and sources of power to solidify their influence. Weber's identification of specific authority roles that solidify the power for certain societal structures of authority is important. This not only because it gives scholars archetypes by which to identify different actors as authorities. It also draws attention to the fact that authority is established and maintained by leaders because followers buy in and affirm their leadership positions, consciously or unconsciously, by taking part in the social structures they create.

Weber's classification of types of authority roles has frequently been used to differentiate the types of relationships that can exist between various leaders and their communities, both online and offline. His work is often used to highlight the importance of identifying and studying specific authority roles at work within internet contexts (i.e., Campbell, 2007), as well as a way to describe the difference and intersection between online and offline positions of authority (i.e., Kluver & Cheong, 2007). This characterization of authority as a distinctive role has by far been the most common way to discuss and investigate the question of authority within Digital Religion Studies. For example, Turner (2007) considered how traditional forms of religious authority are disrupted by networked forms of social engagement and communication, and how new forms of online authority may reflect traits of charismatic authority. Hoover (2016), in the introduction to his edited collection on media and religious authority, argued Weber's approach offers scholars an important and useful way to distinguish between and discuss the different ways authority is conveyed, especially by key religious actors and organizations in media contexts. Horsfield (2016), in this same collection, went on to argue that Weber's three types of legitimate authority have become a core way for scholars of media and religion to discuss authority. They use this approach to identify how different religious structures and leaders have responded to and utilized media in relation to the positions of authority they have established and seek to maintain in religious social–cultural contexts.

Weber's approach to authority as distinctive roles that position specific actors and/or structures in places of influence and control culture helps scholars discuss how established religious authorities may respond to media innovations that challenge those positions or their social standing. Studying authority as a role has thus been central to discussion about the connection between online and offline forms of religious community, as well as how emerging charismatic authorities threaten traditional religious authorities. Focus is placed on how established offline and new online leaders garner attention from their followers and seek to build their authority in hybrid spaces where online and offline religious communities intersect. Weber's approach also has proved useful for scholars seeking to identify specific strategies used by religious leaders to establish their right to rule or muster influence among their membership in these new contexts.

However, there are also limits to the usefulness of focusing on authority as a distinctive social-cultural role. This approach, and the ways it has been used, tends to either overemphasize the role of traditional or legal authority as the most powerful leadership positions or over speculate about the influence of charismatic leaders to undermine these positions. This points to two extremes noted by Cheong (2013), suggesting early research tended to speculate that only the power of either the logic of disjuncture and displacement or the logic of continuity and complementarity could be at work at any one time in a religious context. Furthermore, seeing authority as roles fails to account for informal authorities that exist within religious organizations with specialized expertise and knowledge, especially those related to digital technology and communication that can garner them influence online. As this study suggests, these informal leadership positions can trump the influence of the formal leader in certain contexts because of direct contact with other organizational and community members. Therefore, while authority as roles as expressed in the work of Weber provides one way to define who can be seen as an authority in online and offline contexts and how they garner these positions, it does not capture the full picture of how RDCs enact and engage authority.

Authority as power

Authority as power pays attention to how control is established in certain social settings, especially related to the social and cultural rules or structures put in place to give a certain group of individual's power over another. Discussions of authority in terms of power are often linked to the work of Michel Foucault, a French philosopher whose close study of politics and political systems led him to a new conception of social power. For him, power is omnipresent within society, and all individuals are influenced by it through its existence within the multiple social forces that surround them. Rather than seeing authority as tied to specific social institutions, rules or systems, he saw authority as based within power, a structural condition that shapes human relations and responses toward one another. In *Discipline and Punish*, Foucault (1977) further described power in terms of "strategies" produced by various power relations existing within and throughout wherever people interact. For him, power is all around us, constantly shaping and influencing our social interactions and contexts. As humans, we are pulled into a position of unmasking these power dynamics, resisting them and positioning ourselves against or in relation to them.

Closely linked to his conception of power is the idea that power is entwined with knowledge and discourse. In other words, power produces knowledge and certain forms of discourse. He sought to resist the idea of totalizing ideologies, which limits or bounds certain contexts to prescriptive understandings. So his study of discourse as a way of enacting power put emphasis on revealing how given discourses produce certain "effects of truth"—i.e., a discourse creates a certain reality rather than dictating a specific true or false narrative used to evaluate and constrain the social relations and context. Much of Foucault's philosophical understanding of power is dense, informed by his Marxist and Freudian leanings, so that a full exploration and explanation of its intricacies is beyond this brief introduction. What is of importance here is to note his discussions of authority were framed in terms of how power is exercised and what techniques and tactics it engages in a given social context. For Foucault, studying authority as expressed through power draws attention to how discourse creates certain social relations that determine how people act and respond. This requires paying attention to what people say and the strategies they enact to respond to the power relations they identify within the social contexts in which they find themselves.

Describing authority in terms of power relations and the social conditions these create has become a common way to discuss the impact of authority on different groups of individuals, both online and offline. Drawing on conversations originating in Organizational Communication, scholars have seen how authority can be discussed by unpacking how it is established through power negotiations between different actors. Here the work of Gert Hofstede has been useful, seeing authority as formed through ideas of power distancing. Hofstede (2011) defined a power distance as "the extent to which the less powerful members of organizations and institutions accept and expect that power is distributed unequally" (p. 9). In other words, power distancing refers to how individuals posit themselves in relation to different solutions to the basic problem of human inequality. Authority is thus described in terms of both the relation between the balance of power between different groups or contexts and the identification of specific power-balancing strategies evoked. Authority is established in terms of short or long distancing between different individuals and powerbrokers. Hofstede argued that that when religion stresses the equality of believers, it is advocating for short power distancing between individuals, whereas the idea religions are based on a hierarchy of religious leaders and structures pushes for a larger power distancing.

Scholars within Digital Religion Studies have also explored power distancing as a strategy for studying how authority is performed online. In power distancing, actors employ different strategies in order to establish influence and control with their audience in that respective culture. In high-power distance cultures, the cultivation of power is encouraged and conveyed visibly by actors through external symbols (such as uniforms, status or artifacts) or recognized social positions. However, in low-power cultures, such signs of power are discouraged in order to promote equality among society. Altenhofen (2016) used the ideas of high and low power distancing to consider how Catholic priests consciously and unconsciously construct their position of authority through their profiles and use of Facebook. As he asserted, Catholic priests "secure authority by matching a casual style of ministry to the intended network of family and friends with whom they already have relationships established offline" (Altenhofen, 2016, pp. 99–100).

Framing authority as power can be useful for drawing attention not only to how authority is negotiated in the ways established leaders online enact strategies to establish their leadership and control. It also can be used to show how autonomous social actors, such as RDCs, navigate and contextualize different digital contexts. This approach is useful for studying how the authority of various actors frames their activities and influence online. By decoding their actions and identifying implicit and explicit intentions, we can see how RDCs' or established religious leaders' use of digital media becomes part of establishing the continuity of their authority between online and offline contexts. However, seeing authority in terms of power also has its limitations. This approach tends to emphasize a visible enactment of authority or articulation of an explicit intention to do so. This suggests specific actors are conscious of how they enact their authority and have concrete goals in mind when they do so. Yet in the case of RDCs, I would argue these individuals often emerge as unofficial authorities in specific contexts within their organizations. In other words, RDCs do work that makes a social or structural impact on their institution due to its online visibility and the public relations focus of their communication. However, they would see themselves as unintentional authorities' online, enacting discourse or strategies that challenge assumptions about their institution, while not intending to engage in power-based activities. Discussions of authority as power often assume some level of awareness by the individuals engaged, either in shaping or being shaped by power negotiations. However, this research suggests this is not always the case, so this approach does not illuminate the full picture of how authority is understood and enacted in the religious contexts under study here.

Authority as relational

While the relational model of authority is new in Media Studies' approaches to authority, it has been common in Social Psychology since the 1990s. Social psychologists used this model to look at authority in terms of individuals' voluntary compliance with the decisions of leaders in social settings and the willingness of group members to accept a leader's directives and assertions of power (Tyler & Lind, 1992). This marked a shift from an instrumentalist approach and an approach looking at authority as established power structures or roles where attention is focused on the negative side of these associations, such as coercion and behavioral control (Elliott, Thomas, & Ogloff, 2011). The relational model of authority sought to highlight positive authority relationships, where individuals gift their attention and legitimacy to others based on those associations being mutually beneficial (Tyler & Lind, 1992). Other scholars have used this approach to authority to highlight the dialectic that can result in a complex interdependence between leaders and followers in many social and political contexts (Lake, 2009). Relational authority argues that rather than seeing authority as a "thing," such as a role someone holds, or a condition we are subjected to such as an outworking of power as constituted, we see it as a negotiation of reciprocity and agency between different parties. Authority as based on relationships puts our attention on individuals' and groups' decision-making and navigation of their interactions and commitments within a given social order. Here authority is focused on the communicative process between actors. This makes it an interesting starting point for scholars studying online conversations and communication and seeking to discover how these digital texts frame social relations online and create structures of attention and influence.

Scholars in Digital Religion Studies have used this approach to move the discussion of authority from a focus on leaders and followers to one that considers the relationship between a speaker or author online and their audience. As Lövheim (2019) argued, a relational-based perspective places attention on how individuals such as bloggers create confidence, respect and trust between themselves and their audience. She suggested here authority is dependent on an individual's communicative skills in the digital environment. Authority is established or earned through an individual's ability to express personal authenticity and exhibit certain values and qualities in communicative relationships.

Bruce Lincoln, whose work focused on how authority is conferred through certain relationships and associations, has become an important conversational partner for considering the relational authority model. He suggested the strategic use of media empowers certain groups and actors with the right and ability to speak out in a public setting. Here relationality is established through discourse. Lincoln (1994) stressed that while some forms of discourse strengthen a set or central authority, other "corrosive discourses" break down or dismantle established spaces and patterns of authority. Overall, his approach stressed that authority is not an entity but is actually an effect of the communication process, which creates a relational connection between different actors, groups or systems. He stressed the idea that without the horizontal distribution of power created by a speaker addressing an audience and seeking to maintain favor with them, authority cannot be enacted. This approach to authority has been used especially to study how the language of religious leaders online sets the boundaries of a communicative relationship. This act creates a sphere of relational authority, where patterns of online textual communication can be used to initiate or ratify a discourse structure that creates a pattern of communal authority. Lincoln presented authority as the relationship between an individual and their subordinates, where power granted through action is seen as either supporting or corrupting this relationship.

This approach to authority as relationship initiated through discourse is seen in Cheong, Huang and Poon's (2011a) work on how Asian pastors and priests have become savvy in their use of Twitter in order to affirm their positions as religious experts within digital culture and in relationship to their members. They offered the phrase "epistemic authority" as one way to define religious authority in terms of focusing on systems of communications relations. They suggested religious leaders use online platforms to create and present global personas that affirm their positions as purveyors of religious wisdom in local and transnational contexts (Cheong, Huang, & Poon, 2011b). In this work, authority focuses on the relationship between religious leaders and followers that is constituted and upheld by communication patterns that seek to affirm a set framework of communal and ideological practices and values. The use of social media by religious leaders is not simply a communicative act but a relational one seeking to establish trust and the dependence of members on leadership. Their relational discourse explicitly affirms the core norms of the perceived relationship; this in turn establishes the legitimacy of church leaders as moral guides and even moderators of technology for their congregation. Authority as relational is also used to analyze how organizational online discourse and texts can build or undermine authority through the communicative processes utilized. Seeing authority as constituted through relational discourse draws attention to the need for scholars to pay close attention to language and symbolic patterns that build and/or undermine how authority is enacted between leaders and audiences.

Roles, power and relationality as framing RDCs' authority offline

Seeing authority as roles and power highlights the dominant approaches to authority found in Media Studies, with Weber and Foucault becoming primary discussion partners to how authority can be defined or perceived. These perspectives offer scholars different ways to investigate expressions of authority among contemporary religious institutions and actors online and offline. Yet, because these theoretical perspectives initially emerged from the study of authority in offline institutions, they do not provide an exhaustive framework for exploring how authority may be constituted within digital cultures. Seeing authority as role- or power-based tends to focus attention on either a single or central individual, or layer of discourse at work within religious institutions. These perspectives do not always recognize the fact that multiple actors hold authority in religious institutions or that appointed religious authorities may not be those with the most public visibility or social capital in digital contexts. The singular focus of these perspectives may fail to allow scholars to map the multilayered and multifaceted aspects of authority structures and negotiations online. Overall, I argue these approaches function on a different logic, based on assumptions of traditional authority grounded in an offline reality where authority roles are clearly identifiable and authority systems tend to have a clear hierarchical structure. However, this study suggests authority, when enacted through online and digital environments, may function differently. Therefore, we turn to two more recent conversations about how authority can be approached in a communication environment dominated by digital technologies and platforms that have become essential to the life and work of religious institutions. Authority as relational and as algorithms will, I believe, help us address important aspects of how authority is constituted in this newer technological-cultural milieu.

Approaching authority as relational is helpful for scholars seeking to study the patterns religious leaders employ as they seek to establish or affirm their positions of authority. This means paying close attention to discourse used by these leaders and how they use it to create certain social dynamics and perception of the norms. Relationship-based authority suggests when individuals enact a certain cultural pattern, the group is shaped by that performance. This highlights the need for scholars to identify both key discourses and the actors who introduce and affirm them as part of the authority-negotiation process. There is a tendency within this approach to focus on official or institutional discourses produced by organizational leaders as the core basis by which authority is enacted in a specific community or context. This perspective means those using this approach may not account for how individuals who are not central to a given institution's authority structure may consciously or unconsciously subvert this authority in the ways they interpret and communicate this discourse to others inside or outside the group.

At the beginning of this study, I assumed that by studying RDCs I would clearly see one of these three understandings of authority dominating how they framed discussions of their work and its influence. However, close examination of the narratives of RDCs revealed a much greater complexity and variation in their understandings of what authority meant to them. Their definitions of authority were closely connected to their perceived relationships with their respective religious communities or affiliated organizations. What we will see in this study is that different categories of RDCs draw on one or more of these approaches to authority in their attempts to describe their position relative to specific offline religious communities and institutions. Therefore, rather than arguing that RDCs primarily draw on a single understanding of authority, this study shows how RDCs enact personal technological apologetics to justify their religious work in terms of the position, influence or relationships this work created. This is explained in more detail from Chapter 3 onwards.

Another issue revealed in the interviews was that RDCs need to negotiate constantly between online and offline institutional and social contexts. This requires them to draw on new logics to describe their digital work and positions that give them community prominence online and offline. This leads to an exploration how RDCs navigate these cultural dualities through drawing on notions of algorithmic authority, which is explored next.

Approaches to authority in digital media studies: Authority as algorithmic

Another important framing of authority to consider for this study is seeing authority as algorithmic based. Discussions of algorithmic authority have gained traction within Internet Studies and Digital Religion Studies, as a way to talk about how information and individuals garner authority within certain digital or technological contexts. Algorithmic authority focuses on structures of information as authoritative for determining truthful or trustworthy data. It is an argument most commonly associated with media scholar Clay Shirky. He suggested institutional trust has diminished within society; individuals turn to what they perceive as more neutral or unbiased systems of verification, such as using Google's PageRank algorithms to help determine the credibility or authority of sources in digital society. However, I argue Lustig and Nardi's understanding of algorithmic authority is most useful, showing how computer-based systems promote a "logic of algorithms, which present authority as an environment framing our social reality in digital culture" (Lustig & Nardi, 2015).

In the past decade, discussions within Media and Internet Studies have suggested the concept of authority may require a new focus in an age of digital media, due to the type of culture these create. Scholars have suggested that the interactive nature of digital networks and systems of information sharing introduce new social dynamics and create new systems of influence and power in a network society. As Manuel Castells asserted, the network society on which Western society is now based, is a unique social-technical system. It is "a society whose social structure is made up of networks powered by micro-electronics-based information and communications technologies" (Castells, 2004, p. 3). This network society encompasses all aspects of modern life as our social lives, education and political systems—and, I would argue, even our religious institutions—have become influenced by our information-based economy and the social-technical infrastructure that supports interpersonal and institutional interactions. Our network-based society has become the model and reality for how we interact with one another and build community. The ever-growing embrace of the conceptual model of network society within many aspects of American culture creates a new cultural reality framing more than how we see society functioning and our role within it. This information-based society brings with it number of new logics that shape how our social world functions and how we understand core concepts of what constitutes community, identity, and indeed, authority in contemporary culture.

It is argued that the structure of the network society is increasingly based on the idea of algorithmic authority. This marks a move from looking at authority as a purely human-enacted or social category, to showing that digital technologies and environments are grounded on a different logic in which computer systems and individuals assert influence and create power structures. The concept of algorithmic authority states authority is based on numerical algorithms used to sort and organize information and communication online. Thus, computer-based rankings and formulas have become the new way to evaluate and direct human action by defining what information is considered true and trustworthy.

Here I draw on Lustig and Nardi's definition of algorithmic authority as "the trust in algorithms to direct human action and to verify information, in place of trusting or preferring human authority" (2015, p. 1). This differs from Clay Shirky's often-cited notion of algorithmic authority as, "the decision to regard as authoritative an unmanaged process of extracting value from diverse, untrustworthy sources, without any human standing beside the result saying 'Trust this because you trust me'" (Shirky, 2009). Shirky relied heavily on the idea of Google's PageRank algorithms to show how computer processes generate information that most people blindly trust as legitimate due to the perceived unbiased and reliable nature of computer processing.

Lustig and Nardi, however, argued the need to broaden this definition to emphasize how people give computer-based systems and environments authority by accepting the logic of their "algorithms to not only decide which information is true, but to also direct human action" (Lustig & Nardi, 2015, p. 1). For them, algorithmic authority is defined by the ideas of logic and control, where a set of abstract instructions based on numerical computations (the orienting logic) creates the conditions for a set of specific instructions and actions to be accepted based on the culture and rules of how computers operate (and assert control). This means algorithms "[give] authority to not only 'do things' to software, but they cause human actors to respond accordingly" (Lustig & Nardi, 2015, p. 1). Let us look at these components of logic and control as central factors shaping notions of what constitutes authority in digital culture. Lustig and Nardi suggested the design of software, computers and digital platforms runs on a certain logic. This is a logic where authority is based on a computer command structure—what is considered authoritative is whatever computer output and results tell us is so. This is a logic based on numerical privilege and rankings; it is important because our search engines and social media feeds tell us it is what deserves our attention. This kind of media logic refers to the technological, organizational and aesthetic aspects of the media that create a process by which messages are constructed and meaning is decoded (Krotz, 2018). This media logic in turn shapes our expectations and understanding of the world.

This leads to Lustig and Nardi's notion of control, where we put our trust in computers and the culture they create. This new culture is based on algorithms as the chief decision makers for what is influential and valuable, where technology is privileged over human and given authoritative status. Striphas argued, "Algorithms have significantly taken on what, at least since Arnold, has been one of culture's chief responsibilities, namely, the task of 'reassembling the social'" (2015, p. 406). This, he claimed, shifts our attention to an algorithmic culture based on a "privatization of process: that forms decision-making and contestation that comprise the ongoing struggle to determine the values, practices and artifacts" (Striphas, 2015, p. 406). In other words, we place our trust in technological and corporate culture to tell us what voices to listen to, which topics are important and which structures to give weight to in evaluating credibility.

Thus, an algorithmic-based authority is given based on numerical ranking—those who have the most followers, likes, friends or citations are seen as those with the most authoritative voices. This means we turn to search engines and other sorting systems to tell us who is considered an authority in a given area. In digital platforms, leadership is determined by one's visibility and prominence in a given online context; in other words, it is determined not by what they say, but how often it has been quoted, or linked to. Authority is based on the value of the contribution judged by the public audience and not the institution within which it emerges. The logic of algorithmic authority thus challenges previous understandings of authority, such as those suggested especially by Weber and Hofstede, Hofstede and Minkov. Authority is not, as Weber argued, based on the establishment or performance of an institutional or even self-appointed role but on the numerical and quantifiable affirmation of the community members within the group. Authority is also not based on the mastery of power distancing, which enacts strategies that seek to affirm authority by highlighting traditional markers or symbols of institutional expertise and influence, as Hofstede, Hofstede & Minkov suggested. Algorithmic authority thus provides an interesting alternate framework for discussing how authority is constructed in digital contexts, especially in relation to individuals or structures online who leverage the high profile that algorithmic rankings afford them. This is true in the case of some RDCs who have been able to use social media outlets and ranking systems to their advantage to create a fan, friend or follower base for their work and ideas shared online. Digital media literacy and expertise have allowed some individuals who hold no official institutional connection or position to rise as prominent voices for their respective religious communities. The work of digital creatives online, especially on public discourse platforms such as blogs and social media, creates opportunities for them to rise in prominence online so they become seen as the public face of a given religious belief or community in ways that present them as a sort of religious authority. How algorithmic culture and the orienting logic of a numerically driven authority that allows a certain category of RDCs to be intentionally and unintentionally presented as authorities online will be explored further in this study.

However, basing our understanding of how authority functions within a digital culture solely on the notion of algorithmic authority is highly problematic. Here authority is based on an external system of connotation that is perceived as neutral. However, research has shown that algorithmic authority is a system laden with bias, privileging a numerical orientation over a human-centered one (i.e. Lustig et al. 2016; Dörr & Hollnbuchner, 2017). It has also been shown by those in the field of Marketing and Advertising that it is a system that can be easily manipulated (i.e., Wilson-Barnao, 2017; Kitchin, 2017). While algorithmic authority has drawn attention to individuals who are often labeled as the new leaders or authorities in different contexts, it is important that we further interrogate the claim what kind of authority they actually have. This involves looking at the distinct ways in which algorithmic authority is utilized by digital media workers.

Algorithmic authority as lived out by media influencers, thought leaders and digital leaders

In the past decade, in the fields of Business Studies, Digital Marketing, and Public Relations, discussions of authority in digital contexts have often involved highlighting a number of new actors emerging through engagement with digital platforms and environments. These individuals are aware of their ability to influence others online and understand that in digitally mediated networks this involves understanding algorithmic culture and its ability to leverage traits of this culture to their advantage.

It is also important to note that, in this study, we explore the extent to which RDCs with places of prominence online have actual influence within specific religious contexts, as well as what this authority is and looks like. Therefore, while algorithmic authority provides a framework for considering how new types of individuals have gained prominence or influence online, it does not provide an exhaustive or complete way for explaining how authority is being constructed in new ways in a digital age.

Employing algorithmic or online authority is often described in terms of individuals taking on the role of a "thought leader," "media influencer" or "digital leader." These terms have become popular descriptions of who has authority within online–offline organizations and digitally driven communication spaces. While there is no firm agreement on the exact definitions of these different terms, or how these roles should be distinguished in current literature, a brief review of discussions in popular Business and Management seems to suggest there are some consistent factors.

Central is the attempt for scholars and business consultants to try to make a distinction between individuals who are seen as having authority, and those who have influence in digital contexts. As seen in previous discussions in this chapter, the concept of authority is often associated with traditional notions of leadership, as in, those who have power derived from recognized institutional positions and structures (Grimes, 1978). In such contexts, leaders seen as having authority are marked by their ability to facilitate actual change in a given organizational context by having subordinates or support structures who follow their advice and instructions and act accordingly. This is differentiated from the notion of having influence, which equates to having a public platform for sharing ideas, but not necessarily having committed followers willing to act on one's ideas (Grimes, 1978). Simply put, within current discussions of authority versus influence, especially in popular Management and Business Studies media, authority is associated with traditional notions of leadership within a company or organization, where social, political and institutional structures grant an individual the right and ability to make decisions that are heeded by others, whereas influence is used to describe individuals who have power due to their visibility, especially digital media prominence, afforded to them by strong communication skills and wide ranging social networks (Kuhel, 2017). This helps frame our understanding of the distinctions and different leadership roles taken on by RDCs in this study.

Media influencers

Media influencer is a title often given to individuals who use social media such as Twitter or Facebook, or even bloggers, who have achieved a notable following online. In other words, they have strong algorithmic authority because what they say or do online has gained a large audience or group of followers. Their social-media accounts become a metaphorical megaphone through which they are able to broadcast their thoughts and opinions to a larger audience. As Booth and Matic (2011) argued, "the 'nobodies' of the past are now the new 'somebodies' demanding the attention of communication professionals who seek continuous engagement with targeted consumers throughout the various channels of the social web"

(p. 184). Thanks to digital media, everyone has the potential to create a platform for themselves. Media influencer may also refer to individuals who may have had a strong media presence before social media, and whose use of social media has simply solidified their prominence as a special topics expert. Yet while it could be argued these individuals have algorithmic authority based on the attention their ideas can be given by a large audience, this may not be reflective of their actual sphere of influence. In other words, their ability to actually influence individuals to act on their shared beliefs may be much harder to determine and achieve. Thus, these media influencers are often criticized for having a large reach for the message but a small reach in their ability to facilitate action in others related to that message. Also, their importance can be judged rather ephemeral; since their position is awarded by a fickle public, it can be easily lost if their position or work comes under criticism or their source of credibility is labeled as suspect.

Thought leaders

The term "thought leaders" is often associated with idea of media influencers, as they frequently gather their audience and gain prominence online and through other media outlets. However, they are distinguished by their expertise. Whereas media influencers' expertise lies in their ability to network and leverage digital media to gain an audience, thought leaders possess recognized specialist knowledge in a specific field that makes them the go-to person in that area (Prince & Rogers, 2012). Brosseau (2014) described thought leaders as those who are able to build a tribe of followers and create a clear blueprint of how they can influence their followers to enact change, whether that be in terms of change within an industry or social change, such as in an activist context. Thought leaders focus more on the knowledge they possess, which draws their audience to them, rather than the technology they use to build their sphere of influence. Yet a large part of the platform of the thought leader is linked to their algorithmic authority, and their status is closely linked to the size of the audience they are able to garner and leverage. Therefore, it can be argued that a notable portion of their influence is dependent on their digital presence and visibility as means to garner the investment of others in their ideas and positions.

Digital leaders

Unlike the previous two positions, the category of digital leaders is presented as a leadership role that relies on combining new and established notions of authority in digital contexts. This, I argue, offers a more robust characterization for discussing ideas of how authority is moderated between online and offline contexts and between traditional and digitally driven institutions. The concept of digital leaders is drawn from Management Studies literature and is based on a hybrid notation of how contemporary leadership functions, stressing the need for leaders to combine traditional management strength with digital skills and fluencies (Kane, 2018).

Digital leaders are described as leaders or movement makers who do not just have a media platform that garners public attention, as is seen with social media influencers. They are like thought leaders, seen as those who have a group of people committed to their ideas and willing to be led in accordance with them. Yet management scholars stress that digital leaders are those whose authority begins from a place of exhibiting traditional leadership skills (Kane, 2018). Digital leaders are described as first possessing core leadership strengths, such as those highlighted by French and Raven's (1959) classic characterization of expert power, where leadership is based on factors like individuals possessing organizational, skill-based and communicative expertise. This means digital leaders hold a credibility drawn from their position and reputation that reaches beyond media visibility and prominence. In other words, digital fluency did elevate them as leaders, but they were recognized as having expertise that was only magnified with their use of or gained expertise in technology. This means they have referent power, where one's followers trust the leader's knowledge and decision-making abilities. This knowledge and these competencies become the base upon which newer digitally influenced skills are developed (Larson, Miller, & Ribble, 2009).

Peladue, Herzog and Acker, (2017) stated that digital leaders must also possess traits exemplified by the nature of digital culture, including creativity, experimentality and highly developed collaborative and network abilities. This means digital leaders must know how to work on and facilitate team projects, as work has become more decentralized and collaborative within may work sectors. They must also be willing to experiment and not be embarrassed when new technologies or strategies do not work out as planned. Finally, they must be able and willing to facilitate collaborations across institutional and organizational boundaries so that their initiatives and teams remain dynamic and adaptable to changes within their industry and organizational context.

This combination of drawing authority from both traditional and network or digitally influenced leadership skills becomes very evident in the digital strategists studied extensively in Chapter 6.

So presenting the media-making narrative entails also identifying RDCs' perception of authority drawn from their engagement with and perceptions of the digital environment. These digital actors of the social media influencer, thought leader and digital leader become concrete ways to talk about RDCs' perceptions of authority in digital culture related to their work. I suggest we must consider not only how they describe their work in terms of institutional positions and knowledge mastery but also how they see the digital sphere as a place of authority performance.

Contextualizing authority in the study of RDCs

So where does this leave us, and how should we understand authority online and offline in relation to the study of RDCs?

As we discussed, seeing authority as a role offers us a way to describe how specific actors establish themselves as leaders and allows us to pinpoint the techniques used so that their followers buy into their leadership position and expertise. Weber's classic categories of leadership become helpful tools for defining who are seen as leaders and how they establish their influence and loyalty. This approach is helpful when discussing how certain individuals seek to function and maintain their religious authority through how they interact with others online and offline. In Chapter 5, we shall see how this notion of authority as a role is crucial for understanding a specific class of RDCs called digital spokespersons. These RDCs frame their work in relation to the leader–follower model. Even though their digital work gives them a public platform, they describe it in such a way that shows they seek to maintain traditional roles and allegiances by affirming the institutional structure, which they serve within. Yet role-based authority overemphasizes the idea that authority is embodied by specific individuals, who can be easily identified and are typically tied to formal social structures.

Seeing authority as power places emphasis on authority as a social system of control that pervades our world and everyday reality. For Foucault, power is a condition existing within society that all individuals are subject to and therefore must negotiate with and resist, lest we become restrained by it. This approach focuses our attention on the pervasiveness of authority in culture, where everyone has potential access to, if they only understand how to navigate their social context and leverage it for their purposes. We will see this understanding of authority as power clearly manifested in the RDC category of digital entrepreneurs. The notion of power as a condition enables them to see authority as a tool to be leveraged to their advantage to promote their digital expertise. However, seeing authority primarily as power-based tends to suggest that authority negotiations and strategies are clearly visible and consciously enacted. This does not account for instances where individuals emerge as unintentional authorities due to the prominence online of their work, or as invisible authorities when their digital strategies have broader religious impacts than they intended.

Seeing authority as relational focuses our attention on the process of communication between different actors or groups within a given social context, establishing a discreet relationship. For Lincoln, relational authority is established through patterns of discourse that frame the social reality and interaction between specific individuals, such as the speaker and audience. The relational model of authority draws our attention to how discourse can be used to describe and justify certain actions or affiliations. In Chapter 6, we will see that RDCs referred to as digital strategists engage relational-based authority as they describe how their institutional affiliations, coupled with their technological expertise, garner them a unique position within their religious communities. It is this dual enactment of authority, which grants them institutional, and digital attention and recognition for their work, though emphasis on relational authority as derived from narratives presented by the dominant members of a given relationship may not accurately portray the nature of the relationship. Embracing digital media affordances can introduce uneven social dynamics to offline affiliations, or even unconsciously subvert this authority in unforeseen ways.

Finally, seeing authority as algorithmic presents a view of authority specifically identified as emerging from computer-based systems and structures. Algorithmic authority focuses on the notion that digital data is trustworthy because computer algorithms offer an unbiased presentation of the most reputable information sources available online. Lustig and Nardi defined algorithmic authority as a technological framework that reinterprets the structure of the social world through these numerically driven and reputation systems. This means that technological culture is privileged over human culture as the basis for determining what is authoritative. It is true that all three classifications of RDCs emphasize their levels of technological fluency and expertise as part of the basis of their authority or influence in digital contexts. The importance they place on embracing digital technologies and its embrace by digital creatives also seems to suggest they place a great deal of trust or privilege in the culture created by computer networks. However, algorithmic authority suggests technological fluency is the sole basis for understanding authority in a digital world, a view that fails to acknowledge how digital creatives also rely on other skills and capabilities to build their digital profiles and proficiencies as reputable experts online. We explore this more in the next chapter, where we introduce in more detail the three categories of RDCs briefly noted earlier. Also, in Chapter 3 and onwards, I explore how digital entrepreneurs, spokespersons and strategists rely on offline or traditional forms of know-how and leadership traits to frame themselves as digital professionals with authority. Detailed descriptions of their work and the relationships they seek to build or maintain with their religious communities show how many digital entrepreneurs exhibit traits of media influencer, digital spokespersons perform as thought leaders and digital strategists use the logic of digital leaders in their online–offline negotiations.

This overview shows each approach to authority—as role, power, relational or algorithmic based—has its strengths and weaknesses, and its advantages and disadvantages. This is especially true when considering which approach is best applied to the study of how religious authority is viewed by different categories of RDCs in this study. This is because a key finding of this research is that each group of RDCs perceives their relationship to traditional religious leaders and established religious institutions in very different ways. There is no one-size-fits-all theoretical approach to authority that can be applied evenly to all types of RDCs interviewed in this study. Rather, the approaches to authority discussed in this chapter provide a toolbox of resources from which to draw, and set down key conversational partners with which to engage. Ideas expressed here help us identify and discuss the differing views of authority performed by digital entrepreneurs, spokespersons and strategists investigated in this study.

Chapter 2

Defining religious digital creatives

As noted in the introduction and last chapter, this book explores how a specific group of actors, religious digital creatives (RDCs), can be seen as religious authorities by the ways they engage technology within specific religious communities and contexts. In order to more fully understand the ways religious authority is conceived of and practiced in the life and work of RDCs, this chapter focuses on describing these actors in more detail. RDCs in this study fit into one of three categories: Digital entrepreneurs, digital spokespersons or digital strategists. Each performs a distinctive kind of digital work and has a unique identity that needs to be clarified. However, before we can describe these three types of RDCs in detail, a little more contextualization is necessary.

This chapter begins with an overview of how authority has been approached within Digital Religion Studies. This exploration then moves to providing an overview of the main approach scholars have taken in this area of study, i.e., to study authority online in terms of the challenges and opportunities the internet poses to specific religious leaders and structures. This then leads to describing a new authority role I identify in this study as surfacing within many contemporary Christian communities, that of RDCs. Defining who these RDCs are and how they function as religious authorities requires a close reading of an early essay from studies of religion and the internet that talks about new religious interpreters emerging within digital culture. Jon Anderson wrote prophetically in 1999 about the rise of three types of religious interpreters he saw emerging through Muslim use of the internet. His classification becomes the basis for describing and defining the different types of Christian digital creatives investigated in this research: digital entrepreneurs, digital spokespersons and digital strategists. This also enables us to consider how they perform and can be seen as new forms of religious authority within their respective faith communities and organizations.

Perspectives on studying religious authority in digital religion studies

Within the three decades of research on digital religion, a clear continuum of responses has surfaced in regards to how religious groups, especially leaders, have perceived the internet. This has ranged from religious groups viewing the internet as a threat, an opportunity or a medium requiring uneasy alliance. Pauline Cheong (2013) offered the best assessment to date of dominant responses traditional religious leaders and communities have made to the internet. She suggested that three core logics have been at work within various religious groups' responses to the internet. These logics inform how religious leaders understand internet technologies and the cultures they create, and can be described as the logic of disjuncture and displacement, the logic of continuity and complementarity and the logic of dialectics and paradox.

Cheong suggested most religious groups are initially influenced by the logic of disjuncture and displacement in their response to the internet. Here the internet is perceived as a place where traditional religious authority, be it religious leaders or hierarchies, is primarily challenged. Established religious structures encounter disjuncture when their authority intersects with new media technologies and spaces which create "upheaval and/or disconnectedness" to their functions and ways of being (Cheong, 2013, pp. 74–75). Displacement occurs as traditional leaders see themselves as being replaced by webmasters and online discussion moderators as the new religious gatekeepers of knowledge and religious identity within digital culture. Scholars have noted the internet facilitates the rise of "instant experts," allowing people to rise to positions of influence through perceived expertise online while bypassing time-honored training or prescribed initiation rites that would establish their position offline (i.e., Berger & Ezzy, 2004; Krogh & Pillfant, 2004). The internet is seen as a sphere that alters ideas about what constitutes valid or accepted sources of religious authority, because it offers individuals the ability to push back against offline religious power hierarchies by introducing new forms of authority online (i.e., Herring, 2005). Internet users are seen as being able to override the influence of offline authority systems by taking advantage of opportunities to explore and share private discourses or information that they may not have access to offline (Helland, 2007). This enables individuals and groups to create sites of alternative community discourse challenging traditional, legitimate sources of sacred knowledge (Turner, 2007). Essentially, this logic frames the internet as a threat to established authority roles and structures, as individuals have the opportunity to communicate their own interpretations, bypassing recognized offline religious authorities.

Next, Cheong suggested that as internet use became more integrated into society, a second logic surfaced, which she described as the logic of continuity and complementarity. Instead of seeing the internet primarily as a place where religious authority was undermined, she noted religious leaders began to conceive of it as a space where they might be able to leverage technology in order to reassert their influence and power in a new context. This is done when religious groups and strategic actors achieve digital media literacy and learn how to use digital platforms and tools to their own ends. When this happens, religious authorities begin to see their relationship to digital media as one of continuity "characterized instead by connectedness, succession and negotiation" (Cheong, 2013, p. 78). Thus, the internet is now framed as a space of opportunity enabling offline authorities to perpetuate and augment their established practices and positions of control. This can be done in a number of ways. Offline religious authorities may survey their members' online practices, monitor members' presentations of communal beliefs and identity and even infiltrate online forums created to offer alternative spaces of discourse outside traditional structures (i.e., Barker, 2005). Others may establish official policies or filtering tools in order to define acceptable internet use and thereby control online behaviors, including putting public pressure on community members who seek to be the face of the community online (i.e., Campbell & Golan, 2011). Yet as recognized religious leaders have become savvier in their understanding and use of digital media, we see the internet also aids them in maintaining and reasserting online authority that they already possess offline. Religious leaders may act as strategic arbiters of religious information and interpretation online and so affirm online a previously established relationship between leader and follower (i.e., Cheong, Huang, & Poon, 2011a). So the internet reinforces previously established offline leadership roles and structures, creating a continuity of authority between offline and online contexts.

Finally, Cheong described the logic of dialectics and paradox, a response that lies between the extremes of fear of technology and enthusiastic embrace of the internet. This highlights the simultaneous "weakening and strengthening of religious authority" offered by the internet to religious groups (Cheong, 2013, p. 82). This logic stresses that the internet simultaneously challenges and affirms offline religious authorities. The dialectic is "understanding the management of conflicting tensions, uneven games, multiple opportunities, ambivalences, and challenges that new media users, like religious leaders, face within their online and offline experience" (Cheong, 2013, p. 82). The paradox lies in the fact that both new online and old offline authority figures must negotiate between the unique technical and social affordances offered by new media and existing patterns of authority defining religious contexts. This logic can be summed up by the concept of "shifting authority," coming out of my previous work summarizing what scholars of digital religion have learned about the nature of religious practices online after 15 years of research:

> Shifting authority notes there is a shift occurring within traditional understandings of religious power structures through the institution of new gatekeepers and authority roles and structures online. This means authority within a networked structure creates challenges for both new and old authorities, as offline leaders seek to solidify their previously established power and new digital creatives vie for influence online. This raises important issues of legitimacy, authenticity and status of authority online within digital social spheres.
>
> (Campbell, 2012b, p. 84)

Here I argued many traditional religious authorities encounter a shift as they are forced to negotiate with new practices and relationships occurring because of interactions between online and offline spaces and cultures. New forms of religious leadership, such as webmasters and theological bloggers, emerge in digital contexts, and these actors must negotiate their place within long-established religious systems of knowledge and influence. In addition, conventional religious authorities are forced to adapt to patterns of communication and being within new digital culture, which is based on an algorithmic authority that runs counter to previous status systems (Clark, 2011). This can be seen in work conducted by Cheong & Poon (2008) on Buddhist communities' negotiations with the internet and how these shape communicative patterns and practices between religious leaders and members of associated organizations. They argued the internet can create perverse or fraught relationships within religious communities, in that digital spaces decrease religious organizations' monopoly of control over religious knowledge. Though digital spaces create unique networks of communication between groups and actors, they found these new configurations may not be as effective in maintaining close relationships for these groups in comparison to established offline patterns of interaction. This dialectic encountered by both online and offline forms of religious authority raises important questions regarding who represents the legitimate voice for a particular religious community in the digital age, what processes must be in place to constitute these positions and how such status is solidified and maintained.

So when the question is posed, "Does the internet challenge or empower religious authority in digital culture," the answer is yes, it does BOTH. It challenges AND empowers emerging and established authorities simultaneously, but in different ways. New authority roles online can challenge and undermine the position of traditional religious leaders, while alternative voices are challenged to negotiate with already established religious structures and practices. Digital content creators and technologists are empowered as people grant them influence due to their prominence in online religious settings; traditional religious leaders may also be empowered to establish their offline influence online as they embrace digital tools and platforms.

This paradox is at the heart of this study, where we seek to explore the relationship between RDCs and recognized religious leaders of the communities in which they seek to operate. However, careful readers of the above will note that the term authority still remains slightly vague and amorphous. In the discussion above, we see scholars in digital religion have used authority to refer to religious leaders, organizations and structures, often with little differentiation made about what specific form of authority is being referred to. This is a problem frequently noted in much early work in Digital Religion Studies, where scholars emphasized the fact that religious authority is often challenged or empowered, but what they mean by authority is often not clearly articulated. So before we can unpack the particular authority roles under exploration in this study, we need to further consider how different approaches to what constitutes authority online and offline have informed digital religion scholars' study of the nature of authority.

Attempts to differentiate authority online in digital religion studies

While authority has often been studied in Digital Religion Studies, in most works it has been a poorly defined concept. Dawson (2000) provided one of the first attempts to outline key areas where authority was being challenged within online religious activity. These included the potential "proliferation of misinformation and disinformation" (p. 43) by opponents of particular religious groups or disgruntled insiders, the "loss of control over religious materials" by religious organizations and providing "new opportunities for grassroots forms of witnessing" (Dawson, 2000, pp. 43–44), thus encouraging the rise of unofficial or alternative voices in contrast to traditional discourses. While Dawson did not explore these questions beyond simply noting their importance, he clearly drew attention to the fact that religious roles, structures and texts are distinctly challenged by online culture and practices. This supports my argument for the need to clearly define the study of authority online, as the term can encompass multiple forms.

I have argued for the need for a more nuanced approach to the study of authority online. In "Who's got the power? Religious authority and the Internet," I identified several different layers of authority influenced by religious activity online (Campbell, 2007). I suggested each needs to be explored separately, especially authority in relation to hierarchy, structure, ideology and text. First, I suggested the need to pay attention to religious hierarchy, which refers to the authority figures and roles existing both online and offline that may influence users' relationships to the internet. Recognized religious leaders (such as imams, clerics, rabbis and pastors) who typically serve as community interpreters of religious knowledge and practice are often challenged by new authority figures (such as webmasters, forum moderators and bloggers) emerging online and performing similar roles. Religious practice online raises important questions about how much influence these new actors have and how their roles may shape a given religious community offline as well as online. Paying attention to how officially recognized religious roles respond to the internet or seek to culture it in particular ways also becomes crucial. Scholars studying religion and the internet have paid particular attention to the ways new religious leadership roles online influence traditional authority figures. For instance, Thumma (2000) found the internet had the potential to change congregational hierarchies, as previously marginalized "techies" take on new leadership roles when they serve as church webmasters. Similarly, Anderson (1999), whose work is explored in more detail later in this chapter, examined the roles of webmasters and online moderators as new agents of authority with the potential to influence traditional authority structures. Thus, I argue attention should be given to the character, perception and role these religious interpreters may have within the local faith communities and tradition as a whole. This approach will be central to this study; however other approaches exist and are worth noting briefly here.

Authority can be approached as the study of certain religious or organizational structures that support conventions of community practice, such as how the community worships, trains leaders, passes along information and stays connected. Online we see traditional religious structures both being imported to or reinvented on the internet—e.g., educational institutions and even worship spaces—as well as new or alternative structures being created, such as independently created study or meditation groups. Thus, it is valuable to explore the relationship between structures or channels of authority created by established offline groups and those formed by independent groups online. This requires careful consideration of the background and roots of various religious structures established online, as well as an examination of how they function compared to traditional organizations or comparable offline forms. Also, because the collaborative and interactive nature of the internet can make church structures and gatekeeping processes transparent, traditional networks and protocols may be challenged by the fact that private conversations easily become public and/or are quickly disseminated. This may lead some groups to seek to control their online presence or monitor the behaviors of those engaged in alternate religious spaces and structures. Barzilai-Nahon and Barzilai's (2005) and Livio and Tenenboim's (2007) studies of ultra-Orthodox Jews' use of the internet found that rabbis often expressed fear concerning the internet. Online spaces undermine their ability to control community members' behavior by removing that behavior from the community's watchful eye and placing it in individually controlled spheres. Thus, the internet may especially challenge the structures of fundamentalist communities, as it offers community members the chance to create alternate spaces of discourse and social engagement.

In my initial mapping of different approaches to authority, I also noted exploring religious ideology as a distinctive form. Religious ideologies refer to narratives or discourse used by a religious group to reflect and help establish a certain system of belief and support specific patterns of behavior within a given religious community. The internet can play an important role in confirming, controlling or countering a group's religious identity construction. It is important not only to pay attention to the patterns of discourse generated within a setting or by a particular group online, but also to consider the language used to frame the internet in a particular light. Language is a powerful tool for shaping views about technology, and a group's discourse about technology often reveals their core religious beliefs and thus the identity they seek to project in a networked context. Scholars are recognizing the need to pay attention to the orienting narrative used by groups to justify their presence online or their engagement with specific digital media as part of their identity management or public relations strategy. For example, Lawrence (2002) found that expressions of Islam online potentially affected traditional forms of Islamic authority by preferencing the notion of global community or structures over local ones. He also found many Islamic websites employed metaphors from traditional, conservative Islam as a way to reinforce global structures and perceptions and suggested that "cyberspace, like social space, to be effectively Muslim, must be monitored" in order to ensure its proper use (Lawrence, 2002, p. 240). Thus, we see discourse plays an important role in promoting a particular outlook regarding the internet and correlating behaviors.

Finally, I suggested focus could be given to seeing authority in terms of the religious texts within a given religious community. Here authority is enacted in the way these texts guide and structure the life of the group. In this approach, attention should be paid to the role traditional religious texts (i.e., Bible, Quran, Torah, etc.) serve in the offline community, and whether they play the same role in the online religious contexts. Consideration is given to how traditional texts are portrayed or interacted with online, as well as how interactivity may shape community members' relationships with the text in positive or problematic ways. The role of texts in a digital information society has become an important area of conversation, though little scholarly work has been done. A notable exception is Charles Ess's edited collection, *Critical Thinking and the Bible in the Age of New Media* (2004), which investigated how the written word may be transformed as traditional approaches and interpretive processes to religious texts are revamped online. The internet raises many issues concerning the role the internet can play in validating religious texts or "canonizing" new ones.

Distinguishing between these different layers or types of religious authority, I argue, is essential for studying the role the internet plays in creating new possibilities and challenges related to religious authority. Only by recognizing the specific form of authority at work within a given context can we uncover the specific issues and challenges the internet raises for a given religious group or context. Thus, identifying the distinct *form* of authority being investigated—such as hierarchies or roles, structures of authority, official ideologies or beliefs of a community and official texts that serve to legitimize a specific group—becomes essential. Such differentiation helps scholars more accurately address and make claims about what specific forms of authority are being destabilized or supported by online practice and internet culture.

I argue this perspective is central to investigating the influence of RDCs, as they represent both a new type of authority role within religious institutions and signal the potential for new types of authority structures to emerge through opportunities created around digital platforms. In this study focus is placed on RDCs as expressing new authority roles. This also draws attention to relationships between these actors and established religious authorities. In this book, I show how RDCs can both act as gatekeepers of information and shapers of identity for religious groups they work with or for.

The remainder of this chapter introduces the work and role of digital creatives as unique actors enacting new understandings of authority within digital culture. On the basis of the overview provided in the introduction, I assert the dynamic technological features of internet technologies and computer-networked platforms facilitate and even encourage the rise of new actors of authority within religious communities. These RDCs can serve as public voices or create platforms that influence how religious institutions function and are conceived of in digital culture. In turn, these religious authority actors are faced with unique challenges when they intersect with established offline forms of religious authority. This means understanding the rise of different forms of RDCs, the religious and digital practices they engage in and the responses religious leaders and institutions have to their presence and work is essential.

The predicted rise of new religious authorities in digital culture

As previously noted, scholars of digital religion have argued the internet can facilitate and create unique classes of religious leaders. Dawson, Cheong and others have suggested engagement in digital environments enables the rise of new gatekeeping roles, which can either control or provide new levels of access to institutional knowledge. The online forum manager, moderator, webmaster and social media-content producer all become types of information brokers that can influence what is known about the different religious traditions and communities and how they are seen by a larger public. While many studies over the last two decades have analyzed numerous ways internet users can bypass or challenge traditional gatekeepers online, little systematic analysis has been done to identify the specific types of authority roles found online and their defining characteristics.

Anderson, in the book *New Media in the Muslim World: The Emerging Public Sphere* (Eickelman & Anderson, 1999), wrote an essay wherein he noted several challenges the internet could pose to religious authority. He argued special attention needed to be given to considering how the internet constitutes a new public space, giving rise to new forms of Islamic interpreters who have the potential to reframe religious discourse and authority in ways that impact Muslims both online and offline. He went on to discuss a range of ways the internet facilitates, and even encourages, new types of religious actors and authority structures to appear through computer-networked platforms and suggested this could have a far-reaching impact upon the Muslim *ummah* and society as a whole. A careful reading of Anderson's essay illuminates predicted areas in which the internet would give rise to distinct classes of religious interpreters and forms of religious interpretation. Many scholars of digital religion have referenced Anderson's work, an important contribution to early discussions of the potential challenges the internet posed to accepted notions of authority within religious communities and traditions. Yet to date, no careful analysis of the specific themes he highlighted has been conducted. As noted earlier, authority online has remained an uncritically explored category in much scholarly work. Yet Anderson can be seen as a prophetic voice noting some tangible issues and areas related to authority online in need of further exploration. Thus, this chapter interrogates Anderson's arguments more closely, in order to identify the concrete, predicted classes of religious authority he saw as online. These different classes of religious interpreter become the basis for the categories of RDCs investigated in detail in this book.

It is important to note the Anderson essay highlighted three ways in which religious interpretation could emerge and be facilitated by the internet, specifically in the form of unique authority (1) roles, (2) spaces or systems of discourse and (3) discourse strategies. This understanding of authority as either roles, systems or discourses acknowledged very different ways of conceiving and explaining how authority may be enacted in digital culture. This also harkens back to arguments in my previous work (Campbell 2007, 2010) that called for a more nuanced approach to studies of what constitutes authority online and treating each form as behaving and constituting itself differently. Here I suggest that Anderson's work presents us with a useful way to distinguish different categories of authority emerging online. His focused reflection on early Islamic expressions of what he saw as new types of religious interpreters online provides a valuable starting point for identifying new categories and outlining some concrete examples of how different actors, structures and discourses found online can be seen as enacting religious authority found in digital platforms. While I have written elsewhere about the religious structures and discourse strategies that can be drawn from Anderson's essay (Campbell 2016), the purpose here is to discuss on the interpretive roles Anderson presented, which relate most closely to this study of RDCs and their work in online and religious organizational environments.

Anderson's religious interpreters as a new class of authority

Anderson began his discussion by arguing the internet is giving rise to unique classes of interpreters. In other words, the internet's technological affordances—such as interactivity, asynchronous communication, and the ability to transcend the time, space and hierarchies found in traditional mass media communication—empower new individuals and ways to speak out on behalf of Islam. This gives those who do not perform or hold traditional authority roles recognized by "Islamic organizations and activist intellectuals" new communicative opportunities (Anderson, 1999, p. 41). These "new interpreters of Islam" arise from different sectors of digital culture. Anderson's study focused on the dominant online mediums of the 1990s—the period in which his study took place—which were mainly online forums such as email lists, BBSs and newsgroups, and the authority roles that he saw emerging within these contexts. Most notably, he suggested the internet encourages three types of actors to speak out online, each type of which he described as taking on a specific role or authority. These were: "creole pioneers," "spokesperson activists" and "reformer-critics," which he described as acting with very different intentions and realms of influence online.

Creole pioneers

Creole pioneers, Anderson argued, represent individuals with professional-technical qualifications and ready access to the internet, who "bring religious interest on-line as after-hours interests" (Anderson, 1999, p. 50). He drew on Benedict Anderson's discussion of creolization, which maintained new identities are created for individuals and groups through the mixing of traditional and modern cultures, to highlight how the internet offers opportunities for new forms of identity to be constructed. Anderson suggested the internet creates new cultural actors who, due to their expertise, serve as mediators between technological culture and their religious community. Creole pioneers establish "intermediate communities of discourse" or mixed communities in which their instrumental and technical skills elevate them to levels of prominence online that can spill over into other spheres. These individuals may spend significant amounts of time online because of their work as computer scientists, programmers or webmasters, but they also bring with them their passions and hobbies, which can include their faith. Thus, they represent a growing presence in online forums like the dominant social media of the 1990s—email lists and newsgroups—allowing them to serve in multiple roles and contexts simultaneously. Creole pioneers represent a blending of identities that can also lead to blurring between professional roles and personal activities (Anderson, 1999, p. 43). In the case of Islam online, most of these individuals initially came from the West, where internet access was less regulated and readily available. Creole pioneers may use their technical skills in their free time to facilitate or create religious online discussions, such as how to lead a Muslim life in a non-Muslim society. Also, as early adopters of the internet, they may be innovators in building platforms or software that facilitate not only their work but also their hobbies and religious interests. Creole pioneers represent a mixed class of both skills and interests; they can become unintentional religious interpreters by default by simply being first online to represent their religious community in a given online context.

Spokesperson-activists

The second category Anderson noted is that of the "spokesperson-activist of established institutions" (Anderson, 1999, p. 44). The spokesperson-activist draws on established interpretive patterns, techniques and structures—e.g., those used by the *ulama* (recognized religious leaders) from a given Muslim community in their engagement with Hadith and Quran—in order to establish their rhetorical authority online. In other words, they may defer to or draw on recognized interpretations of religious law, moral codes or other discourses to justify their activities or positions online. These individuals may be *imams* or a teacher in an offline Muslim community and seek to use the internet to affirm Islamic teachings and practices. However, spokesperson-activists hold strictly to the dogmas of the specific organization or group they represent (Anderson, 1999, p. 44). Spokesperson-activists primarily seek to replicate or advocate offline authority structures online, while the reformer-critic mirrors the internet's tendencies toward preferencing flattened hierarchies and collaboration over formal structures.

Reformer-critics

The third authority role highlighted by Anderson is the "reformer-critic." These individuals seek to interpret religion in a world of competing voices found both online and offline. The internet offers space where individuals can present a distinctive narrative related to their religious tradition or community, especially through the creation of religiously oriented websites that allow them to extend their religious views into new public forums. According to Anderson, reformer-critics are those with a predetermined reason for going online; they are motivated by a conscious religious or political agenda. They may create a religious website that promotes their religious beliefs, or take a vocal role in a discussion forum to highlight their personal understanding of community theology. They use the internet to recruit others to a specific viewpoint or to gain access to a wider audience online for their message. These reformer-critics can represent alternative groups, using the internet for mobilizing their agenda and witnessing to their belief in the new public sphere (Anderson, 1999, p. 49). They see the internet as a space to recruit others to a specific group or belief, and their work online can be seen as propagandizing, encouraging people to act in certain ways. Thus, reformer-critics often arise as actors of recognized fundamentalist groups, yet are often driven by a personal rather than an official or sanctioned agenda in their online activities. They embrace and leverage new communication technology with a focused agenda, in hope of reshaping the online social sphere to specific ends through their presence online.

Reformer-critics are similar to spokesperson-activists, as they similarly draw from on a broad range of official sources or interpretive forms to make arguments. Yet they also differ in that reformer-critics have a greater freedom to self-select sources and rationale, which they present in ways that meet their particular needs or agenda. Together, the creole pioneer, spokesperson-activist and reformer-critic demonstrate a unique range of different interpretive roles the internet can encourage and facilitate online.

Defining religious digital creatives as actors with authority

In this study of digital creatives, the term is used to encompass a variety of different types of individuals whose digital work places them in public positions within various religious institutions and communities. I suggest that the visibility of their online work elevates them to positions of influence within broader Christian contexts, and as a result, they manifest characteristics of authority. What is meant by authority and how it is understood in these digital spaces and work is a focus of this study that is under continuous interrogation. In the chapters that follow, I describe specific characteristics and actions performed by different groups of RDCs that show many move beyond simply exhibiting agency in their technology choices for personal motivations to work that places them in positions of public prominence and gives them different forms of communal or institutional influence. This means the understanding of authority I am paying attention to here is more than individuals having the ability to act independently of an organizational context. It is when their work gains some sort of recognition and enables them to exert different forms of action that enact change in different ways that can be seen as having influence on or within their respective institutions and their memberships. Thus, this idea is my starting point for understanding what authority tangibly is and how different categories of RDCs manifest this in distinctive ways due to their positions and communal outlook. Therefore, this study starts with the idea of RDCs as having authority based on their digital and/or institutional expertise, having organizational prominence, and possessing the ability to influence decision-making and public perceptions of their religious communities.

Religious digital creatives are understood as those with specialist skills who produce and manage born-digital resources and/or content. Digital creatives are producers of artistic or evocative media content or resources, often motivated by a personal passion or business agenda. Yet due to the algorithmic authority inherent in digital culture—social trust garnered from informational tools and rankings—they emerge as thought leaders and hence, cultural authorities, for particular communities. RDCs are those involved in digital content production and management with the aim of using these skills to serve a religiously motivated agenda or population. They create a variety of online resources and/or content for personal ministry sites and/or institutionally based outlets online in order to influence both personal and communal agendas influencing a wider religious community.

Applying Anderson's categories to religious digital creatives

I suggest that the categories presented by Anderson of creole pioneers, spokesperson-activists and reformer-critics provide a helpful starting point for describing and differentiating the RDCs discussed in this study. However, due to nuances of this context, Christian RDCs, and the fact that the technological environment and forms of online religious engagement have evolved further than the landscape Anderson sought to document, I argue his initial categories are in need of some redefinition. Therefore, I use the nuances of classifications as guides rather than as exact definitional categories in this study. Below I introduce modified definitions of Anderson's initial categories and new labels to identify them.

I suggest three new titles that correlate to the ethos of creole pioneers, spokesperson-activists and reformer-critics, but which more accurately describe the work and motivations of certain types of digital creatives. Here I introduce the labels of digital entrepreneurs, digital spokespersons and digital strategists to more accurately reflect the different forms of work and intentions of Christian digital creatives investigated in this study, while still seeking to correlate them to the roles outlined by Anderson in his essay. Along with providing a summary of these modified categories and their work related to digital media, I offer short profiles of RDCs from this study, which exemplify these roles. I also briefly introduce three Catholic RDCs from this study, in order to help the reader more clearly conceptualize the nuances of these roles.

Digital entrepreneurs

Anderson's category of "creole pioneers" serves as the basis for describing *digital entrepreneurs*. Digital entrepreneurs are similar to creole pioneers—they are computer hobbyists or digital professionals who leverage their technical and professional skills to create digital resources for their religious communities. Digital entrepreneurs do their digital creative work outside their normal work activities. They may use their digital skills to design religious apps, software and websites, or to run online discussion forums they describe as serving their religious community. Like creole pioneers, these are individuals who use their professional-technical qualifications and talents to develop religiously oriented digital resources they see as meeting the needs or goals of their community. In this study, digital entrepreneurs typically work in tech-related industries and often have secular employers, yet they associate closely with a specific religious group, such as a church or ministry. They also describe themselves as being compelled or inspired to create digital resources to fulfill a religious goal (i.e., evangelization) or address an underserved religious outreach opportunity online. In this study, I also show how digital entrepreneurs often draw on distinct algorithmic authority strategies to describe and justify their work and influence in their religious communities. For them, their authority is proven by the reach of their ideas and digital activities to a broader public than just their respective religious community.

Eric van den Berg is an example of a Catholic digital entrepreneur. He runs a small digital media company in Holland where he designs websites and does media trainings, mostly for educational and some religious organizations. However, van den Berg is most well known as a blogger and head of the website Katholiek. nl, which he designed and runs on his own time. It has become a central hub for background information on the Catholic Church in Holland, as well as a provider of news and opinions on Church developments. His blogging and work on the website led him to collect some of his writings into two books, *The Handbook on the Internet* and *The Handbook for Church and Social Media*. These books provide not only practical guidance for how religious groups can use the internet but also a theological basis for his understanding of Church engagement with internet technology. Because of the prominence of Katholiek.nl, van den Berg has become known in Holland as an expert on the Catholic Church and so is often consulted by the media to speak on behalf of the Church about various events. This is especially true because, for a long time, his local Church diocese did not have a website or a media officer that journalists could contact. While he described this situation as somewhat uncomfortable, he understands his position online makes him easily accessible. Also, he sees this volunteer work as essentially representing the Church online, so that gives him a feeling of responsibility to speak when the official Church's voice is absent. As van den Berg stated, "When journalists contact me I tell them what my position is, that it is coming from the website, not the diocese. [I] am not official, but to them I am authoritative" (personal interview, March 7, 2013). Thus, van den Berg displays how digital entrepreneurs can achieve public influence through the online prominence of their digital work.

Digital spokespersons

Anderson's category of "spokesperson-activists" forms the basis of *digital spokespersons* explored in this study. Both categories represent individuals who use the internet on behalf of a specific religious institution in order to present that group's beliefs online. Like spokesperson-activists, digital spokespersons typically come from within a specific religious institution and are appointed or asked to do digital work on behalf of that group. However, digital spokespersons differ in that at least part of their role requires them to function as online identity curators. This involves consciously creating or managing the digital presence of their group online. Religious organizations are increasingly seeing the need to employ individuals to do digital media work related to public relations and to manage the online media or presence associated with the institution. These digital spokespersons hold jobs such as media officers, communication workers, webmasters or even church/ parish assistants, requiring them to regularly act as liaisons between the media, the public and their institution and to oversee the online presence and reputation of the groups for which they work. We will discuss how digital spokespersons draw heavily on traditional notions of authority, where authority is attributed to specific roles and expertise. This causes them to seek to contextualize their positions of authority based on their need to employ strategic discourses in their work in relation to institutional roles their superiors hold. In other words, digital spokespersons are often placed in situations that elevate their work in ways that make their profiles very public, and as such, they are perceived as authoritative within their workplace in ways that make them feel uncomfortable, as if they were supposed challengers to traditional institutional leaders.

An example of a Catholic digital spokesperson is James Abbott, webmaster for the Catholic Bishop's Conference of England and Wales. He is in charge of creating and running the bishop's conference websites, as well as developing podcasts and digital training material for the conference. He gained public attention for his design work in 2010 after winning the People's Choice Award at the Christian New Media Awards for the website he developed spotlighting Pope Benedict XVI's visit to the UK that year (www.thepapalvisit.org.uk). The site offered live web streaming, social media links and a chance to interact with other Catholics relative to these events. Abbott knows that while most people in his office just see him as one of the tech guys who works in the basement of the bishop's office in London, he realizes his online work is having a broader impact than most of those involved in the conference realize. He sees his work designing and maintaining the public online face of the conference as deeply theological. He describes it as telling the story of the Church visually and structurally, and he sees web design work as displaying, in part, what it means to be Catholic online, especially to those outside the Church who may come across the site. Abbott sometimes feels uncomfortable in this role as a religious interpreter, especially since he has no theological training. When he has tried to explain his digital work and its potential impact to those he works for, he is typically met with blank stares. This he says indicate they do not understand his concerns or the potential digital media has for shaping people's understanding of Church identity in a digital age. As Abbott stated,

> Religious websites are often the first place people encounter Catholicism today. That means the information we provide and the design I create must put the Church's best face forward. Websites are how people outside the Church read what who we are as a church, and what we stand for.
>
> (personal interview, May 9, 2011)

Abbott demonstrates how digital spokespersons often recognize the importance and potential public impact of digital work more clearly than the institutions they are paid to represent, a situation that makes their digital influence a sphere fraught with tension and complexities.

Digital strategists

Finally, Anderson's idea of the online "reformer-critic" was used as a basis to describe *digital strategists* in this study. Both use digital platforms and tools in order to accomplish a distinct religious agenda. Both view technology as important, able to help them accomplish the mission of their faith in unique ways. They typically leverage already available digital tools and/or platforms to produce digital content for religious ends. However, digital strategists differ from reformer-critics in that they are typically community or organizational insiders. Whereas reformer-critics are often self-appointed religious digital witnesses, outsiders who seek an "official" role for themselves as doctrinal or religious watchdogs, digital strategists truly hold an official role or position within their religious community or institution. Digital strategists interviewed in this study included denominational missionaries who develop digital evangelism tools, bible teachers who create religious initiatives to promote Bible study or prayer, or seminary students who envision developing websites for religious networking and discipleship. Just as reformer-critics are described as using the internet to draw an audience around a particular religious topic or interpretive stance, digital strategists often use digital media to serve strongly focused religious-based goals such as religious education or evangelism. However, unlike Anderson's notion of the reformer-critic, digital strategists typically have a level of institutional expertise and recognized affiliation, so they are not seen as outsiders but as insiders seeking to reform religious institutions. This means they enact a form of hybrid authority as represented by those acting as "digital leaders" as described in Chapter 1. For digital strategists, authority is based on institutional expertise combined with digital experimentation that raises the profile and impact of their work in their sphere of religious influence.

Sister Julie Vieira is an example of a digital strategist. She is co-founder of the website and blog "A Nun's Life Ministry" (http://anunslife.org/) and a member of the Servants of the Immaculate Heart of Mary (IHM), a Catholic religious institute of sisters. Sister Vieira, along with others in her order, became concerned about the decrease in interest in young women joining their order or considering a consecrated religious life commitment. As an avid internet user, she began to envision how her order could use this as a tool to show people what it was really like to be nun and give people online a glimpse beyond the cloister. What started as a blog evolved into a podcast and now a full online resource center, both for religious brothers and sisters to communicate and share stories of their spiritual life journeys and to engage with spiritual seekers online—those just wanting to explore Christianity or Catholicism, or those wanting to learn more about becoming a postulant for IHM or other order. The website has now become part of her official ministry with the order, and she takes its work very seriously. She recognizes most young people would never approach a nun and have the kind of honest and open conversations about life and faith offline with a leader in the church, conversations she regularly has the privilege of sharing with them online. For her, the internet is more than a tool, it is space of holy and sacred engagement between the world and the Church. Sister Vieira says, "By sharing our life online we are opening what it means to pursue a spiritual vocation for the Church, its integrating and bridging ministry in this internet era" (personal Interview, February 11, 2014). Sister Vieira's work demonstrates how digital strategists use technological engagement as a way to redefine their roles within their communities and give them a different kind of public profile and increased sphere of influence beyond their initial remit.

In Chapters 4 through 6, a more detailed investigation of these RDC categories of digital entrepreneurs, spokespersons and strategists is presented. This exploration will focus on their reports of why they do the kind of digital work they do, how they interpret its meaning and the impact these activities have on Christian institutions, in order to uncover how RDCs can be seen as acting out new authority roles within their religious communities and digital spheres

Comments on studying religious digital creatives

Digital religious creatives profiled in this study were identified using a snowball sampling strategy. This was based on the recommendations of scholars, religious leaders and laypersons I interacted with online and at various conference events from 2011 to 2016, where I solicited recommendations for local individuals they felt were doing interesting independent or institution-related religious-oriented digital media work. Due to funding constraints, this research is bounded by the interactions with RDCs in certain geographical locations. Between 2011 and 2016, I was frequently invited as a guest speaker to lecture on my research at various universities and meetings of religious communicators, mostly in Western Europe and North America. These became opportunities for me to conduct in-depth representative interviews with local RDCs and individuals attending those events. *Ergo*, the narratives collected represent a sampling of RDCs from these encounters—a mixture of Protestant and Catholic and non-denominational contexts and a diversity of religious organizational and cultural contexts. In order to provide structure to this diverse sampling of Christian RDCs, a set of criteria was used during interview selection to help establish some consistency and comparability for the sample.

RDCs interviewed for this study shared the following characteristics: Active in digital work for over five years; have a recognizable online profile; were recommended by more than one source as individuals recognized for their digital work and have an identifiable connection with a specific offline Christian denomination, organization or community. Each interviewee was asked the same set of questions related to (a) describing their digital work, (b) ways they saw this work as an extension of their religiosity/faith, (c) their relationship to a specific religious institution and (d) that group's views of their digital work. Informants included representatives from these Christian denominations: Anglican/Episcopalian, Baptist, Catholic, Charismatic, Lutheran, Methodist, Presbyterian and independent Evangelical/Emergent church networks. They represented select Christian RDCs from the USA, Mexico, New Zealand and the following European countries: Belgium, Denmark, France, Germany, Ireland, Italy, the Netherlands, Spain, Sweden, Turkey and the UK.

Interview narratives provided insights into the RDCs' motivations for digital work, how they framed technology use as part of their ministry, and the relationship RDCs reported with the offline faith communities or groups with which they sought to associate. Careful consideration was given to the extent to which RDCs match Anderson's specific categories and descriptions, to see what such data may further reveal about Anderson's predictions about the influence of the internet on religious communities. This study focused on how RDCs navigate their positions in relation to their offline religious communities and the challenges and opportunities this poses to Christian churches and organizations.

Identifying these three categories of RDCs was key in guiding the types of informants interviewed in this study, as well as in considering how these roles might help interpret their responses related to their motivation for using digital technology for religious purposes. It is important to note study focus was placed on RDCs emerging and at work specifically within current Western Christian organizations and communities. While each category of RDCs does different types of work and serves different audiences, each does this digital work by drawing on a common range of assumptions about the nature of technology and its relationship to religion and religiosity.

I recognize any attempt to offer a typology of RDCs comes with its limitations. The intent of this study is not to suggest that all RDCs easily fit into the rigid and mutually exclusive categories presented here. Indeed, it could be argued that some RDCs in this study could be described as straddling more than one of the categories in how they frame their identity and work. This study also does not suggest RDCs can be limited to or categorized only by the three categories identified here. Rather, I assert the informants within this study could be identified as primarily representing the categories of digital entrepreneurs, spokespersons and strategists. Follow-on and further studies of RDCs could indeed find new types of RDCs or variations of these actors. My hope is that the introduction of these specific categories provides a basis for a focused analysis of the work, intentions and authority negotiations of RDCs within this study. I also hope this will serve as the basis for further exploration of RDCs beyond Christian contexts to consider their presence and influence within other religious traditions. I assert the study of RDCs' language and discourse related to technology is vital, as it both reveals distinctive views of how each group sees themselves as religious actors within digital culture and how they understand their relationship to their religious communities. Chapters 1 and 2 provide crucial background information and contextualization for the introduction of the theoretical method used in this study for exploring how RDCs perform as religious authorities.

Chapter 3

Christian digital creatives' performance of authority

Enacting media-making narratives and a technological apologetic

Thus far, RDCs have been presented as a new actor perceived as possessing some form of religious authority within their religious communities or organizations in which they work. Because the technological skills and public communicative tasks these RDCs take on, their digital work often gives them public prominence online that can grant them internal or external influence within their religious institutions. In the previous chapter, I introduced three types of RDCs at work in many Christian religious contexts today, the work they do, and the impact it can have. However, while I suggest identifying RDCs as a new form of religious authority through the roles they take on, this does not fully answer for us what constitutes authority in digital culture in such contexts.

The aim of this chapter is to present the methodological framework used to study Christian digital creatives as those who perform authority through digital engagement. This understanding begins with an introduction to the work of Erving Goffman who, I argue, offers a useful conceptual metaphor to guide this research. His performative approach offers guides for identifying how different Christian RDCs enact various conceptions of authority in their digital work. Goffman's study of individual identity and agency took a dramaturgic perspective that helps us understand RDCs' understanding of authority as a kind of performance. It also focuses attention on how their performance of authority can be identified through careful analysis of what they do and how they speak about their digital work.

During my interactions and interviews with over 120 RDCs interviewed over a six-year period, I discovered two key narratives emerging from the interview transcripts. First, RDCs emphasized the breadth and impact of their digital work, which I call their media-making narrative. These media-making stories reveal the fact that they see their work as embedded within a distinctive understanding of authority drawn from those discussed in Chapter 1. Second, each category of RDCs offers a justification narrative for their digital work, or what I call a technological apologetic. Here they seek to justify their digital activities and their institutional or community impact by framing their activities within a distinctive rationale about how they see or seek to position themselves relative to their religious affiliations. Paying close attention to RDCs' discussions of their work—especially the language used to frame it in terms of being a ministry— and their underlying motivations helps reveal the distinctive interpretation of authority held by each category. This chapter unpacks and outlines a concrete method for reading these media-making stories and their technological apologetic.

While Erving Goffman is not often thought of as a theorist who talks about authority. I will show that his work offers a useful framework for considering how RDCs draw on different understandings of how authority is enacted in both offline and online contexts. This theoretical method, inspired by Goffman, is used to show how, through action and language, a distinct performance of authority is enacted by RDCs.

Approaching authority as a performance through Goffman

I assert a method for studying the ways authority is enacted and understood in digital culture can be found in a very unexpected place—in the work of Erving Goffman and his dramaturgical approach. Goffman was a social psychologist who studied symbolic interactionism, i.e., how humans use various symbols to communicate and represent themselves in society. He is most well known for his work, *The Presentation of Self in Everyday Life* (1990), in which he presented a theoretical discussion of identity using the metaphor of the theater in order to describe human social interaction. He offered the image of humans as actors on a social stage, where they act out certain presentations of themselves. Just as an actor presents to the audience a crafted performance of the character they take on in a play, humans make choices that offer a specific presentation of who they are and how they want to be seen. Important to Goffman's theory are the ideas of the front stage and back stage of the theater. On the front stage, the actor is in performance mode—through language, dress and action they offer a specific image of who they are seeking to portray, an "idealized self." He argued this performance of the self is planned, controlled and consciously constructed for the public. However, backstage—behind the curtain, props and stage set—the actor moves out of performance mode into a representation of their authentic self. This is considered a performance of the self in the private sphere, where individuals' identity become more transparent or, arguably, reveal their "authentic self."

This theoretical approach is known as Goffman's dramaturgical analysis of the self. He used the metaphor of the theater and how actors relate to the stage as a way to describe how identity can be seen as a performance. Goffman presents how individuals negotiate and present their sense of self in their daily lives as if they were actors in a drama. This has become a significant approach within sociology and communication to help understand how one can study people's actions and interactions, by suggesting scholars need to engage in participant-observation in order to study individuals in the backstage. Here, when they stop performing, we see and hear people's true feelings. The dramaturgical perspective is complex, as human performances are complex, and the line between the front and back stage can become blurred, but I argue this approach has helped scholars consider how people perform and maintain their social identities in different public and private settings.

Goffman's dramaturgical approach has been important to scholars who study the internet and investigate how individuals interact and perform their identity online (Miller, 1995). Initially, scholars focused on how the internet may be seen as a new hybrid space, being both public and private, where the private backstage of acting out an authentic self becomes mixed with a public performance of the self (Pinch, 2010). Thus, it can be argued that individuals are able to reveal parts of their authentic self through their combination of and interaction between performances in various digital platforms, from social media to gaming environments. Digital play and communication highlight for researchers' aspects of an individual's true self, as these blurred contexts, along with anonymity and the presentation of multiple selves, can give individuals more control over their performances, while creating a safe place for transparency (Bullingham & Vasconcelos, 2013).

Scholars have however critiqued Goffman's work and interactionism as so focused on the performance of the self and individual identity that it overlooks larger social structures and forces that inform and shape such performances. Some have suggested a key social condition he ignored in his work is the theme of power which, as seen in Chapter 1, is closely linked to discussions of authority contexts and structures. However, recently, scholars have begun to observe that Goffman's work offers some important tools and concepts for understanding what power is and how it actually works in the twenty-first century. Jenkins (2008) argued Goffman is a significant theorist of power, but his understanding of power as seen in everyday contexts is diffuse, ubiquitous and dynamic, an outworking of public performances of the self, thus making it harder to differentiate his discussion of power from the cultural conditions that influence normal performances of the self. Manning (2008) suggested Goffman's approach to power takes into account how various actors are often oriented toward sustaining and making a visible authority and "can only be understood by close attention to detail, in terms of realized context and practices 'done'" (p. 682). In other words, Goffman said power can only be identified by observing what people do and how they react in a specific context.

Scholars have suggested Goffman's works tended to overlook discussions of authority, but I beg to differ. Rogers (1980) was one of the first scholars to recognize Goffman as offering interesting insights into the question of how authority is enacted in society. She suggested Goffman had not been regarded as a power theorist, not because of his lack of attention to power, but because he saw power in a different way. She argued that, for him, power, hierarchy and social structures are intertwined, so that he was not as vocal as other scholars in highlighting the importance of power as the central trait manifestation of authority. This means references to authority in his work were often implicit, inferred from his discussion of how the stage of life is framed by visible and invisible forces and structures of the social order.

Rogers went on to stress that Goffman talked about power in terms of social influence and control rather than as a value or a belief; for him, "Power is see-able (p. 396)." This means authority is to be approached as something to be observed. Actors can be seen as influenced by the conditions of the culture in which they are situated. These cultures have embedded views and frameworks of authority that further condition the extent to which people are able to act in solitary, self-determined ways or are subject to the conditions of being interconnected to others or structures. She suggested using Goffman's dramaturgical approach for studying how individuals are subject to and shaped by various manifestations of authority requires paying attention to two aspects of their performance in tandem—their actions and language. By viewing an actor's front- and back-stage performances, paying attention to what they do and say, a full picture of authority emerges—of how it is understood by the actor and so performed. I argue that such a reading of Goffman offers us the basis for a concrete method to apply this approach to authority to the study of RDCs.

Toward a dramaturgical view authority of RDCs' work and discourse

By using Goffman's metaphor of the theater, we can see authority as something that is performed by individuals as they take on a specific role that is subject to certain power dynamics, organizational structures and relationships. In order to see what authority is in such a context, we must pay attention to how it is manifested in what the actor says and does. Because status, hierarchy and power are all parts of everyday life and closely interconnected, we must recognize that authority is both implicit and explicit. Authority is seen in an actor's actions and heard in their speech. However, it can also be implied, as it becomes embedded in the stage and the actor's response to the props and boundaries of the theater. I believe this understanding of authority provides a useful and tangible framework for studying authority.

Discussion of Goffman's dramaturgical approach to authority offers us the metaphor of the actor on the stage, which helps us conceptualize authority as something performed within contemporary society. This performance of authority is subject to multiple factors and, as discussed in the previous chapter, includes certain roles, power dynamics and relationships. This performance of authority is also influenced by a new social reality, a hybrid context that brings technological and religious spaces and structures into collaboration, where online and offline contexts and conditions intersect. That creates interesting complexities relative to our reading of RDCs' actions and speech.

This enables us to spell out a theoretically informed method, shaped by Goffman's notions of performance, for studying RDCs' response to authority. I suggest that in order to grasp and distinguish these particular performances, which take place both within the technological spaces and religious institutions they navigate, we focus on the action and language of these negotiations. The sections that follow spell out how we can identify the story RDCs tell about themselves through their perform-ance and discussion of core aspects of their work, indicating a specific performance of authority.

Performing authority through doing: Media-making stories in digital work

Mapping RDCs' performances of authority begins with focusing on the digital work they undertake and how they frame it. Here attention is placed on observing and describing RDCs' engagement with specific digital and networked technolo-gies and how these are selected, used and formed into media and ministry outlets. This means identifying what I call the media-making story revealed through their front-stage performance of digital work. In this study, the process involved paying close attention to what digital media they work with, the content they create, how and for what purposes these are used, their media audience and the perceived impact of this work. Some of this information was gleaned through direct questions asked during interviews; other insights were gained through digital ethnography or personal online engagement with the software, platforms or content different RDCs used/created. In most cases, this also involved observing of how RDCs engage with their digital media tools or resources by asking them to provide a tour of their app, website, blog, etc. during interviews and closely observing how they engaged, framed and presented their work. I suggest paying attention to media-making stories requires attention to three aspects of their work performance.

Naming RDCs' performance of work

First, identifying RDCs' media-making stories requires identifying the work these actors undertake and for what purpose. This begins with a summary of the tan-gible work they do and observations of their engagement with the specific media resources and/or texts produced. Coupled with insights gained from interviews about the technological and development aspects of their work journey, this reveals how they view digital media as both a tool and a form of ministry. These media-making stories also reveal RDCs' convictions or assumptions about their work, i.e., what they see as its purpose and potential to affect their faith communities or broader society. Describing RDCs' work is similar to describing what the audience sees of the actor on the stage. Actors are given certain cues for the role they are to play from director's notes in the script that guide their performance. Yet they also have a certain amount of freedom to interpret that role based on their interpret-ation of the script and the method of acting they decide to employ. In the same way, RDCs' choices about the practical aspects of their work are framed within a specific identity performance; RDCs use their digital work to create and portray a certain persona. This speaks to how RDCs see the relationship between tech-nology, religion and their respective communities, what is important and valuable in terms of digital work, that which may be considered problematic, or the limits of technology used for religious purposes. The mapping of the media-making story begins with a description of what RDCs do; that leads to insights about who they seek to be as an actor within digital world and the religious world. This naming is both of their work and their identity. It allows the researcher to assess the RDCs' idealized self they seek to portray through their work. This process also helps reveal the assumptions about authority embedded in these performed work identities.

The naming of the work performance and identity of each group of RDCs is introduced at the end of Chapters 4–6. These chapters introduce in detail the variety of digital entrepreneurs, spokespersons or strategists interviewed in this study. The final section of each chapter highlights common themes that characterize the work each group of RDCs seeks to do, as well as the idealized self they present as digital creatives through their activities. Here RDCs are shown to act out a unique identity, framing their work and intentions as digital workers in distinctive ways. These performed identities are introduced in the title of each chapter, in brief discussions in the introduction, and then fully defined in the conclusion of each chapter. These media-making stories do not just help reveal RDCs' performance of the self; they also point to how these performances are grounded in distinct understandings of authority.

RDCs' work as negotiating authority with institution or community

Second, it is important to recognize that the work portrayals RDCs enact are grounded in a dual conception of authority. By this I mean RDCs see and describe themselves and their media work in ways that impact digitally mediated contexts. Yet they also understand their work intersects with the offline-grounded institutions they work for or the communities they are a part of. Thus, their work identities have embedded within them assumptions about authority drawn from engagement in both traditional offline and mediated online contexts. Analyzing how they relate to or frame the religious organizational and community commitments in their media-making stories helps us unpack the definitions of authority that underlie their work. This process begins with identifying the way their work positions them relative to established religious cultures and groups.

One of the findings of this study is that there are noticeable themes and similarities found in the media-making stories within each category of RDCs. By comparing individual media-making stories among the three RDC categories, I was able to identify the common understandings of authority these groups seemed to rely on. Each group of digital entrepreneurs, spokespersons and strategists had very different connections to their affiliated established religious institutions or communities, both conceptually and practically. Their unique framing of those associations, as revealed through their media-making stories, pointed toward a shared conception of what constitutes authority for a specific group of RDCs. In light of descriptions of their digital work and performance of RDC s' identities in relation to their community and organizational affiliations, we are able to identify which of the three traditional notions of authority introduced in Chapter 1 they relied on to frame their idealized selves. Discussion and comparison of the traditional conceptions of authority applicable to each RDC group draws our focus at the beginning of Chapter 7.

Digital work as the making of digital influence and/or leadership

As noted earlier, media-making stories capture how RDCs present their work identities. This story of what they do is filtered through two different understandings of authority. One is grounded in RDCs' understanding of their work as it relates to a religious community or organization; the other is grounded in their comprehension of how digital media work grants them a form of influence. This is the third and final focus of the identification and reading of RDCs' media-making stories.

RDCs' media-making stories reveal a distinct understanding of authority that correlates with how they situate themselves and their work within digital culture. These perceptions of authority, drawn from their engagement with and perceptions of the digital environment, speak to the notion of algorithmic authority, as discussed in Chapter 1. Algorithmic authority recognizes one's prominence and potential ability to influence others as grounded in technological expertise. Leveraging their skills and influence created via social networks and resources enables RDCs to position themselves as actors able to influence their audiences' opinions and actions. The researcher must pay attention to the ways RDCs talk about digital technologies and spaces, the value they place on these, how they situate themselves within them and the perceived social outcomes or impact of their work. This research shows that a description of their digital work enables us to link them to the strategies and practices of one of the three types of digital actors within algorithmic culture as described in Chapter 1. Mirroring the work strategies of a media influencer, thought leader or digital leader helps us talk about the way RDCs perform algorithmic authority in digital culture relative to their work. These connections can be made by paying attention to what they see their as their position, to their technology mastery and to the prominence of their work online. Together these components guide a distinct performance of authority online and the extent to which they also connect this to their offline expertise. I argue RDCs' media-making stories provide the researcher with tangible examples and connections to show how the digital work produced manifests understanding of both algorithmic and traditional authority at work in their identities.

Studying RDCs' media-making stories seeks to capture how RDCs present their work as an identity performance. Initially, it is a story of RDCs living out a distinctive public persona, that of digital expert and servant-leader within a specific religious community. Yet upon closer examination, we see the work narrative also reveals the fact that their performed identity is filtered through two different understandings of authority—one grounded in their understanding of their work's relationship to a religious community or organization, and another grounded in their comprehension of how digital media work grants them a form of influence. Mapping this dual performance of authority enables us to see media-making stories as clear, and often fraught, negotiations between traditional and new online and offline grounded views of authority. As RDCs negotiate between these different perceptions with their work, they are typically led to offer a justification narrative, framing these negotiations and the tensions within their work performance. This leads to the discussion of RDCs' technological apologetic, what it is, and how it can be studied.

Performing authority through discourse: Creating a technological apologetic

As noted in the introduction to this chapter, RDCs' performance of authority is not only revealed by what they do and how they describe this work on the front stage. Attention must also be given, as Goffman noted, to how authority is performed in the back stage, or in this case, how it is revealed through their language. I found that during RDCs' interviews they often offered a narrative that framed the aims and motivation for their work in a particular light. I call these "justification narratives," moments where RDCs attempted to explain how their technology engagement relates to their core religious beliefs and convictions, or the sense of responsibility they felt at individual and communal levels to actively demonstrate their faith commitment. These justification narratives can be seen in the ways RDCs use language to frame their technology work into a story of their personal faith, strongly associated with a sense of purpose they draw from digital work. These narratives reveal the fact that they also seek to frame their convictions in terms of their institutional ties and commitments.

In this study, RDCs interviewed were asked to reflect on a number of areas, including their motivations for using digital media for religious purposes, which digital arenas they felt were essential, and what they saw as the beneficial impact of their work for their religious community or organization. In the justification narratives emerging from my interviews, I noticed the narratives also revealed a broader understanding of how RDCs perceived and performed authority. These confirmed observations I made while identifying their media-making stories, which pointed toward a dual integration of traditional and digital framing of authority. Careful attention was paid especially to how RDCs framed their religious affiliations and perceived the relationship between those and their digital work. RDCs' initial discussions of their use of technology quickly went on to contextualize this work both in relation to what they saw as a personal spiritual calling and in relation to their work/community affiliations. This justification seemed to be based on a notion that relationships between religious groups and technology were often perceived as problematic, either because religious culture or structures were often framed as resistant to change, or because of institutional resistance to media or technology that introduce new structures of control and gatekeeping.

I further noted these justification narratives seemed to follow a similar discourse strategy commonly found within Christian communities, that of the apologetics argument. Apologetics is an area of argumentation found within many Christian traditions, which tries to use evidence and logic to justify and explain certain religious beliefs or the very notion of a religious outlook. I describe these narratives of RDCs as a "technological apologetic," a manifestation I had noticed in my previous research on religious communities' responses to newer forms of media.

Defining the technological apologetic and its relationship to the religious social shaping of technology

Apologetics is a form of study and rhetorical argumentation directed from the perspective of a specific belief system. The term comes from the Greek word *apologia* (ἀπολογία), which means "speaking in defense," as in to defend a particular position (Geisler, 1999). It is often associated with a specific branch of Christian theology that bears its name and seeks to provide a systematic explanation of and support for Christian doctrines. Thus, the work of apologetics is to provide a rational response to potential objections voiced against a specific viewpoint. I have coined the term "technological apologetic" in order to describe the structured attempts made by individuals and groups to clearly explain and defend distinct forms of technology use (Campbell, 2010b). A technological apologetic seeks to present a particular position about the nature of technology and perceptions of how it should be engaged, so that its use affirms recognized core values of the community from which it emerges. Thus, while the technological apologetic is centered on justifying a particular view of technology, it also innately articulates a unique understanding of the identity of the community from which it emerges. In other words, the defense of a particular view of technology is grounded in uses, core values and motivation. Therefore, the technological apologetic has a dual role—to present a clear argument about the nature of technology and to construct a certain understanding about the group that engages with the technology.

The concept of the technological apologetic emerges from my previous research on and analysis of how religious communities negotiate their uses of new media and their decision-making processes regarding the adoption or innovation of different forms of media (Campbell, 2010b). In *When Religion Meets New Media*, I presented a unique theoretically informed method called the "religious social shaping of technology" in which I argued,

> Religious communities are unique in their negotiations with media due to the moral economies of these groups, and the historical and cultural settings in which they find themselves. Therefore, what is needed is a distinctive approach that draws on the social shaping of technology approach, but also extends it in order to look at the special qualities and constraints of religious communities.
>
> (Campbell, 2010, p. 58)

This narrative is informed by the social shaping of technology (SST) approach, which focuses its study of technology on the use and consequences of media use by taking into account their interactions with institutions and cultural contexts (Kling, 2001). The SST approach can be seen to challenge medium theory approaches to technology, which suggest media are ingrained with core assumptions and values that inevitably shape social spaces and media environments in which they are found (i.e., McLuhan, 1964). Such positions have often been critiqued as technologically deterministic, in that they privilege technology over other factors as the ultimate social force and cultural determinant within society. SST challenges these assumptions by arguing media space and technologies are shaped closely by the motivations and values of their users, so user decision-making largely informs how technologies are perceived, and their innate values can be altered through these processes (i.e., Williams & Edge, 1996). SST is a broad conceptual approach, which encompasses a range of media theories. These include "domestication," which argues technologies are conditioned and tamed by users to fit routines of the daily life of households (Silverstone, Hirsch, & Morley, 1992), and social construction of technology or SCOT, which states people and things have agency and thus are connected together in a network that coproduces meaning, so technology is seen as a socially constructed medium (Callon & Latour, 1981).

The religious social shaping of technology (or RSST) is a theoretical method emerging from the SST approach. It argues religious communities undergo a unique negotiation process in their decision-making regarding how new technologies should be used. Specifically, RSST suggests scholars studying technology within religious contexts must undergo four stages of reflection. First, researchers are asked to *pay attention to the history and tradition*, in order to uncover the background of the community's position on technology. This can be uncovered by paying close attention to how that group defines its understanding of what constitutes the community and their established authority patterns and structures. It also involves considering historic responses to the group's sacred texts as early forms of media requiring the formation of use protocols and interpretive process.

Second, researchers are asked to *identify core beliefs* clearly related to the community's beliefs about media and how it should be used. This means defining the dominant social values of the group, which have shaped previous interaction with technology, in order to consider what platform this presents for future decision-making. After these two initial stages have been disclosed, researchers are ready for the third stage, that of *considering the media negotiation process*. Here it is recognized that religious communities typically do not often fully accept and/or reject new forms of media outright. Rather, religious groups' use of technology is constrained by community-specific values, meaning they must reflect on and negotiate what aspects of the technology itself or the message it produces can be embraced and what features may need to be resisted. This may lead religious groups to reconfigure particular technologies, changing and altering their functions or features in order for them to align more closely with the values and social or moral ethos of the community. Finally, researchers are asked to *consider processes of communal framing of technology.* This requires investigation into how discourse about technology presents the community in a particular light. In other words, technology talk within a religious community often represents more than just discussing the practical application of technology or ethical boundaries for its use. Instead, close observation of technology talk produced within religious communities reveals strong identity narratives are often constructed about how the community sees itself or wishes to be seen within broader contexts.

Studies of communal discourse have shown technological-negotiation strategies often involve the creation of community-specific framing discourses about media—e.g., Protestant (i.e., Becker, 2011) and Catholic (Campbell, 2012; Guezek, 2015). These discourses spotlight core communal values and self-perceptions the community seeks to project both internally and externally. In order to show that technology engagement promotes and exemplifies the behavioral boundaries of the group, this technology talk must demonstrate that technologies are appropriated in ways that complement the communal beliefs and patterns of life. For example, study of the Israeli Orthodox community's response to cellular phones and their eventual creation of a "kosher" cell phone illustrate how some groups may need to alter the way technologies are used, or features of the technologies themselves, in order to avoid use that would violate the moral boundaries of the community (Campbell, 2007). It is from the RSST's fourth stage that the identification of technological apologetic emerges.

Defining the technological apologetic

Within the technological apologetic, focus is placed on what religious community members say about HOW and WHY they and their group use (or should use) technology in specific ways. This process involves highlighting motivations behind the choices or positions advocated and the ways members defend or justify their choices, then reflecting on what these narratives reveal about how members feel their community should present itself internally and externally. Internally, the technological apologetic is aimed at members and leaders within the religious community. This offers a particular story about the nature of technology and how it relates to the goals and values of the community. The internal apologetic is offered in order to affirm community beliefs, build community cohesion and encourage buy-in from members relative to choices presented or advocated about technology. Engaging modern technology often requires religious groups to create a framing discourse that sets internal boundaries for how technologies are to be appropriated so they complement communal beliefs and patterns of life.

Externally, the technological apologetic is aimed at those outside the religious community. It focuses on stressing how technology choices affirm the group's religious convictions and identity. The external apologetic serves as a sort of public-relations exercise, providing the group an opportunity to create a cohesive narrative that can be used to solidify and re-present their unique identity within the public sphere. In other words, it reveals to those outside the community the in-group's understanding of what it means to be a religious person from their specific group (i.e., Christian) by how they use and speak of technology, projecting a specific identity narrative. The externally focused apologetic gives the members of the group an opportunity to solidify and re-present their chosen religious affiliation within the public sphere, communicating their communal values in light of technological choices. Thus, attention should be paid to both internal and external technological apologetics and how they contribute to or support one another.

Identifying the technological apologetic of RDCs

Together, the internal and external narratives make up the technological apologetic, a structured discourse that can be either personally or corporately focused. When employed by individuals such as RDCs, it allows the user to uniquely position themselves in relation to a specific religious tradition or grouping. When the apologetic emerges from a religious community's technology talk, it becomes part of their process of communal religious identity construction, enabling them to present themselves as being in a certain relationship to contemporary society. Thus, RDCs and religious communities utilize technological apologetics in order to rhetorically create a space in which they can justify technology use and the blending of aspects of the digital with offline culture and to enable them to contribute as an intentional role model or unintentional leader. So by focusing on reports of "why" specific RDCs do the digital work they do and how they interpret the meaning and impact of these activities, we are able to discover where and how RDCs act as new authority roles within their religious communities and digital spheres.

Attention is given in Chapter 8 to presenting the technological apologetic used by each group of RDCs to frame their digital-media work. Here discussion of their internal narrative involves highlighting the "self-talk" used to justify their work on an individual level. This necessitates paying attention to how descriptions of what they do also speaks to their religious identity—in other words, how they see their digital work in relation to their understanding of their personal religious faith. This includes digital work being described in terms of one's religious vocation, where technology use or development is described in terms of a spiritual calling to serve or minister to those in the church or even in broader culture.

Discussions of the technological apologetic focused on the external narrative pay attention to how RDCs related their work to their specific religious community or organization. These narratives emphasize why religious groups, and theirs in particular, should embrace digital media and for what purpose. While talking explicitly about their motivations for media use, they often also address why Christians should appreciate and value their work. These external narratives are directed to their faith community, but often sound like validation discourses seeking to justify the importance of what they do and how it affects or influences the religious groups they are affiliated with. Identifying the internal and external narratives of the technological apologetic is also important. This is because they reveal some interesting and important dialectical and institutional tensions RDCs must manage, and how they frame their perceived relationship with their religious community or institution.

The technological apologetic as revealing relational dialectics

Overall, the technological apologetic of RDCs presents and defends particular views about technology and religious community. Their attempts to justify their positions can be seen as an attempt to mediate perceived tensions between the individual and their community or institution. Therefore, this requires identifying how RDCs mitigate or make peace between these groups and any conflicting positions in which they see between themselves and their religious context. I suggest a relational dialectics approach to studying discourse helps us highlight the perceptions of competition or tension RDCs perceive between these groupings.

Explaining relational dialectics theory

Relational dialectics is a communication theory developed by Baxter and Montgomery (1996) and is based on several core assumptions. First, it assumes relationships are not linear, and the relational life is characterized by change. It also argues contradiction is a fundamental fact of relational life, and communication is central to organizing and negotiating relational contradictions or incongruences in meaning experienced between different individuals. Relational dialectics is a useful theory for studying the relationship and dialogic patterns that emerge between communicative partners. In the case of this study, the communicative relationship under study is between RDCs and their religious communities, especially recognized religious leaders of those groups. Individual motivations and digital practices often create tensions around actual and perceived intentions of their digital work. These are incongruences that must be negotiated by RDCs if they seek to remain in relationship with their established groups, which have static perceptions of how group members or the true believer should behave.

Because relational dialectics assumes contradictions will exist between parties due to their different backgrounds and communicative expectations, this theory helps highlight core oppositional patterns that frequently occur during dialogue and attempts to create a shared conceptual map of meaning. Specifically, the theory highlights three common dialectics within communicative relationships. First is the tension between *openness and closeness*, as partners in a relationship expect openness for a healthy relationship to be maintained, yet may also desire privacy on an individual level. Second is the tension between *certainty and uncertainty*, where constancy offers those in a relationship a close bond and sense of security that can, predictably over time, make the relationship seem stale; elements of surprise, on the other hand, help partners stay interested and invested. Third is the tension between *connectedness and autonomy*, where the longevity of a relationship is based on close physical, mental and emotional connections being maintained, though too integrated a connection can seem to blur or suffocate individuality. Within this study, focus is placed on how RDCs frame and negotiate this tension between connectedness and autonomy, and the extent to which they seek to justify their digital work and frame it as building up rather than undermining the religious community they seek to affiliate. Secondary reflection focuses on tensions between certainty and uncertainty, or how the technological apologetic of RDCs seeks to shore up tensions created by their digital work within their community. Here they seek to not be framed as religious competitors or agents causing too much institutional change.

Baxter and Montgomery also noted that the relational dialectic can be applied to studying the external dialectics a specific pairing may experience when seeking to frame or connect their relationship to a larger community outside themselves. This speaks to the relational negotiations RDCs undergo between not only themselves and traditional authority roles or structures of their religious communities, but the need they see to contextualize their work and position in relation to their broader religious community, church or institution. These communicative relationships involving RDCs' rhetorical negotiation of their place within their religious groups may lead them to encounter tensions related to three key areas. The first centers on the ideas of *revelation and concealment*, where the desire to self-disclose in order to gain group acceptance may be tempered by the need to keep some information private to retain a close relational bond. Also noted is the dialectic of *conventionality and uniqueness* that pulls them to adapt to the group's identity in opposition to the desire to retain a unique sense of being, and *inclusion and seclusion* related to the feeling of being an insider or an outsider within the new group. These last two tensions are most influential in the rhetorical framing and negotiations certain RDCs enact relative to their relationships with community authorities and the community as a whole. They must navigate between the novelty and uniqueness of their digital work and the conventional practices and boundaries of their community. In addition, they must decide to what extent they are willing for their work being seen as counter cultural or supporting the group's identity, and thus being seen as a boundary pusher, leading to their seclusion from the in-group or even group membership.

When considered together, the tensions and contradictions presented within relational dialectics theory highlight key areas of decision-making individuals must engage as they seek to situate themselves in relation to key-pair and group-based relationships. Baxter and Montgomery summed up these negotiations in relation to (a) *integration vs. separation*, as some autonomy must be surrendered in order to connect to the other; (b) *stability vs. change*, because balance between the expected and unexpected must be achieved to maintain the relationship and (c) *expression vs. nonexpression*, so agreement is reached between the parties about what is allowed to be public and what in the relationship should remain private.

Relational dialectics revealed in RDCs' technological apologetics

All three of these dialectics of relational negotiation come into play as key areas influencing the technological apologetics of RDCs explored in this study. However, different dialectics come into play for certain categories of RDCs more than others, as will be explored in more detail in the next three chapters. Baxter and Montgomery further suggested that individuals draw on a variety of different strategies in order to achieve balance between these dichotomous values parings in their communicative decision-making. They outlined a number of specific strategies often used by individuals and groups to manage these core relational dialectics. Of the negotiation strategies they present, five are most evident in the technological apologetics of the three categories of RDCs within this study. These include RDCs using denial, disorientation, balance, reaffirmation and integration as ways to frame their relationships to community leaders and authority structures for the sake of affirming their place in and connection to the broader religious community.

Denial happens when individuals become overly focused on one side of an argument or position when confronting a problem or contradiction, while ignoring other potential explanations or justifications. In this case, RDCs seek to establish their position above that of community authorities by citing their expertise and point of view as superior. Disorientation involves attempting to avoid the communicative problem all together by terminating the relationship or downplaying its importance. Here RDCs may say that their technological expertise, knowledge of digital culture or sense of personal calling trumps the attitude of their community, so they need not adhere to these perceived uninformed or unskilled positions. Balance involves individuals attempting to keep a balance within a communicative situation, while seeking to solve the communication problem at hand. This means RDCs seek to listen as well as be heard, for their positions to be clearly communicated and recognized by their community while equally acknowledging the views and constraints of their religious group. Reaffirmation involves individuals accepting the reality of the problem and the challenges the contradiction creates, thus indicating a willingness to relax their convictions or constrain their actions in order to maintain the relationship. Here the RDCs hold the area of disagreement in tension with their own goals and desires, and for the sake of a sustained relationship are willing to put their agenda to the side. Finally, in integration both the parties are satisfied by working together to develop collaborations or methods that enable them to solve communicative contradictions and reach a mutually agreeable way forward. RDCs seek to collaborate with their communities, serving as both teachers and servants in building digital strategies and facilitating the work of the community.

Applying theory to RDCs' words

The chapters that follow reveal how various digital entrepreneurs, spokespersons and strategists speak of their digital work, from which conversations we will see distinct technological apologetics emerge. Each employs a different tactic to frame their work and relational affiliations. Applying a relational dialectic approach to these technological apologetics not only helps spotlight the communicative tension RDCs highlight but helps reveal specific rhetorical strategies they employ to frame their institutional and communal relationships. Overall, these tensions can be generalized to three core categories of how each category of RDCs uniquely responds to tensions they encounter between their work and mission and their religious affiliations. They can be summed up as RDCs opposing, intermingling or co-opting certain claims about media and ministry into their technological apologetic response. Oppositional strategies focus on resisting ideas or responses seen to run counter to the core values of the individual or pair placed in a position of negotiation or justification. Co-opting strategies focus on adopting certain arguments or beliefs of the other for one's own purposes. This may include redefining the highlighted values or positions presented by perceived relational outsiders. Intermingling strategies focus on the conscious integration of competing positions in order to create new hybrid positions.

In Chapter 8, focus is placed on how RDCs create a technological apologetic and frame their positions vis-à-vis technology and their community in light of the three categories of dialectics presented earlier: integration vs. separation, stability vs. change and expression vs. nonexpression. Consideration is given to the specific types of rhetorical strategies each group of RDCs seeks to use. This includes identifying whether they (a) highlight oppositional views between the RDCs and their community, (b) represent a co-opting of beliefs or agendas of the community into the work and motivations of RDCs or (c) evidence attempts to intermingle competing views or tensions to create new ways of viewing community, authority and religious identity within the technological apologetic.

Summary: Mapping the performance of authority through media-making stories and technological apologetics

This chapter presents a theoretically grounded method for studying RDCs' performance of authority. It is based on a number of key assertions. This begins with the premise that RDCs' use of reports, indicating their technology work and digital activities are explicitly linked to unique religious motivations and desires. This motivation is key, because it frames how they understand the positions they take on and how they relate to their respective religious community or organization. Also, key is recognizing the fact that RDCs' beliefs about and enactment of authority should be approached as a performance that can be identified by paying to attention to both their actions and words. Researchers must consider what RDCs do and say in order to reveal what is happening on both sides of the performance stage. This approach also argues that RDCs' beliefs about and performance of authority are grounded in both traditional and digitally influenced ideas about culture and authority. As actors negotiating between dual realities of mediated/online and institutional/offline contexts in their work, it is important to recognize the fact that they draw from both arenas in justifying and acting as new forms of religious authority.

Finally, this theoretically informed method stresses the importance RDCs' language. Their interviews often include a rationale framing their tech work as essential to the life of their group in the digital age. Thus, they create a space in which they can function and contribute as intentional role models or unintentional leaders. RDCs' technology talk is understood as a form of God talk, a public discourse that enacts their religious beliefs. Here descriptions of individual or communal technology use and integration for religious purposes offer a distinctive narrative revealing how RDCs see their faith positions and traditions. Ergo, studying RDCs and authority requires attention to the fact that their technological apologetic, or religiously informed justification discourse, presents more than a certain understanding about technology.

Naming media-making stories

I suggest RDCs' performance of authority can be revealed by paying attention to two areas: (1) RDCs' media-making stories and (2) their technological apologetics. Identifying the media-making story involves observing what these creatives do and produce online, as well as listening to how RDCs describe their digital work and the resources they create. From this, researchers are able to identify how they name this work relative to both digital and religious cultures. Within this story lies an identity narrative that is closely connected to certain assumptions about the nature of authority in relation to the dual contexts in which they function. Each group of RDCs draws primarily on one of three traditional notions of authority outlined in Chapter 1—seeing authority in terms of their roles, power or relationships. This is manifested in the ways their work positions them with their affiliated religious group. They also draw on notions of algorithmic authority, as their engagement with digital platforms through technological spaces and tools requires them to negotiate with the structures of digital culture. Here RDCs often emulate patterns of media influencers, thought leaders and/or digital leaders in these negotiations. Mapping their unique media-making stories thus involves naming the RDCs' work identity. This is followed by identifying how this identity is laden with certain assumptions about authority in the digital and institutional contexts that bracket this work. This chapter draws on these assumptions and offers a systematic method for their exploration.

Identifying the technological apologetic

The naming of RDCs' media-making story then leads us to unpack the technological apologetic of RDCs. The technological apologetic is a created discourse, in which RDCs seek to justify why they do what they do with digital media. They produce a narrative that highlights the motivations that drive their engagement with digital technology. This reveals the assumptions RDCs make about how they see the intersection between faith and digital media, which is seen as an internal narrative or personal rationale for how and why they engage digital media. The technological apologetic also enables researchers to identify the motivations connected to certain assumptions RDCs have about their religious communities and organizations' interaction with digital media. This external narrative is aimed at justifying their work and negotiating their relationship with this external structure. These internal and external narratives involve negotiations with notable tensions they see their work as creating for them and their religious affiliation. Finally, drawing on relational dialectic theory becomes a useful tool to explore how RDCs frame their digital ministry and manage the position it creates for them, especially with external communities or audiences. This negotiation can be described in terms of negotiating perceived as opposing, intermingling or co-opting competing agendas.

This theoretically informed method, which I will refer to as the "performance of authority by digital creatives," informs the chapters that follow. In Chapters 4–6, I provide a detailed profile of the general categories of RDC investigated in this study. Through detailed narratives about these categories of religious digital workers and various examples of how these approaches are manifested in different religious contexts, I show how a diverse group of individuals consciously and unconsciously performs as RDCs. These explorations of the actors, work and language of digital creatives help identify the opportunities and challenges this work affords them, how they perceive their relationship with their religious communities or institutions and what, if any, tensions emerge for them through their digital work. By providing a general overview of each RDC category, offering profiles of select exemplars, and reflecting on the areas noted earlier, we begin to see how RDCs understand and manifest authority online and offline, as they try to negotiate their complex relationships with traditional religious leaders and institutions.

Chapter 4

Digital entrepreneurs

Internet-empowering visionary technology influencers

Now we come to the core of this study, and introduction to the work, motivations and identities of these Christian digital creatives. As noted previously, "digital creatives" is a term that first emerged within the field of advertising in the mid-2000s. It was used to refer to individuals who create or work with digital media such as websites to create internet-based campaigns or messages. This term has become a popular way to refer to those who work in digital marketing and online advertising. Since all individuals in marketing or advertising now engage with digitally based media, being a digital creative has become a catch-all term for many involved in these fields. When I began this research in 2011, the term digital creatives was most commonly associated with individuals developing software or digital platforms. This included individuals whose work focused on website design and/or mobile application development, or those who created social media initiatives for digitally driven businesses and companies.

Throughout the course of this research, I noted that when people use the phrase "digital creative," they often picture individuals who builds digital tools like a website or computer software. However, in the world of advertising and marketing, the term digital creative can also refer to those who create digital content. Through my study of individuals involved in digitally creative practices associated with religious communities and institutions, I found digital creatives include both. Religious digital creatives (RDCs) can be tech designers who create websites or platforms for innovative forms of ministry, or individuals who primarily engage with established media platforms, producing unique content focused on specific religious topics meant to educate, inspire or challenge their faith community.

Through interviews, online observations and engagement with a range of individuals involved in digital-creative work, this study identifies three unique categories of RDCs. In this chapter, I present the first group, what I describe as "digital entrepreneurs." These individuals are frequently involved in a media- or technology-related profession. This expertise motivates them to use their skills in conjunction with their spiritual pursuits or to help their religious communities by creating digital resources or materials that they see can modernize and revolutionize their faith-based practices and goals.

This chapter also serves as a model for discussion and presentation of the next two RDC categories. It begins by offering a more detailed definition of who can be considered digital entrepreneurs, expanding the brief description presented in the initial introduction in Chapter 3. This is followed by outlining the variation that exists within this category by introducing three different manifestations of digital entrepreneurs observed in this research. Each type is described and exemplars introduced, in order to provide concrete examples that can be analyzed according to the performance of an authority theoretical method introduced in Chapter 3. Each digital entrepreneur's description highlights aspects of their media-making stories and hints at aspects of the justification narratives they provide to frame their work and mission. Chapter 4 ends by summarizing shared traits of these digital entrepreneurs and the media-making narrative those create for them. This framing becomes key for unpacking the underlying understandings of authority their work evokes, which are discussed in comparison to other RDC categories in Chapter 7.

Defining digital entrepreneurs

As introduced in Chapter 2, *digital entrepreneurs* are RDCs who use their technology and design skills to create digital resources or content to aid the mission of their faith tradition. Like Anderson's notion of creole pioneers, digital entrepreneurs represent individuals with professional qualifications and technical talents, who aim to develop religiously oriented digital resources they see as meeting the needs of their faith community. Because they are often early adopters of technology, and have advanced technological design or production skills, they often create digital resources that are on the cutting edge. Their work often offers unique possibilities to media users for engaging in religious practices or communicating their faith to others.

Digital entrepreneurs are often professional media workers who use their abilities to serve the mission of their faith community or affiliated church. We typically think of them as having a high level of technical design or coding expertise, and they see these skills as gifts they can and should use to help the work of the Christian church. This may include designing religious mobile apps, software or websites, or even running online discussion forums or social media sites. However, there are other digital entrepreneurs whose expertise lies in digital media literacy and proficiency. Rather than focusing on technology tools, their strengths lie in their ability to envision imaginative digital content or strategies that can be implemented to serve their faith community's goals. Their digital media expertise enables them to rise as external experts seeking to offer guidance on how best to adapt to digital media culture.

Both types of digital entrepreneurs, tool designer and content creator, face a unique challenge. While they desire to serve the church, they are employed outside the religious organization they seek to assist. This gives them a unique level of freedom, as their digital work is driven by their personal vision and enthusiasm, allowing them to think outside traditional boundaries and practices set by religious institutions. However, their efforts can also be viewed with suspicion, or at least a lack of understanding by those inside the official structures. In this way, digital entrepreneurs may be seen as competitors by the very groups they seek to serve. This issue will be explored in more detail later in the chapter. Now we move on to a discussion of the several different manifestations of digital entrepreneurs identified in this study.

Types of digital entrepreneurs

In this study, 50 individuals interviewed could be identified as digital entrepreneurs, the largest segment of informants in this research study. They included web and software developers who tithed their time to help their churches develop digital resources, media directors for secular companies that do free consultation work for Christian organizations and mobile media strategists who develop apps and tools for Christian outreach. Some of these individuals had set institutional connections to various Christian denominations, including Anglican/Episcopal, Assemblies of God, American Baptist, Catholic and Methodist. However, most individuals in this category had rather loose institutional ties. Many described themselves as having previous or inactive links to specific denominations, but are now affiliated with non-denominational, interdenominational or broadly evangelical church contexts. Others preferred to describe themselves as now being either "post-denominational" or "simply Christian." In this chapter we explore three different types of digital entrepreneurs: (1) techies for God, (2) theoblogians and (3) internet evangelists.

Techies for God are digital media innovators who use their design expertise to create websites, software or online resources to fulfill a particular religious mission. These individuals are the ones most often associated with the term digital creatives, as they are professional technologists with high-level computer, hardware and software expertise. Their work is often very innovative and experimental. Techies for God often focus their attention toward what they perceive as an underserved religious market or outreach opportunity online. They often work independently, not afraid to come up with ideas based on what they perceive as a need or potential in their faith community, create a tool or platform that addresses this need and put it out there for others to try, while continuing to work on refining its development. These techies are doers and frame their tech skills in terms of a part of spiritual gifts they feel called to use, even if most churches and religious organizations would see technology development as outside the normal understanding and remit for what constitutes ministry.

Theoblogians are individuals who start blogging, often focused on a particular religious topic or theological perspective. While these bloggers are content creators rather than technological innovators, they usually display a strong digital media literacy and an accessible writing style. This means they know how to create tags and present their online content in ways that make it easily accessible both in style and design to a broad audience. Their blogging can be perceived as provocative due to the topics they tackle and the comments they make, which may make them controversial with not only religious leaders but also other Christians due to the theological positions they take. This only helps their blog gain followers and media attention that can lead to public prominence. Furthermore, their writing may prove to have a lucrative potential. Many times this requires the bloggers to make a choice about whether they will focus on their writing as a personal passion project or take advantage of the potential financial benefits of having a public profile. Indeed, two of the theoblogians presented here have been critiqued as being celebrity religious bloggers, where their controversial choices have been said to detract from their religious contributions online.

Internet evangelists are similar to techies for God in that they feel called to develop websites and applications to facilitate the spread of the Christian gospel to those outside the church. However, unlike techies for God, their reason for using technology is singular—to develop tools for evangelization. These individuals are often early internet adopters, avid computer hobbyists, media professionals or just individuals that just like to stay on the cutting edge of technology use and innovation. While they have notable tech skills and fluencies, it is their heart to spread the Christian Gospel that is their primary motivation for technology development. They are both traditional evangelists, wanting to publicize the message of salvation, and internet evangelists, enthusiastically advocating the use of digital media to do this work. Unlike the media-driven missionaries described in Chapter 6, these individuals operate outside established church or missionary societies to undertake this work. Many start with a solitary passion project, but over time, this can morph into a large-scale, international evangelistic initiative or even a full-fledged incorporated ministry.

Each of these different expressions of digital entrepreneurs is known for their online work and creativity and their ability to turn this digital work into a form of ministry and expression of their religious commitment. Many have earned reputations as innovators within certain Christian networks online and sometimes even offline, not only for their technical skills, but also for their understanding of how internet technologies and digital culture are shaping society and the church. In the following sections, we explore these visionaries and how they use media for religious influence.

Techies for God

Huw Tyler served as founder and creative director for Share Creative from 2008–2012, a digital media startup that does web and design work for a variety of organizations in the charity sector, equipping and providing resources to these organizations with communications material. Yet at the time in which we spoke on 2011, Tyler shared that this work is what pays the bills, but for him Share Creative also offered him the opportunity to pursue other faith-based and social-justice media-based projects. The company was connected to and did promotional media for a mission organization called Share Jesus International. Yet it was structured as an open relationship and Tyler and his team were able to direct their work toward other projects and groups that matched their mission to equip Christians and church groups with media resources designed to fulfill their ministry. Tyler described much of this kind of digital work as an opportunity to "stretch their creative muscles" and go beyond designing eye-catching informational resources to actually offer individuals a creative encounter.

> Our first goal is to engage people who are in the church with social media and the second is to engage people outside the church with church issues through social media. Through our projects, we've really felt proud of the impact of engaging people in their faith and to make a difference in small and big ways.
>
> (H. Tyler, personal communication, April 5, 2011)

One of the ways they did this is in their pioneering work on the Natwivity project. In 2009 they launched a digital storytelling project that presented the Christmas story in a unique format. Using Twitter, which had only been launched 2.5 years ago, they envisioned and created a storytelling experience where people could watch the Christmas story unfold in the voices of key biblical characters as told by live tweets over the days running up to Christmas. As the wise men tweeted about asking directions, and Joseph complained via Twitter about not finding room at the inn, they created a simple yet unique experience online for those following the story. An initiative that garnered a mere 300 followers in 2009 reached over 10,000 followers of the "Natwivity" a few years later, along with over 14,000 retweets and repostings of the events on Facebook per day. They also went on to run a similar Twitter storytelling project around Easter called "Easter Live" during Holy Week, where people could follow tweets starting with story of the Last Supper through the crucifixion and Jesus's resurrection as told from the standpoint of the disciples and other observers noted in the biblical text.

> What we've found is a great way of meeting people where they're at, a way for church-building via technology at Easter or Christmas time. Times of the year when people outside the church are often more open to spiritual things. For us social media has become a space to open the important stories to a wider audience.
>
> (H. Tyler, personal communication, April 5, 2011)

The work of the Natwivity and Easter Live have since inspired many other groups and Christian organization to run similar social media storytelling campaigns around these religious holidays around the world. Tyler said his team was always looking for ways they can use digital media to make a difference and get other Christians involved in social-action initiatives. For example, in 2011 they created a special website to raise awareness about human trafficking in the UK and encourage readers to lobby their ministers of Parliament (MPs) to put this issue at the top of their agenda. Part of this site included a page allowing individuals to create digital valentines that shared the message that everyone is a special someone and share facts about human trafficking. That Valentine's Day, hundreds of these digital cards were sent, including 300 to the then Prime Minister David Cameron, petitioning him to opt into a directive on human trafficking that was before Parliament at the time. When the UK government opted into that directive, Share Creative got excited about the role they had played. "We are seeing there are many really good creative ways of engaging with a justice issue that engages a lot of people, that can be leveraged and enacted through social and digital media" explains Tyler.

> Theologically, I think we have a God who is a God of communication. I think that's rooted in God's DNA, I think that's rooted in the church's DNA, so communication is really important. The church has a lot to communicate ... whether that's a core gospel message or social injustice, there's a lot the church has to speak out on each of those communication technologies differently. In last 2000 years the church has chosen to communicate in very different ways, whether that's been poetry, books, paintings, constructing cathedrals ... our role now is to show the church how they can use these new communication technologies to do the same thing.
>
> (H. Tyler, personal communication, April 5, 2011).

At its height, Share Creative received a lot of support and kudos in the UK for their digital ministry initiative, especially from young people who get excited by seeing digital media being treated as an opportunity for creative outreach. Tyler said at the time that he does worry about the very institutional and hierarchical nature of the church, especially in England, and what he sees as a common resistance to digital media among church leaders.

> I think our leadership is going to need to change drastically in order to become facilitators and mobilizers of people at every level. We have a long way to go to become far more of an open-source church that meets people where they are at and what they care about. Understanding and using the digital that is a core essential to moving in this direction.
>
> (H. Tyler, personal communication, April 5, 2011)

Since then Tyler say has gone one to work for several other religious organizations as Save the Children and Tearfund in the UK in the area of innovation and technology. The lessons he learned while running Share Creative have encouraged him to continue to experiment and model an open-source way of sharing information and creating relationships and investments with others through digital storytelling and social media justice work. He finds that modeling best media ministry practice is the way to go, and then through this example hope other religious organizations and institutions will take note of the potential impact technology can have for the work of the gospel.

Alex Kerr is another techie for God. He has worked in web development, digital video and as a mobile-phone software designer for much of his career. In the early 2010s he started a tech-based ministry called Phone Publish, with the aim to use his design background to help Christian organizations and churches move their content onto mobile-phone platforms and applications. His particular passion is aiding organizations doing outreach in the developing world, where many people still do not have smartphones, but rather rely on lower-end 3G feature phones. He noticed that while Christian mobile-media innovators working with religious organizations were focused on developing mobile applications for smartphones, designing software for feature-packed phones remained an overlooked mission opportunity. He developed Phone Publish as content system that could assist ministries in getting their materials or ideas accessibly translated for access onto the lower-end feature phones used by the majority of their outreach audience.

He at the time of our interview was in the midst of a collaboration with a number of smaller ministries, helping them envision how they could create applications that share stories and resources on mobile phones with the different language groups they seek to work with. For example, one ministry he was working with is using the Phone Publish system to create a mobile platform for a bible concordance project that could be distributed to pastors in Africa via phone connections. In the mid-2010s he noticed a growing awareness of an interest in using mobile phones for Christian ministry. He was encouraged by this perspective and excited to be able to use his professional skills to help Christian groups expand their outreach.

> Churches are just starting to wake up and see that mobile ministry is a powerful possibility, it's like a door of consciousness is opening to the future of what Christian mission and ministry could and should look like. I think there is a huge volunteer army out there of people like me, with the tech skills and vision for this kind work, who are just waiting for others to catch this vision.
> (A. Kerr, personal communication, February 12, 2013)

Kerr described himself as part of a growing group of Christian, skilled technology professionals working in various media industries who see their expertise as a God-given gift. He felt churches need to see people with media expertise not just as people who can run the soundboard at church but as those who hold the potential to open new doors for Christian ministry through creating new tech-based ministry tools and strategies.

> I think church ministries need to wake up and see the potential of mobile media and release the unique volunteer possibilities they have within their congregations. I think most churches do not fully see or understand it, this technology design work as ministry. It is not a normal everyday ministry. But in our churches' services people are often physically getting on their phones and browsing a mobile Bible or other apps, why not capitalize on this trend.
> (A. Kerr, personal communication, February 12, 2013)

Kerr admitted that even the people belonging to his large, progressive Church of England congregation located in central London often "don't get it" when he shares his dreams of making mobile-media ministry a central part of church- and mission-based outreach. However, he remained unmoved in his contention that the future of the church is mobile, although he was quick to temper his enthusiasm for using technology with the recognition that discernment is needed. He says those involved in mobile-ministry work can find it hard to resist the hype of advocating using smartphones just because they are latest wonder gadget.

> Those of us involved in mobile ministry, we are trying to work it out. How do we say to the church as a whole, or individual churches or ministries, we know this is not only a legitimate medium but look at the massive benefits here. The church needs to not get scared off because technology is something that is new and they do not understand it. We also understand the church has got a duty to really think carefully about who they are trying to reach, how they can best be reached, and who also they are missing out when they use these technologies.
> (A. Kerr, personal communication, February 12, 2013)

Still, Kerr spoke of his commitment and conviction about working in the mobile-media industry, both for his livelihood and as an outlet for Christian ministry. He saw the potential and hopes over time the church will too, allowing him to use his professional skills to help build innovative Christian tools for ministry.

While some digital entrepreneurs focus on using internet technology to create innovative and cutting-edge ministry tools, others see this technology as offering a unique opportunity to redefine what church is and could be. Marc van der Woude is Dutch digital entrepreneur whose technological foresight and interest in missions put him on the cutting edge of using the internet for various forms of ministry. He runs a digital media company called eMergeMedia and works as an internet consultant and trainer for business. His story started in 1995 when he was working in the communication department for the Dutch national railways. The internet had just come to the Netherlands, and many organizations were beginning to consider its business potential. At work, he was charged with doing an exploratory study of how the company could use the internet. At the same time, he became personally fascinated with how this technology enabled him to connect with people and stories about what God was doing all over the world. Several spiritual-renewal movements were emerging at the time— related to charismatic Christianity, prayer and church planting—and the internet became a space for him and others to connect with news and stories associated with these movements.

> I met people from all kinds of church backgrounds and I liked that much more than only meeting the same people in my local church. Through the internet I was able to internationally connect to many people from many different backgrounds, from Wiccans and Buddhists to Christians from Africa. I was interested to find out how people think and why they are motivated for their religion even though it is not my religion.
> (M. van der Woude, personal communication, March 8, 2013)

In his free time, van der Woude began to collect these stories of how people's lives were being changed spiritually and influenced others, and share them with his Christian friends through the then new technology of email mailing lists. This soon became a weekly email newsletter that he called "Joel News International," a collection of stories and news events about Christian witness and life he gathered online from all over the world, which were then sent out to subscribers. Collecting content for the newsletter helped him amass a vast network of Christian contacts who shared information with him, as well as a growing database of Christian resources found online. His interactions with readers and international networks also opened many new doors for him. For example, one of his early subscribers from Russia invited him to speak at conference. He showed up with his message prepared, only to learn he had been billed as the keynote bible teacher for a weeklong event.

> That was a really interesting challenge. But you know that is the fun thing with the internet. It opens doors into nations and with people who wouldn't have without international connection. So that is good I think.
>
> (M. van der Woude, personal communication, March 8, 2013)

That was over twenty years ago. Today he continues to run "Joel News International," now on a much smaller scale and on a subscription basis. It is only one of many religious initiatives he has become part of over the years because of the Christian network he gradually formed online.

> I would say that the wireless internet is to me what the Holy Spirit is for the church. You can't do without it. I live in a very boring local town and I have a small study with only a computer and a file cabinet. But being connected through the web I can reach out to the world.
>
> (M. van der Woude, personal communication, March 8, 2013)

Van der Woude has continued to be an early adopter of new internet technologies, seeing how each one can be used for ministry and connecting with other Christians. He started blogging in 2002, was active in the 2000s and then joined social media in 2007. He has long become convinced of the importance of using the internet as a tool for spreading religious information. Blogging and then Facebook became places where, for a time, he and those with like minds could think out loud about the mission of the church in the world, as well as discuss the challenges the internet poses to this work.

> I think the internet has a disruptive potential. The internet is anarchistic. It is by nature not to be controlled by anyone, and anyone can participate. There is no limitation and no border to it. If you take that seriously and realize that, you will end up with quite different approaches to the internet and eventually to seeing the church.
>
> (M. van der Woude, personal communication, March 8, 2013)

It is these interactions and online connections that have become the basis for a nonprofit ministry he helps run called Simple Church Europe. He describes Simple Church as a church-planting movement and a network of mission-minded communities of faith developing throughout Europe, seeking to do church in a different way.

> They are basically groups of people that want to follow Jesus together and serve other people, serve their communities, and improve the world around them. They do that very intentionally. It is different from normal church, characterized by a building and a Sunday morning service, focused on a central place of worship. A simple church can happen anywhere at any time, any place, in any people group. And that is the strength. It can more saturate daily life than church as an activity that you go to once or twice a week.
>
> (M. van der Woude, personal communication, March 8, 2013)

For him. this understanding of church emerged very closely related to his experience of building connections, friendships and ministry collaborations with other Christians he met online. It is seeing church as a network of relationships rather than depending on a centralized event or space as a basis for community.

> When you start defining church differently and more organically, then you experience much more freedom. So for us this new expression of church was related to the internet. The whole thinking behind the internet is that it's a free space. Anyone can participate. Anyone can connect. Meaningful communities can come into existence on the web, as people co-create. They work on stuff together and stay connected, whether through Facebook or other social media. Online you can truly be part of a worldwide body of Christ, instead of limiting ourselves to one little club.
>
> (M. van der Woude, personal communication, March 8, 2013)

Like van der Woude, most of the movement's leaders have moved out of involvement in traditional church in favor of this new missional model of church they have invested in building. The movement sees the internet not only as a model for collaboration and interaction but believes digital resources are key for running the movement. They have a classical resource website that houses articles, testimonies and training resources related to the Simple Church movement. They use Twitter and Facebook for dynamic communication and to spread information to the network. Furthermore, since the movement's core team is International, they use Skype and email regularly for event planning, prayer and strategizing, as they are normally only able to meet once a year face to face.

> To be honest, before we left out local church, I got most of my spiritual nutrition, through the web and through friendships we had with people in other streams of church. When I look at it now, I would say that I maintain daily

connections with more than half of those I see as my Christian community through the internet. It opens up the richness of the whole body of Christ. That is what the internet does.

(M. van der Woude, personal communication, March 8, 2013)

However, van der Woude stresses that he is not arguing for an exodus from offline churches to a new and improved online or networked version. The aim of the Simple Church movement is to expand contemporary conceptions of what church can look like. He says his goal, and the goal of the movement, is to partner with traditional forms of church.

I think that the real challenge is not to see these digital platforms as an extension of church as we know it, but to really try to understand the mindset of people who use this technology and consider how we can revision what it means to be church. That is the real challenge for the church as it is. We don't need more of the same. We don't need more bible studies on the web. We don't need more sermons on the web. What we need are new expressions of community and new collaborative ways of doing the work of the church in a digital era.

(M. van der Woude, personal communication, March 8, 2013)

So van der Woude sees the internet as an opportunity to intentionally redefine church.

And if you see and can embrace the church as a decentralized and empowering movement, as a connection of people who follow Jesus or share a common cause or common mission, rather than those who are part of the same hockey club and go to the same meetings, I think that is liberating. Because I think if you embrace what the internet represents, this understanding of church makes complete sense. Whatever you do on the web is mission, is church, is community.

(M. van der Woude, personal communication, March 8, 2013)

In this way, techies for God see their digital work as more than building tools; they see it as enacting new expressions of church and outreach, challenging previous conceptions and models of practice.

Theoblogians

Tony Jones is a freelance theologian in Minnesota. He is also an adjunct theology professor and social media innovator. For over a decade, he was a high-profile Christian blogger, posting his thoughts on theology seven days a week. He initially gained a significant following online in the mid-2000s due to the part he played as an avid blogger associated with the emerging church movement. The emerging church movement has been described as more of a theological conversation among individuals, than a cohesive church movement or structure

(Gibbs & Bolger, 2005). Scholars have defined it as global dialogue that began online led by individuals associated with mainline Christian denominations (Anglican, Baptist, Methodist, etc.) in the USA and Europe, individuals who were disillusioned "with the structures and rituals of mainstream Protestantism, and the perceived consumerist attitudes of modern Evangelicalism, or 'mega-churches'" (Teusner, 2013). This dissatisfaction with traditional expressions of church drew many people to the blogosphere, a free space where they could share their criticisms and brainstorm new ways to do or restructure church practice. Blogs enable people to share their ideas about how they can create a new expression of church, one more relevant and "missional" to reach postmodern and con-temporary cultures. It was in these global conversations that Jones's theological reflections emerged and thrived.

Jones began blogging in 2004 when he was a PhD student at Princeton Theological Seminary. His commute between his home in Minnesota and school in New Jersey resulted in a lot of time on his own to read theology and think deeply about it. His first blog, "Theoblogy," focused on his reflections about what he was learning during his studies.

> My mind was just a fertile, lush garden that was growing with ideas. I had stuff to write about every day from thoughts on some great theological treatise to commentary on new ideas I was being exposed to in preparing for my exams.
> (T. Jones, personal communication, May 21, 2012)

His blog became a space to discuss his vision for the church and reflect on the role technology and networking played in the development of the emerging church dialogue. Over the past decade, his blog has changed platforms, formats and even focus, from covering more in-depth and controversial theological debates like those over open theology and LGBT (lesbian, gay, bisexual and transgender) issues in the church, to more personal writing about his hunting dogs and personal faith journey.

Even after he earned his PhD in theology, he continued to describe himself as theoblogian, which he defines as "somebody who is trying to do populist the-ology and somebody who gets the blogging medium and the blogging genre" (T. Jones, personal communication, May 21, 2012). He argues that not everyone who blogs about faith or theology issues fits into this category—rather, it is a label he reserves only for those doing "significant theological work." For him, this means people who seek to deeply "understand God's movement in the world," speak publically about this and ground their arguments in a nuanced theology of the church.

As student, he saw the value of theological blogging, which allowed him to share his thoughts and theological understanding as it was being developed. To this end, he made several rules for himself to keep his blogging authentic and show how his theological thinking was evolving. If he made a mistake, or posted something that proved wrong later, he let it stand online without edits.

Early on I made a commitment that if I say something incorrect, stupid, or offensive, I will apologize for it in comments, but I will let it stand. I am going to let this be a record of everything I think going back all the way to 2004.

(Personal communication, May 21, 2012).

He also decided not to engage comments or debate with those commenting on his blog, but let these responses to his post stand as is, whether they be critiques or affirmations.

Jones says his blog is where he does some of his best, most original and honest theological work. About a decade after he began blogging, he was invited to move his blog to Patheos.com, curated by a popular non-denominational online media company, which posts religious information and commentary from a variety of faith traditions. During the four years he was paid by Patheos.com to blog, site metrics reported his writings tracked about a million page views a year.

When I started to get paid to blog, even more people started paying attention to what I said, and my stats, I had a pretty good sense of who is reading me— seminary presidents read me, theologians read me. I am humbled by that. Now I know exactly what I need to do now to get traffic. I know whom I need to write a post about, some Christian celebrity, or if I write about gay marriage my traffic will spike.

(T. Jones, personal communication, May 21, 2012)

Jones has leveraged his popularity as a theoblogian to launch a career as a book author and speaker. Around the same time he began blogging, he began writing books on themes such as postmodern youth ministry and Christian discipleship, as well as devotional books on themes such as Bible reading and study. Different established publishing houses, like Zondervan (Jones, 2001) and Jossey-Bass (2008) printed his first books. He credits his blogging for helping raise his profile as a public theologian and enabling him to gain the attention of the religious establishment, giving credibility to his ideas and writings. As he states,

I do actually think it is a serious vocation to blog theology, especially when I know the number of people who read my stuff. I think others think what I have to say is more authoritative because of that. But I've learned that there is also an aura of credibility that comes with having published a traditional trade book. NPR or the *New York Times* isn't going to call me for a quote because I am a Christian blogger. But if I have a hardcover book out, then suddenly the media gives you more credibility. So I saw that publishing offline was an important strategy."

(T. Jones, personal communication, May 21, 2012)

However, after a few of his works appeared in traditional publishing outlets, he grew increasingly frustrated, both because of the constraints of formal book formats and the limited revenue most Christian authors make on their books. In the late 2000s, he began to experiment with eBooks. His first eBook was on the atonement of Christ's death for human sin. Working with recycled blog posts on the topic, he put together a short 14,000-word booklet for the Kindle platform. By Easter, he had sold 2,000 copies, and the eBook was reviewed and praised on Twitter, via email, and in book reviews on blogs (Jones, 2012).

> It was like as much as feedback as I have gotten from a serious 200-page, eighty thousand-word hardcover book that costs $35. People loved it. It is short, readable, it is digestible and it is for whatever reason on a topic that a lot of people wanted to talk about. The buzz around it made me think, "Man, people really care about what I have to say about theological doctrine. I am not just a pundit who pokes my finger in the eye of the denominations, as I sometimes see myself. People really want to hear what I have to say."
>
> (T. Jones, personal communication, May 21, 2012)

This experience has led Jones to other eBook projects, including one written based on crowdsourcing several ideas to his 5,000 followers on Facebook. In an online survey of his followers, he asked if he should next write about gay marriage, sexuality and the church, or some other topic.

> Overwhelmingly, people wanted me to write on prayer. It was overwhelming, like 80 percent. I am not even like very good at prayer! But that was the overwhelming response and so that is what I am going to write on next.
>
> (T. Jones, personal communication, May 21, 2012)

For almost two decades, Jones has invested in his work as a theoblogian. He is partially motivated by what he sees as the need for publically accessible theology to be produced by the church (i.e., Jones, 2011). He argues that the church no longer sees a person with PhD in theology as "the smartest person in the room," but rather as the one who has the best ability to communicate theology to congregations. He argues people are increasingly looking to accessible theological voices found on YouTube, blogs or social media as the new faith "experts" able to explain essential ideas about God and "what the church is supposed to be about."

> I want my ideas to be part of what populates the internet, which is where people are going to look for theological understanding these days …. I want Google to point to me, not because I want people to think my ideas are that great. I actually don't think I am that much of an original thinker theologically; I am primarily a popularizer of other people's theology. But I think most vocationally trained theologians have abdicated their ability to present popular theology."
>
> (T. Jones, personal communication, May 21, 2012)

Jones argues theoblogians function in the twenty-first century in the vein of the American historical preaching tradition, where pastors are elevated to the status of important theological thinkers, because they translate faith directly to the masses. He stresses the ideas that we need to give more credence to voices that can write and communicate theology at a popular level, because "theology has jumped the shark" as a closed guild dealing in incomprehensible ideas and specialist language.

Jones' popularity as reputable theological voice took a hit in 2015, when accusations by his ex-wife of emotional spousal abuse were made public. Due to the negative publicity this news garnered, which had impact on his reputation, Jones left Patheos.com. He continued to blog on his own website tonyj.net until 2016, when he transitioned to microblogging via Facebook and Twitter. Today Jones continues to work as a freelance theologian, speaker and author in Minnesota where he is remarried and lives with his three children. However, in order to protect them, he no longer reveals personal information on social media as he once did.

Jana Riess is a professional writer, freelance editor and senior columnist for Religion News Service. While she has worked for two decades in the publishing industry, she has only since 2010 established herself as a prominent Mormon blogger through her column "Flunking Sainthood." Her online presence first gained attention through her experimentation with Twitter, which sparked a project that later became known as "The Twible" (Riess, 2013). It was 2008, and she was working as freelance editor overseeing the publication of a handbook on religion and media for Oxford University Press. While at a meeting for the publication, she needed to look up something in the Bible. "I got the Bible out of the hotel nightstand, and I was struck very suddenly with how big the Bible was to compared to how much of it I actually know and read" (J. Riess, personal communication, October 12, 2013). She had recently joined Twitter but had quickly become annoyed by people who used Twitter for things she considered very inconsequential, like what they just ate. Then she had a thought. "Wouldn't it be interesting if I could use Twitter as a way of reading the Bible out loud." Riess had tried several times before to read the Bible from cover to cover, but had always given up. She thought, "If I could do it in community, with other people who held me accountable, and maybe if I could make it fun in some way, the process wouldn't feel like something that I 'had' to do" (J. Riess, personal communication, October 12, 2013).

So on October 4, 2009, Riess began tweeting the Bible, summarizing one chapter a day in 140 characters or less. In January of 2013, she concluded her first draft summary of all 1,189 chapters of the Old and New Testaments. Over three years her Twitter following grew from a few hundred to over 3,000, who encouraged, critiqued and offered feedback on her summaries of chapters and interpretations of scripture.

> Not everybody actually liked this project. There have been some people who have been offended by different things I wrote. One of the first controversial passages came in Genesis not long after I had started tweeting. It was when

Abraham rents his wife out for money; he does this twice with Sarah, and his son Isaac follows his example, renting out Rebecca. I called it pimping out, which is harsh language, but so is the concept that a patriarch of the Bible would be okay with rich men having sex with his wife. The concept in itself ought to be troublesome.

(J. Riess, personal communication, October 12, 2013)

Through this experience of tweeting the Bible, she discovered the value of crowdsourcing her ideas online. Her interaction with Twitter followers, propelled by comments received on this project, showed her how the internet could become an interactive collaborative space and a place of conversation about issues of theology and the church she deeply cared about. As a convert to Mormonism, Riess was deeply invested in issues related to how the Church of Jesus Christ of Latter-day Saints (LDS) was framed by media. Her experience around "The Twible" project and a desire to provide an alternative view of the LDS church pushed her to begin blogging in 2010. What would become her first blog post was initially a personal essay she wrote in response to a comment Glenn Beck made on his show, saying Christians had no place in social-justice-focused churches.

I was really angry with that, because the Book of Mormon is all about social justice, so I sat down wrote out my thoughts on this. I also pointed out that a few months before, the president of the LDS church had revised the church's threefold mission statement, which was to preach the gospel, redeem the dead, and perfect the saints. President Monson had added a fourth, which was to help the poor. I sent my response to Glenn Beck to a friend of mine who worked at beliefnet. com. He said, "Great! We'll put it up today!" because it was timely. The traffic for my first post very good and it showed them, I think, that it was sustainable to have a Mormon blogger on the site; they asked me that same day if I would be interested in doing a regular blog for them. So that is how I got started.

(J. Riess, personal communication, October 12, 2013)

Riess quickly gained a reputation as a progressive Mormon blogger on beliefnet. com, a religious lifestyle website that hosts content from authors representing many faiths. At the time, there were few Mormon voices in the blogosphere, a fact that made her take on current events and religious topics she found unusual and interesting. She clarifies, pointing out that as a "progressive Mormon blogger," her position is also atypical within her own faith community.

I am progressive within the predominately conservative Mormon community, in that I identity with some liberal politics and that I agree with homosexual equality and women's ordination. But by the standards of the rest of the world, the non-Mormon world, I am very much right in the middle. For a Mormon, I may be seen as a flaming leftist, but for ordinary people, I am not.

(J. Riess, personal communication, October 12, 2013)

She says her writing is born from a desire both to reflect on issues of Mormon faith in contemporary society and to respectfully question key social and theological issues that are not being addressed by the LDS church and its leaders. She describes her column as part of the "bloggernacle" community online:

> Within progressive Mormonism there has been a veritable explosion of podcasts and websites. We call it the bloggernacle, a place we can find community with other people asking the same questions, so it is this tabernacle online of voices.
>
> (J. Riess, personal communication, October 12, 2013)

Riess says that, in the last few years, the bloggernacle has made a significant impact in addressing issues surrounding the democratization of hierarchy and power in the LDS church. She says this is especially true for the part it has played in incremental changes that have increased women's visibility and leadership within the Church. Although women still do not hold the priesthood, within the last several years they have been granted the right to serve as official witnesses to temple ordinations and sit in on some of the previously all-male meetings that govern church administration. Mormon girls now receive the same budget for their activities that boys receive, and the adult temple endowment ceremony was updated in 2019 to remove or change some of the language that had been troubling to women. All of these were changes that feminists in the Church had lobbied for online.

Riess argues that the internet and voices in the Mormon blogosphere continue to play an enormous role in shaping decisions and discourse within the church. In 2013 an online campaign was launched called "Let Women Pray," encouraging women to sign a petition and join a Facebook group that simply asked LDS leaders to consider allowing a woman to pray publicly at a General Conference, an event that happens twice a year in Salt Lake City. Until 2014, there was no record of any women ever praying publicly at a General Conference in nearly two centuries of Mormon history.

> It was in March (2014), the rumor came down that a woman would be praying in General Conference, and then it happened for the first time. The church later stated that it had already planned to do that. So that may well be true, but I can't imagine that the online campaign didn't have any impact in that decision.
>
> (J. Riess, personal communication, April 26, 2014)

Riess functions as a theoblogian in that her online content seeks to facilitate a religious discourse within her faith community about important social issues and to consider how their church tradition and beliefs can allow for new practices and adaptions within contemporary society. She argues that the LDS church has often enacted "classic minority behavior" in that, "you want to control your public image as much as you can," because religious minorities can be easily caricatured or misrepresented in society, and especially in the media. The internet challenges the

LDS's very top-down approach to information, where each Sunday, congregations around the world study the exact same lesson, derived from a centralized curriculum.

> But the internet cuts through the Church-controlled authority and its chain of command, for better or for worse. The church is recognizing that it is a powerful tool for people to tell their stories, like through the "I Am A Mormon" campaign, showcasing the richness of a diverse membership. But it can also be a source of great theological difficulty when the internet shows people the problematic history of the Church, like finding out Joseph Smith practiced not only polygamy but also married women who were already married to other men. The Church itself has always wanted to pretend that didn't happen, or that it was so far in the past that it is irrelevant, but the internet makes this information easily visible. This can be really damaging for some people's faith. So the internet has been both a build and a stumbling block. It is a double-edged sword for the Church.
>
> (J. Riess, personal communication, April 26, 2014)

Riess argues that the Church needs to understand that it can no longer control the message about how it is perceived the way it could in the 1960s or earlier with its broadcast ads and media campaigns about what it means to be a Mormon. While the Church of Jesus Christ of Latter-day Saints remains a centralized institution, the media it seeks to leverage to provide a unified message and image of the Church are not the same in the current digital age. The internet allows people like Riess to think aloud online about their faith and relationship with the institution and share their questions and doubts. Church leaders can see the internet either as a threat or as an opportunity to listen.

> Within the institution are deep thinkers who care very much about some of the same issues that digital creative people care about. I have been surprised, and pleasantly so, by some of the individual notes that I will receive from people who work for the Church and who work for BYU and who read my blog and are grateful for it even if they can't in their position officially retweet what I say. They are thinking about these same challenges, and I find that very encouraging.
>
> (J. Riess, personal communication, April 26, 2014)

Theoblogians represent a new class of religious interpreters who understand how digital media offer them a unique platform for sharing their religious convictions and thinking. Their theology is more narrative based, personal and reflective than it is conditioned by traditional analytical categories and methods of argumentation. It emulates the culture of digital storytelling, pairing thoughtful biblical reflection with accessible language that enables them to connect with a broader readership. It is their engaging style of communication and way they frame their message through personal storytelling, which builds for them in minds of their readers the image of being an emerging theoblogian.

Internet evangelists

Internet evangelists are those who see the internet opening up a new mission field and believe the flexibility of networked technologies enables the creation of new tools for evangelism. Unlike the media-driven missionaries to be discussed in Chapter 6, instead of waiting to collaborate with established Christian organizations to build tools or implement digital media strategies for proselytizing, internet evangelists just go out and do it. They are independent entrepreneurs who embrace the opportunities offered by digital media, experiment with creating content and tools, develop resources or initiatives and then freely share their creations online.

Tony Whitaker from the UK is one such example. He describes himself as an early internet adopter with a heart to share Jesus with others. After spending some time online, he quickly caught a glimpse of how the internet could be used for witnessing to non-Christians. Not only could traditional evangelistic media be easily translated online—e.g., creating digital version of tracks that shared the Christian message of salvation through Jesus Christ—but new forms of evangelism might even be made possible. He also saw the networking potential of the internet offering the ability to connect like-minded Christians with a heart for evangelism so they could share resources and encourage one another.

In the mid-1990s, he spent much of his energies exploring other early internet evangelists who were developing e-vangelism training courses and witnessing websites, and best-practices guides for sharing your faith in news groups or via early web chat. These explorations led Whitaker to found Internet Evangelism Day in 1999, a campaign aimed at helping local churches get over a fear of the internet as a problematic secular tool, and encouraging them to catch the vision of how they could use the internet as a tool for evangelism to spread the Christian Gospel. For him, embracing the internet means Christians beginning to see the positive potential of the internet.

> To me, in this work I am keeping the church aware of what they could be doing, the potential the internet hold for church outreach. From me, it is a gift to give them ideas and suggestions or other positive things they could involve with on the internet.
>
> (T. Whitaker, personal communication, September 23, 2011)

Whitaker also wanted to show churches how their outreach online could not only impact local people, but people from around the globe. The Internet Evangelism Day initiative centered around a website he created, which not only publicized this event but featured pages that linked to witnessing resources found online and suggested activities churches could do during a service or Sunday school to raise awareness about how the internet could be used for evangelism. Over time, the internet Evangelism Day site became a key hub providing links to other Christian organizations involved in training and conducting witnessing online. It also offers an extensive repository of witnessing resources from digital tracts and Evangelistic podcasts found online, even providing inspirational Christian GIFs and images that can be shared with others via social media.

Whitaker says 2005 marked the point when this solo endeavor began to gain public attention among Christians in the USA and Europe. He now not only advertises the annual Internet Evangelism Day but also calls Christians to consider a specific month, usually May, as Digital Outreach Month, and offers suggestions about how churches can integrate the internet into their mission and outreach activities. For him, internet evangelism is a simple and straightforward task and an opportunity the church should not miss. It is "sharing the good news via the internet."

> I get a lot of positive feedback. Lots. I think that the problem is that the Christian mindset can be very traditional, that proclamation of God's word happens through a sermon or maybe through a particular event. The church can be skeptical about new strategies for traditions, like the idea you could share the Gospel on Facebook. That is just not how it is expected to be done.
> (T. Whitaker, personal communication, September 23, 2011)

Despite this mindset, he says he has had little criticism of his work and internet evangelism. However, he did voice frustration about the fact that, in the 2000s especially, many church leaders he shared his vision with treated it with amusement, rather than seriousness.

> When I first started this work, I thought if we could get some denominational leaders on board, then we would have buy-in from the people. But I quickly learned that doesn't work! Church leaders tend to be resistant to change and the internet. It is the grassroots people that are interested and will listen to this potential for evangelism … talking to leaders about this was like speaking to a brick wall.
> (T. Whitaker, personal communication, September 23, 2011)

After two decades he is still very invested in Internet Evangelism Day and continues to run the site primarily on his own, with the help of a few friends and volunteers who also publicize the event online. He feels the project is having a reasonable impact, as the website garners 2,000+ hits a day, and the site's associated blog averages 4,000 reads a month. He also runs a Facebook group connected to his work, posting conversion stories people share with him on his various platforms. His goal continues to be to encourage others to see the internet as more than an information tool or entertainment medium, but as a powerful tool any Christian can use to make a positive impact on the world. Each spring he runs a social media campaign to raise awareness about the annual Internet Evangelism Day.

Many internet evangelists studied in my research had starts similar to Whitaker's. They begin with a revelation of the potential of the internet as a tool for outreach. This leads to personal experimentation online, followed by launching a passion-driven evangelistic campaign or website. However, in a few cases, the solo projects have birthed initiatives with international impact.

Eric Celier from France could well be described as a French-speaking Billy Graham on the internet. He is charismatic, full of energy, an eloquent speaker and overflows with enthusiasm for using the internet to bring people to Christ. Though his name is little known in the USA, his online ministry has made a significant impact in Europe, Africa and Asia over the last three decades. As a teenager, he became a Christian through a Billy Graham crusade in Paris; this encounter lit within him a personal passion to similarly serve God with his life and career. In the mid-1990s, he was preparing to plant a church for the Assemblies of God denomination, when the internet caught his attention. Though he did not have any formal experience with computers, he began to experiment with building a web page for the church he was training with. This opened his eyes to the possibilities of using the internet for evangelism.

In the late 1990s his friend suggested, "We don't have any Christian websites, we should start one."

> Then I caught this vision. I built one of the first church pages in France. It was really an ugly website, but I had no background in IT, so I experimented. I did it. But my vision was bigger than this.
>
> (E. Celier, personal communication, February 7, 2013)

As part of these beginnings, he began to look for other Christians online in Europe with a similar vision. A chance encounter online connected him with a Christian woman in Switzerland who had an internet company, and with her staff's help he build his next website. In 1997 he founded a webpage in French called Top Christen, (or Top Christian) focused on telling people in French about the basics of Christianity and the story of Christ's death for human salvation. While the site was the result of hard work and personal passion, he quickly saw his vision of affecting France via the internet was not something he could do alone.

> In a sense I co-started my ministry with the help of Christians in Switzerland. That is a story that I can tell you […] with internet work you are never alone. I have learned that internet ministry, you cannot do it alone; it is always best do it through teams. I am the visionary guy, but I work now with a team.
>
> (E. Celier, personal communication, February 7, 2013)

Top Christen became a stepping-stone to the eventual launch of an internet ministry in the 2000s, Jesus.net, a full-fledged religious nonprofit network. Creative headquarters of Jesus.net is based in a suburb just outside Paris, where Celier works with a team of 15 full-time people, including graphic artists, online content experts, web specialists and software designers as internet evangelists.

> We do our work like missionaries. Missionaries are people called by God to do this mission, and they raise their own support. Each person who works with us raises their own (financial) support to do this work. Sometimes we employ people because we need special skills for a project, but mostly we live off gifts and donations to do this work.
>
> (E. Celier, personal communication, February 7, 2013)

Besides the Paris team, Celier oversees a network of over 500 volunteers spread throughout Europe, North America and other parts of the world. These volunteers are invested in helping with his evangelistic work online through Jesus.net. Over the past two decades, as each new online platform has emerged, he has asked himself, "How can we use that for evangelism?" He shares the story of how one morning in 2001 he had a brainstorm.

> I was praying and it became very clear for me that we can use the internet to do evangelism in a new way. I saw God give me a step-by-step presentation of the gospel, finishing with a prayer that could be emailed via invitation to people. So I did research on the internet, "What is effective online? What do people like?" I discovered that there were new tools on the internet out there that we could use for my vision if we combined them.
>
> (E. Celier, personal communication, February 7, 2013)

In this way, Jesus.net has grown to offer multiple evangelistic tools and resources. "KnowingGod" is an online digital tract and video experience that shares the Christian salvation message in different languages. "A Miracle Every Day," also offered in multiple languages, is a daily encouragement newsletter aimed at encouraging new Christian believers. MyStory.me is a platform that enables Christians to record and share testimonies of what God has done in their lives and allows them to send these links to others they are witnessing. Their LikeJesus app offers people daily devotional readings and bible-reading plans. Combining all these elements, Jesus.net serves as a hub and portal to these and still other resources, such as bible study courses and Christian teaching videos for those who want to learn about Jesus or grow in the faith.

Due to the breadth of Celier's global vision—to reach beyond French speaking people in France, Africa and Canada—he has seen the necessity for Jesus.net to move from being a pioneering stand-alone ministry to partnering with over 70 established Christian organizations that have a similar desire to pursue evangelism through the internet.

> Our vision is imagining everyone in the world having free access to the Gospel. Everyone! Automatically, when you have this vision of the world having access

to the Gospel, you know that you cannot do it alone. No organization can do it alone. I remember speaking with a big organization in the US, very large, and I said to them, "You think you are big, but the internet is much bigger than you are."

(E. Celier, personal communication, February 7, 2013)

This includes working with many well-known and established international parachurch organizations with long histories of doing evangelistic work, such as the Billy Graham Association, Campus Crusade for Christ and the Christian Broadcasting Network and its ministry partners. These connections have helped broaden his ministry's reach into new countries and language groups, expand their network of volunteers, enable them to do more wide-reaching evangelistic campaigns, draw on external experts to help with specific projects and share content and tools to keep Jesus.net on the cutting edge.

Part of Jesus.net's vision is to be a ministry that helps equip other religious organizations that "have no clue what to do with the internet." As Celier states,

I really see Jesus.net as a movement. It is not just one person, somewhere giving directions on how should do evangelism online. It is a team and partners asking how we can be better at what we do. We have an understanding of technology by God's grace. So we give to others the tools we have, we give them for free; it's the new paradigm for ministry, open-sourced evangelism and resources.

(E. Celier, personal communication, February 7, 2013)

Jesus.net seems to be making its mark online—according to their website, as of July 2018, over 15 million people worldwide representing 35 different language groups have made a decision to follow Christ after coming in contact with one of the site's tools. But for Celier it is not about the statistics. For him, each decision is important.

I am like a full-time pastor, but my congregation is the internet. What is important online is the people. It is not the numbers […] of course, we do count the number of visitors, because if you don't have many visits then you don't reach people. But it is real people whose lives are changed is why I do this, not because of the tool but to reach people with the tool.

(E. Celier, personal communication, February 7, 2013)

He shares the story of a man who contacted him through the site. He was so excited to learn about Jesus, he asked Celier if he could come visit church with him. The man was from Brazil and ended up traveling to France and staying with Celier's family for a month while he learned the basics of Christianity. It is experiences like this, facilitated by the internet, that deepen the passion he has for internet evangelism.

We feel God is really calling people to be internet evangelists. Even Google is now using this word evangelist […] to speak about Google and how certain people who are having a great impact on the digital world, and spreading their message. So even the internet is using our terminology, evangelist. How much more do we need evangelists for the internet? God is calling people with technology backgrounds … any kind of people. I am not a tech guy. But God called me for that and equipped me. So that is special. Now God is calling business people to put their time, some of them their money, into the internet.

(E. Celier, personal communication, February 7, 2013)

One of these people who has joined the ranks of the Jesus.net ministry network is Arjo deVroome, a middle-aged man from Holland. He initially worked for an evangelical television station and then for Campus Crusade for Christ in Holland, but now works for Jesus.net where he works as partnership director. His work involves connecting with and coming alongside Jesus.net's partner ministries and supporting them in planning different evangelistic strategies or campaigns in their specific countries of ministry. He also helps partners develop evangelism strategies related to their organizational websites. One of the main ways he does this is through his involvement in an outreach program run by Jesus.net called "Why Jesus?"

This is a five-week online course that introduces people to who Jesus is and other Christian basics. It was originally based on a booklet of the same name written by a well-known pastor and author from the UK who helped found the internationally known, church-based evangelism program, "Alpha." Interestingly, when the Jesus.net team approached the author about using his book to design what they described as a "pre-Alpha online program," he was not supportive, not wanting to skew or lose control of the "Alpha" brand and its established programming. But the team moved ahead anyway. The Dutch Alpha-director said, "Well, we are just going to do it. Because if it works, Nicky will be happy, and we'll ask for forgiveness. And if it doesn't work, then he will never hear a word of it" (A. deVroome, personal communication, March 4, 2013).

Today, they describe "Why Jesus?" as an online pre-evangelism-to-evangelism course inspired by the booklet but featuring mostly rewritten material and guided by e-coaches who offer support to people taking the course. De Vroome oversees training the e-coaches who run the "Why Jesus?" program in different countries. Individuals taking the online course are offered access to a personal coach during those weeks; the coach offers feedback to participants' responses and clarifies questions they have about material. De Vroome's role is to come alongside volunteers and groups running a language-specific course online and prepare them for acting as e-coach guides that facilitate open dialogue with participants and avoid preaching at them. With over 1,500 participants taking the course per year, that means training hundreds of e-coaches a year. Over the past decade, he has traveled all around Europe, to South East Asia and to other parts of the world, training e-coaches and helping organizations think seriously about internet evangelism.

Since de Vroome works with many traditional evangelical organizations and church-networks that use predominantly offline events and face-to-face methods, he says many could be described as internet adverse or hesitant. He is often faced with questions or concerns from churches about online evangelistic work, most relating suspicions about whether you can really build a relationship with someone through technology and whether or not authentic discipleship can actually happen online.

> I often hear, "What is happening online, it is not as real as offline" […] And this perspective is always the challenge—to make sure organizations, churches, and ministries understand that what we are doing online is really a preparation for offline connections. So we want to reach people where they are at, which is online, to connect them with Christians and then try to make the connection offline […] But many groups still think we are trying to keep people only online.
>
> (A. de Vroome, personal communication, March 4, 2013)

De Vroome describes "Why Jesus?" and Jesus.net as landing spaces where people can encounter the Gospel. For him, the internet is the point of connection, and he stresses the fact that e-coaches are trained to connect participants with an offline local church at the end of the course, if they are interested. He finds it novel that, in an age when the internet is so pervasive, especially in western contexts like Europe, churches are still so adverse to the idea of internet evangelism

> A big part of our work is modeling, activating the church to see the potential for internet evangelism, and that personal spiritual searching is being done online. Through Jesus.net, we have tried to open the eyes of churches all around Europe and outside of Europe. And provide them the opportunity to get actively involved too through e-coaching. The problem is, we find pastors are resistant, because they are like, "Oh the internet, well, I barely know how to use my email. This is too much." But we try to encourage them to mobilize the people in their churches who are online to get involved, even if leaders feel they can't.
>
> (A. de Vroome, personal communication, March 4, 2013)

Working with churches in the former Eastern Europe and places like the UK and Holland, he has especially seen this resistance. However, he believes the coming new generations of younger pastors do understand the role the internet has to play, not only in running a church, but in evangelistic outreach.

> They understand it doesn't mean that every pastor needs to be a techie or following the latest tech things. It doesn't mean you have to do this with the Internet and you have to be online all the time as a pastor, but that this online space is also an important place for ministry. And I tell them it is not about building just your own kingdom online, it is about God's kingdom, we must do this work together, share our talents and gifts for reaching the world online and offline.
>
> (A. de Vroome, personal communication, March 4, 2013)

From the profiles provided of techies for God, theobloggians and internet evangelists, we see that overall, digital entrepreneurs present themselves as individuals with technology skills who find themselves inspired, or even compelled, to create digital resources to fulfill a religious goal. In what follows, I summarize the shared traits noted in the stories profiled here and the challenges they face due to this sense of calling and the associated work they pursue.

Digital entrepreneurs' media-making narrative: Visionary technology influencers

Taken together, these three types of digital entrepreneurs can be seen as media designers and content creators with professional and technical qualifications along with media expertise, all of which they seek to leverage in order to develop new types of religious resources. They have a strong desire to create cutting-edge tools or distinctive content that they believe can make a difference in other people's spiritual journeys or in the practices of their Christian community. They like to experiment with new tools and platforms to see how they can be adapted for Christian ministry. Much of their innovative work is done on their own time and self-resourced, and they are highly motivated individuals set on achieving the goals they establish.

I describe the media-making narrative they present as *visionary technology influencers*. They have a strong desire to create solutions to problems facing the Christian community or meet needs others may not even see. For them, the answer is found in the innovative use of technology for religious purposes. Because their influence comes primarily from their technological expertise, they often fall outside the traditional preview of being a religious leader. Their influence comes from what they make, how they and others use it and the public take-up and attention given to their endeavors. Their religious influence is technology based; they are not bound to an established organization for their positions or influence. This pioneering spirit makes them enthusiastic and inspiring visionaries. Digital entrepreneurs are very focused on seeing technology work as a form of Christian service, and openly talk about how they see their technology skills as a God-given form of ministry. The individuals who rise in prominence due to their online work are often unexpected, but overtime, often gain an audience of admirers who support and give credence to their creative work. While they represent diverse technical backgrounds, skills and goals, analysis of their interviews shows they possess several common traits.

Entrepreneurial spirit as asset and handicap

Digital entrepreneurs, as the name suggests, are entrepreneurial in outlook and actions. They exhibit what they see as valuable skills and insights for building technologies that can have a transformational impact on Christian ministry, yet at the same time, their vision for using these skills can be institutionally challenging. They are creative, trying to look at established practices and emerging problems in new ways with an out-of-the-box perspective. They are independent and personally motivated by their work. They do their digital creative work on their own time, and tithe it, often freely, when motivated by a strong goal.

Their nature as entrepreneurs is to experiment with new ways of doing work and helping people through the tools of their trade. They give attention to what they see as immediate, practical problem solving for specific tasks related to religious practices, rather than to the creation of tools that fit into a set system or institution. Their approach is making and doing new things, not sustaining and solidifying old patterns. All of these characteristics mean they are highly motivated by work they see as having value and are often willing to freely give of their time outside their formal work or religious organizational structures.

However, these motivational strengths of independence, creativity and being business-minded can be seen to be at odds with the nature of religious service. Digital entrepreneurs insist it is imperative that churches understand and adapt to digital culture. Yet as many noted in this study, this perspective is not always understood or welcomed by various religious groups. Digital entrepreneurs are energized by change, direct action and experimentation. Their emphasis on doing something original and readily embracing new technologies can also be seen as a threat to religious organizations that often lag behind in their technological adoption. Their advocacy for change and technological innovation can also be seen as a subtle critique, suggesting they see their communities as backward or out of touch with contemporary culture. So the very character of digital entrepreneurs can create innate tensions with the very people they seek to serve

Digital work as religious calling

Digital entrepreneurs often describe their religious-focused digital creativity as more than an outworking of extending their profession into their personal time. They consistently describe their work of building new media platforms, applications and outlets as a form of service to the church or a tithe of their time and talents to their faith community. The church becomes a site for envisioning new and more efficient or innovative ways of doing core tasks and established rituals related to religious education and witnessing. These RDCs see themselves as equipping their faith community and providing resources that can replace those which are lacking or out of date. They have a strong sense of personal mission and do this work on their own time, typically outside their formal work and religious organizational structures, even if they have close institutional affiliations. Their strong sense of independence, wanting to push boundaries to create new forms of Christian outreach through their digital work, can also lead them to encounter a number of challenges. This is because, while they see their technology work as service or ministry to the church, their work is not accountable to a specific religious organization or tied to a recognized spiritual gifting or ministry.

An unrecognized ministry

Digital entrepreneurs recognize the fact that their digital work is frequently not understood or valued by their religious community as a form of ministry. This can be the case for two reasons. First, they are perceived as institutional outsiders. These digital entrepreneurs typically work in media- or tech-related industries and have secular employers, so their religiously motivated digital work is done on their own time without official authorization or oversight. This challenges the highly controlled structures of religious institutions, as, while they are insiders within the faith community, they are outsiders to the religious institutional structures they seek to serve.

Second, they appear to be self-appointed. Digital entrepreneurs often work independently, creating initiatives or resources they see as useful to the work of the church, then bring these resources to the attention of the religious groups with which they see themselves as affiliated. Thus, they can often be seen as instigating an independent or parachurch ministry that can be seen as in conflict with traditional gatekeeping, vetting or promotional structures.

Digital entrepreneurs as visionary technology influencers

Digital entrepreneurs frame their digital work as very mission focused, or infused with a sense of religious calling. They are motivated to use their skills to meet a perceived spiritual need in the Christian church, whether that be in the area of religious education, community building or proselytizing. They strongly reflect the traits of the media influencer described in Chapter 1, who relates to algorithmic culture by immersing themselves in that space and using its tools and techniques to create a public platform to share their thoughts or passions and gain attention. This acting out of algorithmic authority totally relies on the structures of digital culture to create and sustain their goals and influence. They rise in prominence due to their online work and build an online social network that helps sustain it. It is their audience of admirers online that primarily supports and gives credence to their creative work. Their innovative digital work frames them as visionary and pioneering, and people applaud them for creating new models for religious engagement in digital culture. However, their design of cutting-edge platforms or services that facilitate religious outreach and practices in new ways can be seen as running counter to traditional structures or offline realities relative to how religious groups or cultures function. This creates challenges that must be contextualized through digital entrepreneurs' technological apologetic, outlined in more detail in Chapter 7.

Chapter 5

Digital spokespersons
The rise of institutional identity curators

Digital spokespersons are becoming very common among religious institutions in a digital age. The press officers and media specialists of a previous generation have had to transform themselves into digital experts to meet the communication needs of their organizations and reach out to an increasingly digitally driven public. As was the case in Chapter 4, I begin by defining the shared traits digital spokespersons exhibit within their respective religious organizations. Then I provide an overview of several different types of digital spokespersons I have identified in various religious communities and institutions. This leads to outlining core traits their media-making narratives share, which become important in later discussions in Chapter 7 of how they frame their relationships to their specific religious communities or institutions, as well as their understanding of authority. Through this exploration, digital spokespersons present themselves as institutional identity curators. Their work presents them as servants of their religious institutions, seeking to manage these groups' official digital presences and/or serving as sanctioned representative voices to the digital public on behalf of those they serve.

Defining digital spokespersons

Digital spokespersons, as introduced in Chapter 2, are religious digital creatives (RDCs) working on behalf of a specific religious institution or community. A key part of their work is presenting and representing that group's identity in the media, especially on digital media platforms. This may be done by designing the group's informational website, managing social media sites representing the group online or moderating online discussions related to their institution. This category of digital creatives draws on Anderson's notion of "spokesperson-activists," or those who seek to present the face of an established religious institution online. Anderson's category, as outlined in Chapter 3, included both those who are appointed by leaders of groups to be their online representatives and individuals who become the public face of their community because of the media and technology work they do for the institution. These spokesperson-activists, as Anderson described them, hold jobs such as communication or information officers, webmasters, press liaisons or even personal assistants serving specific religious leaders, positions that require them to regularly liaise between the media, the public and their institution. Thus, they are charged with overseeing the online presence and reputation of the group for which they work.

In this study, digital spokespersons are defined as those who serve as digital content creators, moderators or public media liaisons employed by a specific religious organization or community for the purpose of representing that group within the digital world. This means they are appointed to such roles by a community leader or recognized institutional structures and are thus charged with the task of creating and managing the group's digital tools and environments. They also oversee institutionally sanctioned information about their group appearing on the internet and/or produce the content their group shares about itself through various digital platforms. These digital spokespersons may serve in a number of different roles within their organizations, including community webmasters, social media coordinators, institutional communication directors and digital media officers. They collate and share relevant online content about their group and monitor how its identity and beliefs are being framed online.

Because digital spokespersons are typically paid by a specific religious group to perform a role focused on communicating and managing how the group is represented online, they often experience a strong sense of duty and responsibility to the religious institution and community they work for. Many times, their role is primarily a technical one, as their job remit may include some combination of tasks such as managing websites, overseeing the leader's blog or the group's Facebook page and making sure news items or press releases from the organization are posted online in an accurate and accessible manner. Yet because their structural and technical tasks involve presenting information about their specific group, it may ultimately mean they are responsible for representing the only officially sanctioned voice of the group in digital spaces. This means many digital spokespersons recognize the fact that their technical work carries with it a unique responsibility to accurately portray the values and distinctiveness of the religious community they represent. While these RDCs may recognize the fact that they speak for the larger group online and not themselves, they often lack the opportunity to consult or get feedback that can help them with such tasks. Such challenges and others will be explored in more detail in this chapter.

Types of digital spokespersons

In this study, 30 of the 120 interviews conducted were with individuals who work as digital spokespersons for their religious organizations and institutions. Individuals taking on this role included Catholic webmasters, technology staff for the Methodist denomination, Church of England and Church of Sweden directors of communication, press officers for various Presbyterian churches, Anglican and non-denominational church media officers, and media workers from a number of other religious organizations such as bible societies in both the USA and Europe. From these interviews, we see three common groups of digital spokespersons present within most religious denominations and organizations: (1) media officers and communication directors, (2) webmasters and technology teams, and (3) online ambassadors.

Media officers and communication directors

Increasingly, religious denominations employ communication directors and media officers to play specific roles related to the production and management of communication services within their organizations. For the most part, communication directors take on a number of key roles, including overseeing the production of media resources related to the work and mission of the institution, as well as managing the flow of information within the institution—especially between church leaders, staff and members—and strategic information sharing about the organization with external sources. A press or media officer may also serve as the designated liaison with journalists or institutional spokespersons for print, broadcast and digital media sources, which would include distributing press releases about church affairs and offering official comments to the press on behalf of specific religious leaders about the church's response to media events.

In the past decade, the roles of communication directors and media officers have shifted due to the rise of digital media news outlets and resources. They no longer interact primarily with mass media. At one time, these individuals would have spent much of their time producing literature for communication within their organization and acting as external promotional resources providing more public information about their organization. Media officers in past have often been referred to as press officers, focused on producing print newsletters and press releases, and engaging with media outlets. Now they are often charged with taking on the important role of representing their church's beliefs and positions online and within digital media and spaces. Such positions are appointed rather than elected, and while they may be assigned as the head of a specific institutional department—e.g., an institutional communication department—they serve under a specific leader, such as a bishop or church administrator.

In this research, communication directors from five different mainline denominations were interviewed—Church of England (Anglican), Church of Sweden (Lutheran), Methodist, Greek Orthodox and Catholic—as well as two non-denominational/inter-denominational churches. Communication directors for mainline denominations work in the national office of their specific institution, overseeing communication departments or multiple staff involved in media work and production. While these directors may work within different institutional structures, the roles they perform, their backgrounds and the challenges they face are quite similar.

Former director of communications for the Church of England, Arun Arora, served for five years as chief media officer for the Anglican Church in England and had previously served in other media-related positions in the Church. In his position he worked with the Archbishops' Council, the Church Commissioners and Pensions Board and Lambeth Palace, headquarters of the Archbishop of Canterbury, on communication issues and acted as a media liaison for the Anglican Church. Arora's background was unique in that he was also an ordained priest with the Church of England, which he said helped him understand both the concerns of media professionals and church leaders related to representing the Church in digital and traditional media spaces.

Like many religious media officers interviewed, his primary training and work experience was in mass-media journalism, especially interacting with the press on behalf of the church. This meant he had to learn on the job over the past decade how to integrate digital media into work he oversaw and how to best implement and leverage new media to meet the communication needs of the Anglican Communion.

> What has been difficult is to bring change to an environment based around a predominately reactive press-office model. The Church can no longer rely on a 1990s model of professional-corporate communication that pushes out information and expect press to pick it up.
>
> (A. Arora, personal communication, March 1, 2013)

When Arora assumed his position in 2012, he was quick to see the need for the Church of England to move past its "one-way, transmission model of communication" characterized by his office producing for subscribers a daily email news digest of all stories that mentioned the Church of England. His first week on the job he asked, "Why don't we publish this via Twitter so that everyone who wants access can have it?" and was immediately met with all the reasons "why we shouldn't and couldn't do this."

This led him to challenge both his staff and his supervisors to think differently about the digital environment and develop a strategic plan for mobilizing new media to spread positive stories about the work and mission of the church.

> The digital era requires us to be proactive, producing material rather than waiting for the phone to ring. The challenge to us is how then we are communicating in a way that takes advantage of new media platforms.
>
> (A. Arora, personal communication, March 1, 2013)

One of the first initiatives he helped implement was running several religious Twitter campaigns over Christmas 2012 (#ChristmasStartsWithChrist) and Easter 2013 (#EverythingChanges), which reached over 15 million users. Arora describes these as important initiatives designed to get church members involved in embracing social media for communicating about their faith and religious observance:

> Christmas Day is one of our best days as the Church, it is when people come that we may not see the rest of the year, and generally speaking when we are at our best. The idea of "Christmas Starts with Christ" was taking the message of joy and the true meaning of Christmas outside of our church buildings through Twitter.
>
> (A. Arora, personal communication, March 1, 2013)

Using Hootsuite, and by convincing the Archbishop of Canterbury and several other key bishops to tweet portions of their Christmas Eve and Day sermons, as well as encouraging church members to tweet personal church experiences, they were able to generate 19,000 tweets focused on the Church's Christmas message. Over Easter and during Holy Week, they recruited people to help live tweet portions of the story of Christ's last days using the voices and experiences of individuals named in the biblical accounts of Jesus' death, burial and resurrection. While these efforts of church staff and members to use social media to spread their message of faith were successful, not all of the digital media experiments he suggested were. When the story of a young Welsh girl who went missing made front page news and was the lead story on the ten o'clock news, he gathered a team to strategize how the Church could comment on and speak hope into this situation. The idea emerged to use the Church's newly established Twitter account to tweet a prayer for her family and those searching for her. Instead of supporting this idea, the communication team listed all the reasons this should not be done and expressed concerns over whether this was the proper use of an official church communication channel.

> And there were legal jurisdictional arguments saying, "Well she lives in Wales … we are the Church of England. This is a Church of Wales story." So I said, "Well it is on the front page of every newspaper. It is leading the national news. Why can't we speak into it?" In the end there was so much opposition within the team we decided the media team should leave this up to the full press offices.
>
> (A. Arora, personal communication, March 1, 2013)

Overcoming the fear of new media and the problem of who should do what with it is another challenge faced by communication directors who work within institutional structures and have staff doing overlapping yet distinct media-related jobs. The Anglican Church National Communication Office is charged to interact with local dioceses—most of which have at least one press officer or a communications officer—to provide media training and advice in developing local church communication strategies. Arora also sought to encourage other media workers for the Church to help them overcome their fears about "getting it wrong" when experimenting with digital media:

> One of the things about digital media, especially social media, is that there is an inherent relational risk. There is no safe way really to build a relationship that is authentic, especially online. It requires risk and that is okay. I don't mind that staff take risks and that they get it wrong, as long as it is in set parameters related to their specific roles and the work of the Church. We must embrace new technology in a way that enables us to do that. The difficulty we encounter is that our media mentality has been informed by traditional ways of communicating with the media that aren't creative and the kind required by digital engagement.
>
> (A. Arora, personal communication, March 1, 2013)

Claus Grue is a senior communication consultant for the World Council of Churches. When I interviewed him, he served as communications director of the diocese of Lund for the Church of Sweden, which has links to the Lutheran tradition. He was responsible for the overall production and distribution of internal and external information and communication at the Lund diocese. This means he works closely with the Bishop of Lund and the over 185 parishes within the diocese. He, too, has seen a transition from primarily working with mass media to focusing more attention on digital platforms. As a diocesan communication director, he noticed an increasing emphasis on the speed with which church communication must happen, due to the church's use of new media.

> The emergence of social media is of course a challenge, because these are new platforms that we have to adapt to and use in a professional fashion. It has changed the work in the way that we facilitate internal and external communication and must respond to events more quickly than before. While we cannot comment on everything, it is an increasing challenge to keep track of what is going on in the internet and where the Church could and should respond.
> (C. Grue, personal communication, June 4, 2013)

The move toward digital within the Church of Sweden was prompted by the national office's establishment of a very clear and highly developed national media strategy that many dioceses, including Lund, adopted and adjusted to local contexts. The strategy covers ideological, ethical and practical concerns related to the internet, with advice on digital media use and online protocols to outline the official chain of communication within the Church and the role of communication directors within this chain. Most importantly, the national communication strategy emphasizes the fact that the internet should become the center of church and dioceses' communications, and details what the implications of this might be.

> It does not replace other forms of communication; in many respects the most efficient form of communication is of course meeting and talking to people, two-way communications. Much of the implementation of digital media becomes question of leadership. It is important that we help our leaders within the church, within the dioceses, to be efficient communicators and to help them do that within the internet.
> (C. Grue, personal communication, June 4, 2013)

Grue worked very closely with his boss, the bishop, to develop digital communication opportunities. He felt that since the bishop is the most visible representative of the Church in their community, it was vital that Grue provide her with platforms that enable her to easily reach out to society as a whole.

> We have a quite ambitious media work that we do. As she is, of course, the main figure, we want to provide opportunity for her to take part in the

ongoing debate every day, about issues that are debated in the media. Instead of her writing an article or reflecting through a blog, we have focused on using Twitter. It provides her with a quick and easy way of responding, to be proactive on social events, but also in a reactive way when other people start debates online.

(C. Grue, personal communication, June 4, 2013)

Since she began tweeting in 2012, the bishop amassed several thousand Twitter followers. Tweeting has also become a way for her to "[push] her messages" about faith and the Church. Grue says that's one reason they chose Twitter for her. He said it has significantly raised the bishop's media profile and public voice:

If she has written something in a paper like a debate article, or the diocese published a video featuring her annual Christmas message, we use Twitter to push it and to multiply the effect. She comes to me and says, "How can we get this message across better?" Or, "Maybe I should Tweet something about this event?" So it is a dialogue all the time together about how best to use the media to get her (the bishop's) words out.

(C. Grue, personal communication, June 4, 2013)

While the move toward Swedish bishops using digital media is growing, Grue said internal church structures often inhibit internet use and digital integration:

The church can be very diversified […] a lot of small units everywhere. Small parishes and even bigger parishes have a tradition of doing things related to communication. There is a lot to be gained if the church could better coordinate resources, coordinate know-how. So there is a lot of work to be done there when it comes to digital media and the Church together.

(C. Grue, personal communication, June 4, 2013)

One move toward unifying Church communication has been the construction of a common website for the Church of Sweden coordinated by the national office. Ulrika Wipple, who served as communications officer focused on supervising web communication at the national office of the Church of Sweden, describes this initiative. While it is not mandatory for the churches or dioceses to join, use the national office's website template, or host their sites here, the national offices' site offers them the opportunity to update their web presence and receive support in terms of quality and cost. This and other solutions are being funded by the national Church office as a way to help especially small parishes that cannot afford the upkeep involved with maintaining a website, often the key digital storefront for most churches.

Wipple described work as mostly supporting and teaching others at the parish and diocesan levels about the web—e.g., how they can optimize web searches to elevate their online presence. Wipple said communication strategy at the local level is vital, "because they are the ones that are actually responsible and able to put out most of the information on the Church" (personal communication, April 17, 2017). One of the challenges encountered working for a large church institution is trying to explain to church leaders how the internet does not function under the same structural communication logic. This, she said, is stressed in the national communication strategy:

> It suggests that all the members should carry and can carry the message of the church in a digital age, which can be sort of controversial. It means not just the educated priests can speak for the Church, but everybody represents the Church in some sort of way in an era of internet, so we need to think differently. We need to provide a lot more digital services, because that is where the web is going on what people expect. We need to target the needs of people. It can be simple things like providing parents interested in baptizing their child a space online to discuss this, what it means, and what it involves. Why can't they just go online and book a time to speak with a priest, as opposed to somebody having to wait until their office hours are? Or can we think about what pastoral care online could be, being available for people who are on a spiritual web pilgrimage.
>
> (U. Wipple, personal communication, April 17, 2017)

But such communicative innovations can be unnerving for church leaders, and even members. She noted concerns she has heard to argue against Church use of the internet, especially regarding how such an instruction may be negatively affected by the transparency and lack of control over messages posted online. According to Wipple, they say,

> If you post a discussion on an external social media site, it is a lot easier to share with members but then outsiders can also react to it. So you get more attention within the organization but also outside of the organization, maybe this is not good. Maybe this is a discussion we should keep 'behind closed doors,' because we are a member of the organization and we understand the context and how we should act. But if every church discussion is open and available for everybody, what will happen? So things like this are a new challenge, and we don't really have a routine or standard advice about the internet yet that makes everyone feel comfortable. This has been a big topic of conversation in our organization.
>
> (U. Wipple, personal communication, April 17, 2017)

Communication directors and media officers, as employees of specific religious denominations and organizations, experience a number of constraints on their digital media work, including the need to adhere to institutional communication policies, whom they work for and answer to within leadership structures, and working within organizational climates that may be hesitant or hostile to change.

The nature of digital technologies that create or function within a dynamic, relational, nonhierarchical communicative environment can challenge traditional communication patterns, requiring these individuals to become digital media educators about the benefits of these technologies and the expectations involved in living in an information age their institutions cannot ignore. In addition, the many creative possibilities new media offer them for changing how, what and where these individuals do their jobs keep these digital spokespersons engaged and enthusiastic about their work and what it could do to change how the church is perceived in contemporary culture.

Webmasters and institutional tech teams

Institutional webmasters and technology-team members also work as digital spokespersons in that they are paid to carry out specific digital media work for their religious denominations or organizations. Their work is primarily technical in nature and focused on tasks such as maintaining official media platforms or producing content for media resources. They typically work under the supervision of the communication directors or media officers described earlier, yet their work plays an important part in representing the official identity of their group within the digital environment. Here we look at two specific roles—the webmaster and digital media tech-team member. Webmasters typically focus on building technological infrastructure as they oversee institutional websites, manage content online and design digital artifacts for their specific institution. Digital media tech teams focus on specific tech-related tasks such as software design, digital content creation and/or managing social media accounts for their institution.

Navin Motwani is a digital product manager at Imperial College who served for five years as a digital media officer for the Church of England, a job that encompasses both of the aforementioned roles. He primarily served as the webmaster for the national Church office's site, ran the Church's Twitter channel and Facebook page and produced videos for their YouTube channel. He also advised other departments and church leaders about digital media, especially blogging and social media. When I spoke with him, Motwani was the first person to hold such a role in the Church of England. He was appointed by Arun Arora who he described as having "a strong vision to move the Church from an authoritative and broadcasting model of communication into a relational model with people online." Related to this, his job is to facilitate the work of the Church by helping it move more fully into integrating digital media.

> Digital media is not just the future, it is the present, with growing importance in society every day. Other groups with less altruistic aims than the Church are getting involved with digital media and my worry would be that if the Church doesn't do more in this area in a unified way we will get left behind. As children get exposed to so much media at a young age, it is informing their reality

in ways we cannot predict. So having the Church in the digital space I think is very important, it needs to be ready to speak to the digital generations.

(N. Motwani, personal communication, February 23, 2012)

Motwani was involved in numerous digital projects, from redesigning the Church's website to helping establish a partnership with Google so every single Church of England in the UK is listed on Google maps, with information on each and a link to the church website. While much of his work is very project- and task-focused— e.g., designing and building the Church of England's official mobile app—he saw his role as more than a technical one. Rather, he took on the role of a digital media advocate who shows what effective technology design work can do for the Church.

> The vision I brought to the role was to transform the way the Church dealt with digital media, to give it (the Church) a voice and a place to speak that it hadn't had before. To start with, it was difficult. It was kind of, "Well, I don't really see the importance of this stuff." But now people are taking notice of the work that I have done, the changes to the website and the results in terms of putting something out on Twitter that gets loads of responses rather than just publishing a press release that may or may not get picked up in a paper. One of the issues we have is that the Church of England is a very broad church both in beliefs and expertise, so I view part of my role here to move the whole Church forward a bit in its digital media.
>
> (N. Motwani, personal communication, Feb 23, 2013)

His advocacy work also involved training other church staff in how to use social media in ways applicable to their work and how mobile technology can help teams better communicate with one another. This helped "integrate my tech work more fully into what goes on within the Church." But Motwani said modeling good digital media practice and creating resources are just the beginning of what is needed for the Church in this area:

> The Church need to ask the deeper question, "How can we best optimize our digital presence for greater impact? How do we move away from just seeing websites as a repository to put a sermon? How can we move into creating experiences online that are more interactive and more relational for people?" For example, when a bishop tweets or a priest blogs, it changes people's percep- tion of the Church. This allows people to see and communicate with an actual person, which is different to seeing us, the Church, as an organization […] it is difficult to have a relationship to an organization because, we are broad and we are faceless. So changing how we communicate can be real positive.
>
> (N. Motwani, personal communication, February 23, 2013)

For Motwani, whether it is helping a church leader set up a Twitter account or offering advice on the best design software for building an app, he saw his work as doing more than building the communication infrastructure of the Church of England. For him, tech work is visionary and theological; it is about building God's "kingdom that is not made with hands," and digital media are "integral and core to whatever we do in terms of both mission and forms of communications."

David Webster performed tasks similar to Motwani's when he served as internet communication coordinator for the connectional team with the Methodist Church in the UK. He served as the webmaster for the main site of the British Methodist Church, managed and developed the Church's mobile app and coordinated all the internet work done by the Church's communication team at their national offices in London. His work primarily focused on internal church communication resources and structures.

> There is so much potential for using online for both for external communication between members and the Church, and for internal communication between church staff and teams. For our internal communications, we are trying to move towards being a more collaborative and open-sourced type of organization, using the opportunities that online communication gives us now to better do the work of the Church. But encouraging using digital media in the Church can be challenging. When it becomes too externally focused, it is not really my remit to be responsible for what the Church does online. I mean, I can sort of help and advise, encourage people I come in contact with just to get connected.
>
> (D. Webster, personal communication, February 20, 2013)

This highlights a common challenge faced by digital spokespersons, namely, how they navigate church relationships and structures, especially when it comes to media work. While the Church of England has closer ties between the national office and local dioceses, the Methodist church has much looser social and accountability ties. This means digital media implementation and innovation do not necessarily filter down to the local level, and advocacy work encouraging media may easily be ignored.

> It is a cultural thing, related to the uniqueness of the Methodists. I mean, if we were a corporation we could just say, "Here is your web template, you use or else." But we are lacking in that sort of relationship or way of doing things. But we have found local churches have very unique opinions and do not like top-down input on how to run their church communication. People at the local level want to remain independent. So even the most basic things like branding or offering technology advice is hard to do. It is challenging, because part of my role is to try and be as connected as possible with the people and the website, and our website resources.
>
> (D. Webster, personal communication, February 20, 2013)

While most of Webster's time was spent managing the website, during his time in the connexion office he had some opportunities to assume the role of digital media educator. He and the team he worked with have been involved in running workshops aimed at church youth and lay workers, training them on how to practically use social media and teaching them to reflect on the implications of this technology on those they serve. At the end of the day, though his days were spent with fixing code and managing web content, he sought to remember his work is ultimately about resourcing and empowering people.

> I think that in the end, with all the technological changes […] what remains important is people and not losing that connection. We think that if technological changes are implemented they should be meant to help people communicate, or engage and encounter other people. I try to remember in the work I do that it is all about people, and not to lose sight of that.
>
> (D. Webster, personal communication, February 20, 2013)

Digital media staff focus on content creation for their institution, producing literature for communication within their organization and external promotional resources informing the public more about their organization. At one time, these individuals working with digital media would have been press officers and publication staff, focused on producing print newsletters, brochures and press releases. Now they focus their attention on digital projects and managing their organization's social media accounts.

Tom Scott was another media team member who worked for a time with Holy Trinity Brompton, a large Anglican church in London, where a key part of his job was managing the Worship Central website. Worship Central is a separate online ministry that operates under the auspices of the church. It is an online resource center for church music and worship leaders designed to "equip the worshipper and empower the local church" by providing access to new worship music that can be used in church services, advice on best practices regarding leading a worship team or preparing a music set and providing teaching on the theology of worship leading. Tom oversaw the design work for the website and produces the instructional and music video resources housed there. With a combined degree in music and design, he felt these skills and his attention to digital media trends make him well placed to do unconventional work for the Church.

> In a day like today that involves digital media in all of culture, we need to be on the top of our game with that. If we aren't engaged, neither is the Church going to be. So digital media for us is a massive investment, especially as we are focused in reaching out to the "i-generation" who see technology as a way to personalize their lives, who are focused on the "What can I get out of this?" mindset. I think that worship music has the power to connect people as well, and yeah, it is just a great place for us to gather and create community, and young people really want to get involved in this ministry. So our target audience is the eighteen-year-old worship leader who has just started leading

worship and wants to get trained up, wants to go into church ministry and start leading worship and a worship team.

(T. Scott, personal communication, February 28, 2013)

One of the largest projects Tom was involved in is Worship Central's worship-leader training course. It offers free instruction to worship leaders in music, leading, technical skills and developing a worship environment within church services, and it has been run online for over 1,400 church groups around the world. At the time of the interview, much of Tom's time was being spent redesigning videos for a revamped version of the course and online guides and promotional materials.

So we are in a time where everything is being simplified in digital tech. We have found that the talks were too long for people, so now we are trying to aim for the twenty-minute mark, shorter more concise videos, clean content that is easy to access. These trends influence how we prioritize the products that we are bringing out on the site [...] we need to create a place people can connect and keep in touch, to resist the whole "i-generation" thing ... Ideally, we want people involved online who are also in the local community connecting and running with worship from their churches ... what we see through Worship Central is that the Church can be on the frontlines of creativeness and edginess.

(T. Scott, personal communication, February 28, 2017)

Tom was also quick to frame his tech work as religious or spiritual work. He recognized that being employed by a church to produce digital media is a unique position with unique responsibility, requiring him to be in tune with latest digital-media trends and the religious vision of the site and the church it is connected to.

I guess one thing that has always stayed in my mind is a little motto we have at HTB, that is, "Aim for perfection, and settle for excellence."... While I am designing and writing music or doing anything at work, this is always in my head. How can I aim for the best I am doing? Because the best I am doing is ultimately worshipping God ... And I think web design and graphic design can be Holy Spirit filled. And people can be filled with the Holy Spirit looking at something, like watching a video online. I guess that is my hope with my work ... I use design inspiration for God.

(T. Scott, personal communication, February 28, 2013)

The work of Worship Central is closely linked to the broader mission of Holy Trinity Brompton (HTB) and their desire to provide a variety of resources to help other churches in their ministry. Holy Trinity is known as the birthplace of the Alpha Course, a popular ten-week evangelistic course introducing people to the basics of the Christian faith and offered by churches all over the world. The church also hosts numerous training conferences each year and produces teaching and music CDs and books on a variety of theological and practical Christian-ministry themes. In the last decade, the church has placed increasing emphasis on developing digital resources and leveraging social medial platforms for getting their work out to other pastors and laypeople.

Their growing digital and communication teams of several dozen members occupy a large floor of the church offices in central London. At monthly meetings, members of various teams are able to provide advice to each other on best tech practices, to brainstorm together on new projects and to offer feedback on each other's creative design work. This makes HTB's approach to digital media work novel, as they strive to see digital media as a vital helpmate in their overall ministry. This perspective informed the way staff see their digital work and the opportunities it can provide. Tom shared about how the Worship Central team has begun to offer opportunities for more people with tech skills to get involved in their work and "empower them for ministry:"

> Something we have realized is that we have a lot of talented people in this church. So now we are starting to think, "Okay, how do we use them? How can we get them involved in this?" And for Worship Central that has been a real thing. So that is why we are trying to create a creative team of volunteers who come in [...] on average a half day a week. We use people around the UK and people around the world, which is really cool. It shows no matter what you are gifted in, you can get involved in ministry, and it is actually amazing to see because people want to give so much and can often get frustrated when their gift isn't being used.
>
> (T. Scott, personal communication, February 28, 2013)

This observation, that digital media skills can be seen as a spiritual gift able to benefit and build the work of a church, is a rare perspective. The above-referenced felt frustration of often being overlooked by their faith communities is a common experience among digital creatives, as noted in this research. This issue is explored in much more detail in Chapter 4 on digital entrepreneurs.

These narratives from webmasters and tech team members demonstrate the fact that these digital spokespersons emerge as individuals influencing the work and image of the religious institutions they work for, due to their digital expertise. They recognize technology skills as central to their work, and many of their tasks are very mundane, focused on keeping technology tools and platforms functioning and increasing their accessibility or visibility for their organization. Yet they also see their technology work as serving very important communicative goal that speaks to or promotes a specific religious identity for their group. This means technology work includes a theological element, an area they often have little or no training in and are often given even less instruction from supervisors or superiors who ask them to create or maintain their institutional digital presence. In this research the tension between technological expertise and performing theological identity work is a pronounced theme among many of these and other digital spokespersons I interviewed. This theme and its implications will be explored later in this chapter.

Online media ambassadors

A third type of digital spokesperson also identified in this research can be described as online media ambassador. These individuals play the role of digital spokespersons within online or other media forums. Like the others described earlier, they are directly employed by denominations and religious organizations, but their primary role is not focused on church communication or media production. Rather, online media ambassadors are recognized high-level church leaders, such as presiding bishops or other denominational leaders who oversee other church leaders, essentially serving as a pastor to pastors in their church organization. These individuals' oversight role requires them to be institutional experts. Part of their role involves internal institutional communication with individuals under their oversight. Their position, combined with these communication skills, means they are often called upon to speak on behalf of their institution or area of oversight when public issues emerge of interest to those outside the church. Their typically high-profile leadership positions within their denomination or religious organization can contribute to their building a prominent public profile. Also, once they are identified by media outlets as colorful talking heads or articulate experts able to give interviews on topics related to their religious institution, they often become go-to media informants for journalists looking for official comments on the church's position on key public news stories, especially those dealing with social crises or controversy surrounding the church. These individuals differ from digital entrepreneurs such as theoblogians, who are self-appointed experts seeking to speak on behalf of their religious community or tradition. They are given legitimacy as digital spokespersons because of their recognized leadership position; their media skills are personally developed, rather than ones they are professionally trained for.

These online ambassadors also have heightened public prominence as media commentators due to their activities online. They become bloggers or active social media users in an effort to increase the visibility of the official church roles they hold. As they gain large followings interested in their opinions, these online ambassadors take on both official and/or unofficial roles as mouthpieces for their denomination or community. Within the Anglican Church, there is a recognition that church leadership roles increasingly demand individuals to play a public communicative role. This means they become the face of the Church for wider society through their social media use.

An example is Nick Baines, Bishop of Leeds in England, and previously served as the Bishop of Croydon, as well as the Bishop of Bradford. During his time as the bishop for diocesan communication officers, he learned the importance of understanding how media work and leveraging their potential to share alternative messages about Christianity and churching. This has given him important insights into both the media policy and strategy of the Anglican Church. He is a frequent guest on commercial and religious radio and television programs and has written several books and radio scripts for mainstream radio programs.

He says he has been described as "one of the church's main social media bishops" over the past decade. He began blogging in 2008, when he was asked to write a blog for the Fulcrum website during the Lambeth Conference. He uses the blog, Twitter and Instagram as a way to speak about his areas of interest such as music, the arts, politics and, of course, religion, always writing from a personal rather than official position. However, he is always a bishop and cannot avoid occasional confusion between the personal and the official. Some public and media outlets see him as speaking on behalf of the Church, even when posting personally on his blog.

> What I am trying to do is give people access to what I am doing through my blog. I can also put a different story about faith to the media, because a lot of journalists are reading my blog. It enables me to share my personal perspective, so I have a bit of control over the message that gets shared. The other thing is that I learn a lot from it, because a lot of people comment, sometimes very robustly. I don't engage with them all, I don't have time, but I learn a lot. It is a good mix. Recently, when I preached in Germany in German, I put the text on my blog, about a week later.
>
> (N. Baines, personal communication, December 6, 2012)

Being a bishop, he says, gives him a very public voice, and his use of the online sphere provides a unique platform from which to speak about his ideas and work. Besides raising his media profile, his online presence has given him the ability to transform his ministry. His media presence allows him to transcend time and space, transforming the ways he is able to share himself and engage his constituency.

> It helps me create the illusion of presence. It is important because I can't be in 169 parishes in my region at once, even in a year I can't visit them all. But online I can let people in on what I am doing and where I am and what I am thinking. It also lets me have a national and international role; online I can give insight and access to what I am doing to a limited degree.
>
> (N. Baines, personal communication, December 6, 2012)

However, Bishop Baines has learned that giving people more access to himself and his thoughts is not always an unmitigated success. Because tweets and blog posts are short and succinct they often lack context, which inevitably allows for misunderstandings. But amidst these challenges he feels it is still worth it for the Church to make itself available to people in this new way.

> In a world where there are so many voices competing for a hearing, I think social media has expanded the noise. It is even harder for people now to determine what is of value and which voices should be listened to. But the Church

is called to engage in the world, where the world is and to get involved, and you can't do that and ignore social media. I do think we can try to model what might most effectively be used and a certain discipline.

(N. Baines, personal communication, December 6, 2012)

Bishop Baines states that in past eras, the role of the bishop was to stand in the pulpit and preach or issue statements of behalf of the Church to the congregations and communities under his oversight. Bishops no longer have such control over their or the Church's message in the new media. For him, the digital age is marked by features of interconnectivity and interactivity, where communication mediums are closely connected to and feed off of one another.

The archbishop once said to me, "You know the twenty-four hour media monster demands feeding, you know it is not our job to feed it." That is right, but it is also wrong. If you don't provide content in a way that is appropriate to the media, and you don't engage it, do not be surprised if they ignore you. The Church is having to wake up to our process—sometimes it is thorough and really good, but in a new media age it can be too slow.

(N. Baines, personal communication, December 6, 2012)

He stresses one of the biggest difficulties individuals in the Church of England face in embracing digital media use is the challenge these media pose to authority. What has contributed to his rise in social media, Baines feels, is his willingness to engage and learn from digital culture:

You honestly see the interconnectivity of digital media as a threat, or you see it as an opportunity. This is of particular concern to the Episcopate. If you see the Church as authorized to offer an authoritative judgment, then you are going to have a problem if you expose yourself online to people able to come back at you with their differences of opinions. The other way is to say, I am human, I am limited, and I might need to learn from this interactivity. So you put it out there and you learn from what comes back. It shines a different light from a different angle on the scene, so you see it differently. I need to keep learning and keep growing that is why I keep doing it.

(N. Baines, personal communication, December 6, 2012)

Other leaders in the Church of England have also been willing to experiment with the new possibilities offered by digital media. Institutional online representatives see this as a positive way to facilitate speaking in both official and unofficial ways on behalf of the Church and their faith. This experience has been similar to another of the prominent "social media bishops," Alan Wilson, the Bishop of Buckingham for the Church of England. He began blogging in 2007 while working for the diocese of Oxford, when one of the diocesan communication staff noticed that most of the traffic received on the official website was in reaction to a small blog posted by the youth officer.

> She thought that it would be good if I had a go at blogging, and that I might enjoy doing it. So she took me out to lunch and explained what a blog was, and I gave it a go. I went after that to a conference at Willow Creek, which is when I started to put something up on the internet. I quickly saw the potential.
>
> (A. Wilson, personal communication, November 27, 2012)

His blog soon gained a following, and over the past decade he has used his blog and social media as a public platform where he records and shares his personal and professional thoughts. Over the last decade, his attention has switched from primarily blogging to mainly being invested in Facebook and Twitter. Initially he used his blog as a space to regularly comment on social or church-related issues. He then moved to offer conscious response a couple of times a month. However in the past few years, he has transitioned to focus solely on social media as a tool allowing him to microblog his thoughts throughout the day—on news, items of personal interest and things that come across his radar in his work as the bishop.

> It is like a kind of record of stuff that my attention has been given to, and it is a way of collecting stuff. I am particularly interested in Facebook when you can develop a kind of conversation that would not happen in any other way … I have been rather frustrated on the blog with anonymous comments. I understand that sometimes people need to do it, but I think it is a much healthier conversation when people are willing to take responsibility for who they are and what they say. I think that is where Facebook does score well in generating a public conversation.
>
> (A. Wilson, personal communication, November 27, 2012)

His experience on Facebook especially have made it clear that because he is a bishop, people give his comments online with an air of authority, and he has seen how his causal comments can have consequences. On one occasion, when the Church of England announced their appointment of a new bishop, he made an off-handed personal comment on his Facebook feed questioning why such a tiny constituency would even need a bishop. He later learned that an hour after he posted this comment, a journalist referred to it and used it to criticize the Church's organizational structure as outdated. Yet this was in no way what he intended by his online post.

> I realized that there was nothing private about Facebook and you would be silly to think there was. So it is kind of like a conversation that is held in a public space that everybody is identified. This showed me that it is a medium

that is extremely and potentially powerful in ways that I did not fully understand at the time.

(A. Wilson, personal communication, November 27, 2012)

One thing Bishop Wilson appreciates about social media is that they challenge traditional communication structures and patterns within the Church. He described
church communications as taking a very conventional broadcast approach to get
the Church's message out. He described this as focused on "massaging our image
so we look okay in public, and then reading newspapers to see what people think
of us."

While the role of bishop within the Church of England was set up to primarily
provide pastoral care for clergy and oversight of church parishes in a specific geographic area, Bishop Wilson reported that there is an increasing need for bishops
to understand they also play a role in representing the Church in the media. As he
stated, "Bishops in a sense are a kind of custodians for the Church," i.e., of its image.
He states that interacting with the media used to involve a much more regulated
format. The head office of the Church in Westminster would designate a "lead
bishop" to be official person to speak with the media on specific subjects, based on
their geography, background and areas of expertise. They received media training
and were given a media formula telling them to be prepared with two good talking
points on the issue at hand related to Church policy and teaching, and to stick to
that script.

> It was basically stated that if you say anything else, then it is going to be a real
> problem, because you are going to make the organization look silly […] to
> a world that runs on dialogue not spin doctoring, and not used to having to
> accept a processed point of view from an organization.
>
> (A. Wilson, personal communication, November 27, 2012)

So the era of instantaneous and highly interactive communication brought on by
the internet and digital media immediately challenges these old processes and strategies of sharing information within the Church. Bishop Wilson explained that if
the Church is to meet the demands of this new communication culture in which
it finds itself, major changes in how the media are approached and what messages
are shared are required.

> The non-hierarchal means of communication it offers means you actually do
> hear people roar online. Very often in a hierarchal-minded society like we have
> in England and the Church, everything that goes to the bishop is vetted in a
> way. It goes through various stages of being prepped before it is shared. So it is
> actually quite good to find out what people are actually trying to do and say
> instead of receiving an indirect, filtered message.
>
> (A. Wilson, personal communication, November 27, 2012)

Bishop Wilson described his embrace and use of social media to share official positions and personal opinions has not always gone down well with his fellow bishops. He suggested the concerns expressed to him about his online presence and openness are essentially rooted in a basic culture-class worldview found within the bishopric.

> I think some of them think I am kind of weird or dangerous … there is a lot of fear around technology amongst the bishops of the Church of England, because they don't get it. Most of them are educated within an arts culture, a classical education at English universities, who have been trained or thought that technology and science did not matter … I think I am an unusual character.
>
> (A. Wilson, personal communication, November 27, 2012)

He stressed that, like many old and established institutions in society, the Church is being forced to change due to the cultural and communication brought on by computers and the internet. These shifts will be uncomfortable and be seen as bothersome and inconvenient to many in Church hierarchy who have failed to recognize technology's impact on all areas of society. He stated one of the biggest problems the Church now faces relates to its communication mindset, as "power of habit" or "doing things the way we have always done them" so often drives church structures. His prominence online and related opportunities to serve as an official Church mouthpiece to the media have taught him much about what it means to be a bishop in a digital media world. As a result, he has been a strong advocate of the idea that church leaders must embrace communicative possibilities presented to them in this new culture and be proactive in representing the Church through digital media.

Online media ambassadors serve as the public voice for their institution in online and offline digital media spaces. Their role as digital spokesperson emerges due to their notoriety as engaging interviewees, so the media often call on them, seeing them as official mouthpieces on social and institutional issues of public interest. Their positions are focused on serving their institution in a pastoral role that focuses on internal communications between clergy and other leaders. Yet the media skills they have developed over time and their ability to creatively articulate religious and official church views through digital platforms move them into spaces that require them to speak to audiences beyond their positions and official constituencies.

Digital spokespersons' media-making narrative: Institutional identity curators

From this review of different types of digital spokespersons encountered in this study, these digital creatives are shown to work inside specific religious institutions and hold positions that involve doing communication or media work for that group. In this case, their creative work is done for the express and paid service of that group. From monitoring online discussions to building media platforms, digital spokespersons' work focuses on presenting and managing their intuition's identity online. At least part of their role requires them to manage the digital presence of their particular group online or create digital content focused on representing these institutions. Increasingly, religious organizations are seeing the need to employ individuals who do digital media work, whether that be building or maintaining their organization's online presence, or producing content related to their group's public online profile.

Digital spokespersons can also be described as institutional identity curators. Their jobs require them to represent and frame the identity of their particular religious group online through digital content and resources. Increasingly, religious organizations are seeing digital media work as related to their institutional public relations, requiring them to hire spokespersons to manage their online media or presence. Identity curators mirror what Anderson described as "spokesperson-activists," talking heads of religious groups that draw on established interpretive patterns and structures from their institutions to build the presence and identities of those groups in public digital spaces. The above overview of three types of digital spokespersons described in this chapter highlight a number of shared traits and tasks focused on their institutional identity curation online.

DIY digital media experts

First, many of the digital spokespersons interviewed for this study did not have formal or professional training in the digital skills or work that comprises much of their jobs. As noted, most communications directors, media officers and even some tech staff came to their jobs either from a journalism background or from business communication, with experience working in the corporate world creating marketing materials or doing public relations work. If they did have any formal media training, this was almost exclusively in older forms of mass media such as television, radio or print news production. This means most digital spokespersons' view of media is grounded in the broadcast-push mentality, where the church produces information and the media is supposed to pick it up and distribute it. Digital media and culture required them to actively rethink what communication can and should look like for the church if it is to be effective and capture people's attention.

Many of these interviewees spoke of feeling overwhelmed by being thrust into the world of digital media due to the position they held and often in the middle of their careers. This has meant having to figure out, through trial and error, what kinds of media content and tools work best for their organization in the digital era. Others found themselves charged by their organization and leaders to get entire segments of their religious institution up to speed in digital media. This included being asked to redesign and digitize publications and develop digital media strategies and policies for church workers. They often found themselves thrown into situations that required them to learn how to navigate digital platforms on the job through trial and error, because they had no prior experience or training in these areas.

PR agents for digital technology and culture

Second, many digital spokespersons found themselves surrounded by contradiction. The work they were being paid to do required engaging new technological tools and creating new patterns of communication for their institution in response to the new communicative climate of the digital era. Digital spokespersons often identified significant changes they felt had to be made within their organization's structures in order to meet changing audience expectations and mainstream media demand. Yet these proposed changes were often met with resistance by the very people who hired them to do their job.

Digital spokespersons characterized some of the resistance to digital media they encountered in the workplace as motivated by co-workers' fear of the institutional changes digital integration requires. Using digital media platforms created shifts in flows of information and organizational structure. Both media officers and institutional online representatives spoke of fear voiced by church supervisors and leaders about the loss of control over church messages in the digital age. As the carefully crafted, vetted press release was exchanged for more quickly responsive website postings or tweets of church news, a common fear was that messages would be misconstrued as they spread online. The change from the church being able to push messages in their own time to now being forced to respond to pull-message demands required shortening traditional monitoring processes of information released. Tech team members also noted clergy and church leaders felt uneasy about the shift in gatekeeping responsibilities for such information from higher-ranking clergy or trained press officers to lower-ranking communication staff that now produced or shortened official content and distributed this via institutional social media accounts. So how church information—from official news to social commentary—was produced, shared and distributed was much less of a top-down distribution exercise, ergo its final form was harder to monitor.

Many digital spokespersons also gave accounts of trying to mitigate the fears of those they worked under by sharing how information online can become an important way to access and learn about their public. They stressed how social media, especially, allowed the church direct access to its members and the broader public, instead of having to rely on the press to mediate their message. Social media also allow the church to monitor how the wider public feels about the church and its messages. Institutional media workers stressed that instead of fearing the comments stream or the retweet function, these should be seen as vital resources for taking the temperature of how the church is viewed by members and nonmembers. This internal digital PR work was sometimes awkward, when the focus of these efforts was the digital spokesperson's direct supervisor such as a bishop or archbishop, denominational leader or church administrator. Yet overall, digital spokespersons strived to offer a positive spin to combat the negative reactions and fears voiced within their institutions about digital media and culture.

Training digitally hesitant leaders

Third, digital spokespersons' work often reaches beyond just producing media content and managing new media platforms; they are often called upon to serve as digital media experts and trainers. Their time is not only spent experimenting with digital media and content but creating resources and workshops in new-media literacy for others in their organization and explaining how technology is changing the position and role of the church in society to others in their institution. This could mean providing institutional staff training on new media systems, creating social media workshops for clergy or designing digital media strategies for organizational initiatives. Their digital media experience and expertise elevates their position within the institution as they share their specialized skills and instruct those of higher position and ranking than themselves. As technology trainers, their advice is often sought, as organizations must often revamp their communication plans and structures when integrating digital media into their work. This gives them a level of institutional influence within their organizations.

This also highlights another area in which they often encountered resistance, as co-workers in their institution began to recognize the fact that digital technologies ushered in cultural change as they created new, unique communicative environments and relationships with those inside and outside their organization. Since few of the church leaders that these digital spokespersons work for come from a technology or even science background, they often do not have a framework for fully comprehending the kind of culture the new technology encourages and cultivates. They associate the work of digital spokespersons and their tools with this cultural change, so may view them and their work with suspicion. Church leaders without media or computer experience describe the world of digital media as a foreign land and digital spokespersons as speaking a language they do not understand. This creates a tense relationship between spokespersons and the leaders who must take on the role of the student, required to work under those they oversee in order to adapt to this new culture and the rapid change it is seen as bringing.

Webmasters and tech teams especially provided examples of how they were asked to work with their "digitally hesitant colleagues," who often proudly described themselves as "Internet laggards, Luddites and technophobes." This shift in the power dynamic between supervisors and media staff is also not a one-time occurrence, as each time a new digital media platform is added or software or computers are updated, tech workers step into the role of teacher to leaders who often find the role of the follower a difficult one to adjust to. Implementing digital technologies in these religious institutions was often described as entering a cross-cultural territory. Some digital spokespersons received the message that digital media were seen as a necessary evil—"it is needed for the church to stay relevant to society, to communicate, but it comes with a lot of baggage." Others described having to deal with those who felt the church entering the digital age was like "biting the bullet" or "getting a shot"—it was important for church work, but the whole process was seen as painful. Despite these negative reactions, most digital spokespersons remained positive about their roles and these opportunities to serve as teachers and trainers; they saw their role within their institution as giving them an opportunity to be digital advocates. Besides mitigating fears, tech teams and webmasters tried to facilitate opportunities to show how digital media can be used to create no-cost outreach tools or creative initiatives that can serve the church and ministry by allowing them to reach a greater public. Digital spokespersons took on the role of technology advocates within their organization by modeling how use and fluency in digital media can be seen as assets. Frustration was noted by many digital spokespersons regarding institutional resistance to technology and the uneasy relationship trying to adapt to digital culture could create at the organizational level. However, most digital spokespersons interviewed remained positive about the opportunity their jobs afforded them, enabling them to be "servant-leaders" by modeling, promoting and facilitating digital media use within their organizations.

Seeing digital work as theological identity work

Fourth, digital spokespersons recognized the fact that their digital work plays more than just a functional role within the institutions they work for. While many of their digital tasks serve primarily utilitarian goals for their institutions, focused on information sharing and intra-organization as well as public relations communication, they also recognized the fact that there is a theological dimension to their work. Whether producing a website or mobile app or managing a social media account, these acts create the public face of their organization in the digital context. This means using digital content and artifacts becomes a way to represent the religious identity of their group online. Such work is more than functional; it is narrative building. They recognized the fact that digital work frames public perception of their faith community; it becomes part of how individuals read the organization in terms of its mission, core values and understanding of religion, and how this is to be practiced in culture online and offline.

Many digital spokespersons spoke about how they saw their technological tasks as having a much broader impact on their organization than simply helping them appear digitally literate and relevant. Web masters and tech team members spoke about the responsibility they felt to accurately present the group's religious identity online and the burden of trying to accurately translate theological positions and the beliefs of their community visually, textually and structurally through their work. They saw themselves as digital storytellers commissioned to tell a distinctive faith-based narrative to the online world, and while they felt confident in their technology skills, they often felt ill-equipped to serve as theological interpreters in this context.

Institutional online representatives also noted with frustration how their institutions did not recognize the fact that digital media work is not simply about broadcasting a set static message, but one that is dynamic. They voiced concern that the ignorance of church leadership regarding digital technology does more than just make the church look out of date and out of touch with culture. It means missing important opportunities to engage in cultural conversations and learn from secular and religious voices within digital culture. Media officers similarly acknowledged that digital representations of their organization mediate meaning in ways that communicate distinct ideological and theological messages about their community. Unfortunately, most religious leaders and clergy are either unaware of or seem unconcerned about this. They noted most are well schooled in the power of words and text but overlook how visual elements of digital media also communicate powerful meanings. When they asked their supervisors for advice or input on these attributes, most supervisors just deferred to the digital spokesperson and their technological expertise. But they seemed uninterested in engaging in conversation about how these digital creatives see technology work as a form of theological work in contemporary culture. Some media officers described this as more than just a missed opportunity, but as a handicap preventing them from showing how digital work can communicate in new ways theological truths and church values in culture. Overall, digital spokespersons acknowledged the limits of their theological background and training and said it is through experimentation they work to create digital media outlets and opportunities that, hopefully, showcase the religious identity of their organization in accurate ways.

In the end, the digital spokespersons are appointed by their respective organizations to serve the communication needs and demands for information and opinion placed on them by digital culture. In a time when religious organizations can see and feel their loss of influence in the public sphere, many leaders see digital media as a ticket to cultural relevance. While institutional structures are increasingly embracing digital media into their work as necessity, they most often approach it from a utilitarian position. Digital media workers are called on to build the digital profile and presence of the groups for which they work. Digital spokespersons often recognize the broader implications and impact of their work. They need to become digital trainers and advocates who work with institutional leaders, who are often hesitant or negative about the impact digital media are having on their denomination and society as a whole. Digital spokespersons also see how their work offers a visual representation of their institution's religious identity, a task they may not feel fully prepared to perform due to their lack of institutional knowledge, history and theological nuance. This can put them in difficult positions that cause them to carefully contextualize, explain and justify their work both inside and outside their institutional contexts.

Digital spokespersons as identity curators

The media-making stories shared by digital spokespersons in this chapter present them as performing the primary role of identity curation—they translate the beliefs,

practice and culture of their religious organizations to a broad public through officially sanctioned digital media content and resources. They also see themselves as
interpreters of digital culture to their institutions, as they seek to build bridges
between the church institution and digital media outlets. They recognize the fact
that church officials often do not understand media culture and acknowledge the
resulting need to educate their institution about media values, strategies and communicative styles regarding both new and older forms of media. They must also
become literate in the mission and values of their organization in order to consider
how aspects of digital media may shape their communication of these communal
beliefs. In this way, digital spokespersons emulate the role of thought leaders within
algorithmic digital culture. Their work primarily takes place within online culture,
but they draw primarily on the logics of offline institutional expertise and structure
for the presentation of their work. In this way, digital culture simply is used to amp-
lify and increase the audience for the more static structures and knowledge of their
offline organization. Doing traditional public relations and work in a new communicative environment also requires them to act as translators and bridge builders
between these two cultures. As such, they recognize the need to create resources
such as social media boot camps to help others in the community develop these
skills and a larger awareness of digital culture. This can also lead to cross-cultural
tensions that are manifested in the technological apologetic of these digital spokespersons, discussed in more detail in Chapter 8.

Chapter 6

Digital strategists
Acting as missional media negotiators

Digital strategists are a third type of religious digital creatives (RDCs), who draw their authority from a hybrid positioning between institutional and techno-logical expertise. These are individuals who have an affiliation with a specific religious institution or community. They often hold a position of leadership as part of these affiliations, such as being a priest, religious educator, seminary student or other ministry leader. Yet what makes them different from digital spokes-persons is that their primary position does not require them to use technology or perform media-focused tasks. While digital spokespersons are employed to do media work and curate the official media and digital presences of their church or denomination, digital strategists choose to develop digital expertise for strategic purposes. They embrace digital media in an effort to innovate their ministries and extend their work into new areas. It is through this digital experimenta-tion and their creative leveraging of already available digital resources for reli-gious ends that they gain notoriety and public attention, rather than from their official roles.

As noted in Chapter 2, digital strategists are introduced as associated with Anderson's (1999) category of "reformer-critics," individuals who go online to pre-sent narratives about their given faith community. These individuals use the internet in an attempt to witness their beliefs and convictions in this new public space. Anderson suggested their work gains public attention when it is mobilized around a particular agenda or digital effort. In this chapter, I show how digital strategists similarly utilize the internet for a specific agenda. However, unlike reformer-critics whose media use is motivated by or focused on a personal agenda, digital strategists' use of digital media is designed to extend the sanctioned or commissioned work they are called or employed to do for their religious community.

By providing a clear description of who digital strategists are and the types of work they perform, and offering profiles of several manifestations of these RDCs, we are able to explore how they act as religious authorities inside and outside their religious communities. This enables us to outline the type of authority they enact and the technological apologetic they evoke in explaining and justifying their positions and work.

Defining digital strategists

The idea of a digital strategist is drawn from Anderson's (1999) discussion of the "reformer-critics" who appear online as individuals seeking to interpret and speak for their religious tradition through religiously focused engagement in various internet platforms. He stated these reformer-critics are often motivated by distinctive religious convictions or a self-imposed agenda that seeks to change or promote new understandings of community religious practices and/or beliefs and demonstrate alternative discourses or models of interaction online. Through their online work, they hope to gain access to a wider audience for their religious message, or recruit others to their viewpoint. Anderson described them as typically self-appointed, seeing themselves as serving their religious community through their online presence. They draw on a mixture of online and offline sources to build their position and credibility. Anderson also suggested these reformers often seek to take on the role of exemplar representative of their religious community, where digital engagement allows for religious innovation and new expressions of religious practice to emerge that can invigorate traditional communities. Their innovation and vocal work online, however, can frame them as potential competitors with other official institutional leaders and spokespersons.

Digital strategists identified in this research share a number of the characteristics of reformer-critics suggested by Anderson, with several notable differences. Here digital strategists also seek to serve their religious community through their digital work, with a commitment to technological experimentation and using the internet to expand the reach of their work and their sphere of influence. They take on this digital work by self-appointment, as something they feel called to in order to share their religious convictions with a wider audience. However, unlike Anderson's idea of reformer-critics as institutional outsiders, digital strategists have a clear institutional affiliation and investment.

In this study, digital strategists are individuals with a foot firmly planted in two worlds. One foot rests in the religious organizations to which they are committed, and one foot stands in digital culture where they see the importance of adapting their work and official calling to the tools and opportunities it provides. Digital strategists work within broader religious institutional contexts than that of the digital spokesperson discussed in Chapter 5. Rather than being employed to perform a media-related role by a religious denomination or church, they typically work for a religious institution in jobs focused on a specific form of Christian ministry. Digital strategists may have an affiliation with a specific religious denomination or organization, but they do not serve as an official voice or representative of that Christian group.

The dual commitment of digital strategists can put them at odds with their institutions, which may view technology as suspect, or balk at the idea of altering established communication practices or ministry processes. This forces digital strategists into unique positions where they are constantly negotiating between their religious tradition that is slow to change and a technological society that is constantly being revised. Digital strategists studied here include a new generation of missionaries who develop digital tools for proselytizing their group, church leaders who see the internet as space to encourage religious networking and discipleship and religious educators who see the internet as extending their faith communities' abilities to share religious truth and training.

Types of digital strategist

In this study, 40 of the 120 interviewees are identified as digital strategists coming from the USA, Europe and Australasia. Some of these digital strategists are church leaders, such as individuals serving on the pastoral team as a youth minister of a specific church, who use digital media in order to create new opportunities to facilitate connections with church members or to expand the impact of their teaching. Others are youth workers or religious educators who recognize embracing social media might enable them to experiment to provide new resources for support and ministry beyond their limited weekly face-to-face interactions. In this study, digital strategists came from Anglican/Episcopal, Catholic, Evangelical Free, Methodist, Presbyterian/Church of Scotland and Lutheran denominations. Digital strategists are also found in monastic communities—Catholic monks and nuns who chose to embrace digital media as ways to expand their ministry beyond the confines of their enclosures, or as a way open up the discernment process for a religious vocation to the digital generation. Most digital strategists studied are individuals whose primary work is to serve in religious education, pastoral/priestly training or in ministries focused on religious practices such as evangelism or discipleship. They come to realize that digital technologies and platforms offer them innovative and often more efficient ways to do this outreach, both inside and outside their faith community. Here I spotlight and describe three types of digital strategists: (1) media-driven missionaries, (2) theologians who blog and (3) online ministers. Each type embraces and integrates digital media into their work, not because this is required, but because they see digital media offer them added benefits, helping them fulfill their work in creative and more efficient ways.

Media-driven missionaries

One example of these digital strategists are those who work as media-driven missionaries. Over the last 200 years, Christian denominations in the West have been training and sending out individuals to foreign countries to proselytize those of different nationalities and religious backgrounds with the Christian message. In the last 100 years, many of these groups have developed sophisticated training programs to help equip future missionaries with skills in religious teaching, language translation and cross-cultural adaptation to the new environments they will find themselves in. In the twenty-first century, many Christian missionary organizations still focus their attention on training up individuals as church planters, pastors, bible teachers or itinerate evangelists, preparing them to share their faith in a new culture within established religious institutions and contexts. Yet there is a growing awareness among some mission-focused denominational and parachurch organizations of the role digital media can play, not only in training new missionaries but also in changing the ways missions outreach work is actually done.

While media production has played an important role in missionary work for much of the last century, as various departments or branches of different missionary groups have focused on producing outreach materials such as bible tracts and teaching lessons or religious videos like the *Jesus* film used in local churches and evangelistic events. Only in the last two decades have mission groups moved beyond simply using digital technologies as a means to produce and distribute traditional material to seeing the social spaces created by the internet and computer networks as a mission field unto themselves. I have previously written about the rise of e-vangelism in the West and how traditional religious organizations in the USA— e.g., the Billy Graham Association and Campus Crusade—have begun to conceive of the internet as a mission field and provide training for individuals who wish to preach and reach out especially to the digital generation online (Campbell, 2010). However, what I here refer to as media-driven missionaries are those individuals situated in traditional missionary training and support organizations who seek to develop and use digital skills to create new forms of evangelistic outreach for non-Western cultural contexts and groups.

These media-driven missionaries are often embedded within the missionary efforts of established Christian denominations or are members of an established Christian parachurch or mission organization, meaning they are not affiliated with a single church or religious denomination. While using and developing media resources may be part of these mission groups' work, media work is not typically seen as mission work, but rather as supporting established mission roles and activities. When media-focused mission activities move from being seen as part of evangelism's support structure to the actual focus of mission outreach and become digitally driven, this is when we see the manifestation of what I call here online missions. This is also when missionaries move from being mission workers who used digital media to produce resources to facilitate established practices such as public outreach campaigns or religious education to become digital strategists leveraging digital media in new ways to meet traditional goals. Here I explore two examples of how this type of media-driven missionaries functions as digital strategists through an online correspondence course and a network of internet missions, both of which have emerged in the past two decades in Turkey. Due to increasing discrimination and criminalization of foreign mission activities and the evangelism of Muslims by Turkish Christian converts, the identities of the specific organizations and individuals discussed here are anonymized and aliases used for these digital strategists to protect their identities and work.

In the 1960s, Western Christians living in Turkey came up with a unique way to reach out to Muslims and other non-Christians. Living in a secular Islamic country like Turkey, where preaching conversion to Muslims is discouraged and believed to be criminal even if technically it is not, foreign missionaries had to be careful about how they went about their outreach activities. Most missionaries became "tentmakers," following the example of Paul in the New Testament who worked as a tradesperson making tents, to help support his Christian work in planting and overseeing churches in the Roman Empire. Contemporary tentmakers are often sent by specific mission organizations, but enter restricted countries as professionals performing work such as being teachers, medical personnel or other business professionals. This allows them the ability to give their nonprofessional time to help build and support local churches in their host country. As one foreign missionary who has worked for nearly three decades in Turkey shared,

> In the old days, that was quite difficult for people to learn about Christianity if they were Muslim. I remember people telling me in their testimonies that they went to a church building to try and talk to a Christian or get a New Testament, and it wasn't given to them. People were afraid about outsiders coming to the church; it could be a trap or the police.
> (male missionary, personal communication, July 10, 2014)

One group of foreign missionaries living in Istanbul came up with the idea of creating a correspondence course that allowed individuals a private way to learn about Christianity and discuss these beliefs with actual Christians. Through ads placed in various newspapers and magazines, individuals were invited to sign-up for a mail-based course that offered several educational courses on the origins of Christianity and beliefs about the historical Jesus. Individuals who signed up for these courses would be sent a lesson on a topics such as "Who is Jesus?" which involved reading a prepared pamphlet and articles, answering a set of questions, then returning lessons via traditional mail to missionaries who would grade and comment on the students' answers. Students would then be sent this feedback, and if requested, the next lesson.

> To make a decision for Christ in Turkey means something different. It can be a high risk for people. So for a person to be open to hear about Christ, they need a personal contact. I would say that all people that have become believers through this work have had an initial contact to the course, through an advertisement they saw that was compelling. Over time, we have learned how to shape and share our message so it connects with people through our online communication.
> (missionary male 2, personal communication, July 11, 2014)

In the decades that followed, these foreign missionaries recruited Muslim-born converts to Christianity and other expatriate volunteers to help with this outreach. While this form of evangelism proved to be a slow process, missionaries and volunteers said the in-depth investments in individuals were an effective way to witness about Christianity to specific interested non–Christians, and converts were made. As the missionary who has been active with the project shared,

> There are people we talk to that are in provinces in this country where they are the lone believer, so we talk to them over the years and they eventually want to be baptized and grow to become true believers in the faith. There is no other means that could have allowed us to do this kind of work or sharing. Technology can change the whole idea of discipleship.
>
> (missionary male 2, personal communication, July 11, 2014)

Over time, the correspondence course became a focus of outreach, drawing individuals from different theological backgrounds and working under the auspices of different missionary organizations to work together in this media-driven initiative. Through these collaborations, new features were added to this correspondence course. This included a call-in service, where individuals could call a dedicated phone line at set times to ask Christians theological questions related to the lessons or other religious issues. Fast forward to the 2000s. Foreign missionaries working with the correspondence course began to see the potential of the internet for their work.

> Turkish people are not readers so much anymore, so newspaper ads and paper correspondence is no longer effective. But almost any young person has a Facebook account, sometimes even multiple accounts. Being present there, being searchable through Google, makes it much easier for people who are searching to find us … to reach the new generation.
>
> (missionary male 2, personal communication, July 11, 2014)

In the past two decades, volunteers have experimented with ways to reach out, especially to digitally savvy young people. They see this as important because course designers estimate 40 percent of the population of Turkey is under 25 years old. As a young Muslim-born believer who volunteers with this ministry explained,

> Turkey is a conservative country; most people don't talk about religion because someone can hear when they talk about these things and there can be problems. Because of this, people more will use the internet to explore religion.
>
> (young Turkish volunteer, personal communication, July 10, 2014)

So the correspondence course has shifted in the past two decades to a digital emphasis, and these missionaries see their work as marking a new generation of missions, media-driven missions. The correspondence course is just one part of their outreach, as they have begun to develop new resources such as witness and teaching videos that can be viewed online on private channels, as well as new types of evangelistic websites. For example, this young Turkish volunteer shared excitedly about an apologetics website he was developing aimed at young people with Islamic beliefs and strong objections to Christianity:

> We want to correct the ideas and bad assumptions they have and correct the prejudice in brains of people about what Christianity is. Because people use the internet and Google, especially young people to learn about religion, Christianity, and to find the purpose of life.
>
> (young Turkish volunteer, personal communication, July 10, 2014)

Through creative campaign advertising about these websites on the Istanbul metro and online, they have seen an upsurge in people taking their correspondence course, which is now available via email. Not only did computers expedite and make more efficient these courses and communication with students, they opened up new possibilities for different types of outreach and ministry. An older Muslim-born Christian convert who volunteers with the course described his work with a group who gathered to brainstorm ways they could use mobile phones for Christian missions in Turkey. "Turkey has almost hundred percent mobile penetration, so we wanted to capitalize on Turks' mobile phones use" (older Turkish volunteer, personal communication, July 10, 2014).

In the mid-2010s they designed a campaign called "whatifitstrue" focused around a giant billboard with provoking, edgy questions and statements about the meaning of life. People were invited to respond by text message or via a QR code that immediately took them to one of the evangelical websites.

> In Turkey there are not too many churches available. For that reason, this tech-nology, the new media, gives us great opportunity and opens more doors to have a personal relationship with the respondents and also we can touch their lives through internet access.
>
> (older Turkish volunteer, personal communication, July 10, 2014)

The correspondence course has drawn together missionaries and nationals in Turkey from different Christian contexts to collaborate in a shared mission. Most of these individuals' main training has been in evangelism and church planting, but they recognize embracing media can allow them to create a new form of missionary outreach. Over time, this work has shifted from being pri-marily a mass-media focused, mail-based evangelistic course to one driven by digital missional resources with multiple initiatives. This illustrates how digital strategists use their creativity to cultivate media skills in an effort to expand their ministry opportunities.

A second manifestation of media-driven missions being propelled by the initia-tive of digital strategists is seen in a support and resource network created by media-driven missionaries and evangelists in Turkey. It was formed by members of the correspondence course ministry and set up to encourage and support individuals in different churches and ministries by experimenting with using digital media such as the internet and mobile phones for Christian missions.

As one foreign missionary who had spent over a decade in Turkey and was foundational in helping create this network described the motivation behind the network:

> We wanted to create a platform online where we could share the resources and make connections with others involved in evangelism through the internet throughout Turkey.
>
> (foreign missionary, personal communication, February 10, 2012)

As mentioned previously, Turkey has strict rules on proselytizing. This means the internet can offer an alternative space, for missionaries to connect with and witness to non-Christian Turks, by offering an increased level of perceived anonymity. It also allows digital missionaries new ways to connect with other Christians involved in different ministries across the country. However due to increased digital tracking by national law enforcement of online religious communication, especially on platforms such as Facebook, tight digital encryption is needed for this new form of e-vangelism.

In the early-mid 2000s, both foreign missionaries and Turkish Christians began to see how the internet provides an easy and inexpensive venue for advertising religious events and Christian-witness media. Since then, internet-based mission activities aimed at Turkish non-Christians have increased due to the efforts of individual workers from multiple missionary organizations and churches who have a heart to marry digital media work to missions. In the last decade, the network served as an important online space for Turkish-focused missionaries to share technical advice, internet tools and digitally driven evangelism strategies.

> We are using technology as tools, as a means to share about the reality of our Christian beliefs and the reality that it is possible to be a Turk and to be a Christian. There is strong cultural links that says by definition to be a Turk is to be Muslim. But through the internet, the Turkish Christian community is able to offer a different narrative. The internet basically provides a microphone for them to say look at this public evangelistic site, which is allowed to exist here. These resources help believers share their faith, and for others to be a little less scared about asking questions about Christianity.
>
> (foreign missionary, personal communication, February 10, 2012)

The important role the internet is now playing for a new generation of Muslim-born Christian converts with a heart to evangelize their countries is illustrated by the story shared at a face-to-face gathering of the network by a middle-aged Turk now based in Germany.

He shared the story of being arrested in the late 1980s for doing missions work with a US-based missionary group. He was incarcerated for three days, then sued by the government for unlawful Christian activities. While he was later found not guilty of breaking the law, public threats toward him and his family eventually led him to leave Turkey. A decade later, he found himself in Germany, pastoring a church that had just launched its first website. After people began to leave messages on the site and ask questions about Christianity there, he got permission from the other church leaders to start a discussion forum on the website. In a short time, the forum was drawing several hundred visitors a day wanting to discuss and debate various issues about faith.

Soon overwhelmed by the traffic, he began to invite Christians, especially those with evangelistic gifting, to help monitor the conversations and respond to individuals. Within two years, they had about 5,000 visitors daily and ran live chatroom discussions on different Christian topics about six hours each day. It was when some Turkish Christian believers visited the site that he began to envision how he could use the internet to revive his missionary work in Turkey. He found Turkish believers in the USA and Muslims in other parts of the world who shared his vision were ready to help with this new online initiative, a Turkish-focused discussion forum on Christianity.

> I had pastored a church for seven years, but I am now an active evangelist sharing the Gospel through the internet. I saw we had enough people in Germany who could take on the responsibility as a pastor or leader in the church. But the internet offered a unique opportunity to reach those in Turkey. It was my heart calling from the very beginning to take the Gospel to Turkish-speaking people.
>
> (Turkish expat, personal communication, February 14, 2012)

Since its initial launch, the forum has evolved into an online church for Turkish believers who are unable to fellowship in an offline church. This inability may be due to the lack of a physical church in their area, to being located in rural parts of Turkey, or to the fact that they cannot openly express their faith due to family pressures or local persecution.

> It is a challenge, because as you know, it is a mediated interaction online. Some of those online have never been to a church, so it is their first church experience. I sense a strong responsibility to be a spiritual father for them. We will continue to gather online until we can see that there is potential they can be led to an offline church, or one can be started for them. We are praying for leaders who can take the responsibility so it can be done.
>
> (Turkish expat, personal communication, February 14, 2012)

Thus the internet plays a key role in supporting missionary activities and initiatives like those described here, helping a new generation of missionaries resource e-Turkish believers and reach out to nonbelievers abroad. Whether supporting the creation of interactive online evangelism websites, digital resources to help Turkish believers teach their children about Christ or mobile witnessing campaigns, the network seeks to be a resource hub for sharing technical and design advice, as well as prayerful encouragement to digital strategists. Yet this networking is not without its risk. As the foreign missionary who initiated the original network stated,

> Our network creates a digital trail that people can actually follow that is linking us all together as a Christian community ... by this linking ourselves all together, those in the network could actually be thrown out (of the country) all together. It is a scary reality and something that we pray against ... The internet offers us an opportunity we never had to reach Turkey for Christ, and so we want to go for it now because we don't know what tomorrow is going to hold.
>
> (foreign missionary, personal communication, February 10, 2012)

While the initial network was dissolved in 2015 due to one of its leaders having to leave the country, its mission was reborn through a number of new initiative's still ongoing online. Media-driven missionaries act as digital strategists as they seek to bring established practices of cross-cultural evangelism into the twenty-first century by leveraging digital tools and platforms to reach out to new audiences and bridge gaps between non-Christian and Christian culture. Digital networking helps missionaries create a safe space for spiritual seekers online, especially those living in countries or contexts where proselytizing is illegal or treated with hostility. Integrating digital media helps a new generation of foreign-born missionaries not only to extend their work in creative ways but it also enables them to offer support to like-minded nationals experimenting with digital evangelism. The internet becomes a space for collaborative resourcing and creating links between nationals and foreign missionaries to facilitate mission activities that reach beyond one city or region, creating new local-global mission initiatives driven by dispersed locals.

Theologians who blog

In Chapter 4, we discussed the rise of "theoblogians," informal or hobbyist theologians without formal theological training, whose online writings and the attention they receive elevate them to the level of religious thought leaders. Here we look at a parallel group, "theologians who blog." These are professional theologians, and Biblical Studies scholars, also referred to as bibliobloggers, who are typically not known for their digital fluency or having a tech background. They often work with ancient texts and set methods of interpretation to produce in-print articles and books on focused areas of scriptural teaching. The central role they play in church institutions as religious educators and trainers is one that has been developed literally over centuries. While the church has indeed had adapt to new expressions of culture over time, and their role within these, the main task of the theologian has charge changed little—to prepare students for leadership roles in their given denomination or religious organization. Yet the age of digital media and communication has prompted a growing number of these professional theologians to experiment with public exegesis, or biblical interpretation shared online, especially via blogs.

"Theologians who blog" are professional theologians or Biblical Studies scholars who often work and teach in the theological faculty of universities, seminaries or Christian-focused colleges. They recognize the fact that textual analysis and biblical interpretation should not be relegated to specialist academic journals and dense books that find their only home in the libraries of theological institutions. These RDCs match Anderson's description of reformer-critics as individuals motivated to use the internet to draw an audience around a particular religious topic or interpretive stance. They use their blogs as a space to reflect personally on their scholarly work or developments in their field of study. They also recognize the value in writing for a broader audience, beyond their scholarly peers, in a style that is less technical and more accessible than the average theologically oriented article.

These theologians act as digital strategists not only because they adopt use of the digital platforms as space for theological reflection and education. They also recognize the act of theological engagement and their interpretive process must be adapted to this new digital communicative context. Their negotiations with digital technologies and culture, and the strategies they adopt, are one of the key issues here.

I came across this category of digital strategists by accident. Having a PhD in Theology, and having completed my thesis based at the School of Divinity at the University of Edinburgh in Scotland, I have an international network of contacts and friends now employed as professional theologians all over the world. Over the course of conducting research for this book, I had the chance to interact with many of these colleagues. As I shared stories about theoblogians I had encountered in this work, several asked if I had read corollary discussions on similar themes happening on blogs of so-and-so, offering the names of established theologians whose blogs they followed.

My conversations began with Tim Bulkley, a pioneer in using computers theological education, who passed away in late 2019. For years he served as a Biblical Studies scholar at Carey Baptist College in Auckland, New Zealand. He has been a forerunner in experimenting with using computer technology and the internet in teaching the Bible and training pastors. In my previous book, *When Religion Meets New Media*, I shared about Bulkley's work in the 1980s. While serving as missionary in central Africa, he used computers' help produce inexpensive church resources for national pastors. In the early 2000s, he also discovered the internet could be used to mobilize Christians around the world to help produce an online audio Bible (Campbell, 2010, see Chapter 6). In later follow-up interviews, he introduced me to the idea of "theologians who blog."

Bulkley spent over three decades of his career teaching theology. He was also an early biblioblogger in his theological specialization of Biblical Studies, blogging on and off for personal and scholarly purposes for over two decades. He describes biblioblogging or theological blogging as,

> … a new layer of conversation emerging between the traditional academic research journal and an undergraduate theology textbook. It is more than just writing that is public, or produced faster than traditional writings. It involves specialized language, but is supposed to be publically accessible at the same time. Theology blogging is not quite like traditional teaching, but can't be pure reflective writing like you see in much blogging.
>
> (T. Bulkley, personal communication, September 19, 2009)

The very idea of blogging, or any kind of technology-driven communication, is very challenging for most people who teach theology, Bulkley argues. That is because, he suggests, digital writing operates within a very different culture to the ones biblical scholars typically work and surround themselves with.

> In theology, we currently relate to the Bible in the ways dominated by the print-culture mindset. But digital culture is mix of written, oral, and visual cultures. The written and oral element is somewhat similar to how the Bible was used in the Middle Ages, but the combination with the visual is something new altogether. We now get the Bible on the laptop screen as a hypertext. For example, most Bible dictionaries now come as hypertext document. This changes ways of searching for words or phrases from linear to jumping from text to text, a drastic shift in our relationship to text.
>
> (T. Bulkley, personal communication, September 19, 2009)

This shift in communication style and culture is something Bulkley feels many theologians try to ignore, because acknowledging it requires a huge shift not only in how they study and teach but in how they see communication and texts.

> Most theological teachers are operating with a kind of head-in-the-sand policy when it comes to our current culture. They are trying to pretend that the technology isn't changing culture, that it is just simply an add on, rather than it being a different kind of writing all together and something we in Biblical Studies can't ignore. You see this clearly in the continued reluctance of many to "cite" electronic sources and unwillingness to acknowledge conversations happening online, or even let students use electronic resources in their research.
>
> (T. Bulkley, personal communication, September 19, 2009)

However, he states that in the past decade, a growing theological conversation is emerging online where amateurs, bible teachers whose area is not the synoptic gospels, and some scholars in the field are starting to engage each other online in the blogosphere. This conversation began my exploration of the negotiations of professional theologian bloggers and their roles as digital strategists.

Yet it was not until I ended up on a train in England, seated near a New Testament theologian from my *alma mater*, which I began to see the importance of this trend. As we swapped stories about our current book projects, he was visibly exercised about my discussion of "theoblogians" and the kind of theological discourse he saw going on in the blogosphere in his own area of expertise. As he shared his experience about engaging interpretive debates on multiple fronts, moving between traditional scholarly writing and public theology on his well-established blog, I began to see how digital discourse about religion was transforming both his theological work and thinking.

Larry Hurtado, professor and honorary fellow at New College, University of Edinburgh, started blogging in 2010 when a colleague helped him set up a personal blog about his research expertise in New Testament and Christian origins. His first post generated 1700 hits in the first 24 hours, and nearly 7,000 in the first week. He was hooked and quickly became an avid biblioblogger.

> I noticed a lot of blog sites were run by amateurs; they have other full-time jobs and in their spare time read something to do with the New Testament or Christianity and blog about it. Often, these blogs were erroneous or confused or slanted, yet it also became apparent, if you read the comments, lots of people are reading these sites and treating it as a source of valid information. So I thought I should balance the crazy and misinformed amateurs with a site of my own in my field of expertise, where you can actually hear from an expert in the subject.
> (L. Hurtado, personal communication, March 15, 2013)

Blogging became a means of disseminating information about his field of expertise, the historical investigation of early Christian teaching and artifacts, to a wider public of whoever is interested. In 2019, his blog has over 500 regular subscribers and over 400,000 hits a month. He described his readership as mostly a mix of students studying theology, a general public who are just interested in Christian origins, and a few professionals in the field who wish to stay up to date with current research in this area. Because of this general readership, he tried to be careful about explaining technical language, writing out scholarly abbreviations and clearly describing academic articles. He referred or linked to journals where the articles are found, for those who are interested. However, blogging for the general public on highly dense theological concepts and historical texts is not an easy task, and one where the academic craft of theology and popular assumptions about theology collide and experience dissonance.

> The impression I get is that it is only the minority of people anymore who read books. I think a great many people who read blogs on religion feel, "I should be able to pick up a lot of what I need to know on a topic from a blog posting. I shouldn't have to read a journal article or a book." And they get annoyed if you say, "I am sorry, I took forty pages to explain this in a chapter in a book, and I can't do that in a blog post." There is an awful amount of people

who simply treat the blog process as something that they shouldn't have to do anything any harder than simply Googling something to get the full answer on their screen. But theology is not like that.

(L. Hurtado, personal communication, March 15, 2013)

Hurtado felt that, as a professional theologian, part of his role online is to elevate the theological discussion. He did this by offering accessible abstracts of his scholarly writing, where he lays out the basic ideas behind his research findings and links to published articles. When relevant, he also uploads prepublication versions of particular pages of articles he refers to, in order to speak to students or peers who might want a more in-depth context about his arguments or claims.

It is my way of putting out and sharing more serious substance as well as the blog postings themselves. I feel a certain missionary purpose, where by blogging I am basically saying, "This is an attempt to try and flush out some of the dark, muddy waters with some fresh water, to try to put out there in the blogosphere and on the internet, for those who want it, serious competent information and opinions on a subject by an expert in Biblical Studies."

(L. Hurtado, personal communication, March 15, 2013)

Online, Hurtado has encountered many different amateur theologians, most who seem to want to make their own mark on debates or issues, and some who have a strong bias against theological scholarship. For him, these amateurs fall into three categories: (1) The overly zealous PhD student reporting on their emerging thesis research, (2) the part-time theology student or hobbyist who enthusiastically recounts each book they read or inspiring lecture they hear and (3) what he describes as the self-appointed experts, whom he finds the most problematic. Hurtado describes these as individuals as motivated by the need to ...

By God, they are going to show that all those theologians are boneheads, and it is up to them to put the records straight, as sort of self-appointed Don Quixotes who are going to put the world right and expose all the haughty thinking. They act as if they have some authority, when in fact they are just amateurs. They use very strong opinions to pronounce things as if it is authoritative, often with a certain combative tone. When the internet came along, it was like Shangri-La to such people because you don't have to have any expertise whatsoever. You don't have to go through any sort of refereeing or examining process. You can just get out there and say whatever you want to say, and it can go to the world. It must be just like a kid in a candy shop for some people.

(L. Hurtado, personal communication, March 15, 2013)

He described a particular encounter with a number of self-appointed experts who were blogging on a news story that reported that a number of new lead-based codices of biblical scriptures had been discovered in Jordan and looked like they were from first-century Jewish Christians. This would have made these findings groundbreaking, as they would be by far the earliest artifacts of any Christian finding in existence. As he read these blog reports, Hurtado quickly realized this was a hoax. From his research experience, the only lead tablets from that era were magical tablets used in occult practices and writing. Also, after examining the images reproduced on the blogs about the lead codices, he noted they were supposedly on lead plates sealed with lead bands, which to him looked like other artifacts found in the fourth or fifth century, so these could not possibly be as old as reports claimed. Due to all the hype being circulated online, he felt compelled to blog about his observations.

> I simply said, "Everybody here take a breath." There was a guy who was being cited by a number of people online from the National Museum in Jordan who said, "This is the greatest archaeological find of the twentieth century." And I said, "If this really is what the guy said, then I just have one thing to say, 'Chill dude, this is bogus.'"
>
> (L. Hurtado, personal communication, March 15, 2013)

Within a day, he got a thousand hits on that posting, and it even gained traction in the popular press, especially where reports showed the tablets were indeed a hoax. This for Hurtado shows the importance of having classically trained and skilled theologians be part of popular discussions about religion online, as they have valuable insights to contribute and the ability to spot "fake news," as it were.

> I say to myself, "The internet is about free speech; anybody can say whatever they want …." But obviously, I don't think it helps things for people to put out inaccurate information or misleadingly presented stuff that is being pumped out daily into the blogosphere. While it is not my job, and I am just not interested in spending all my time policing the internet, I think we have a role to play. I feel we are to patiently put out accurate information, to try not to pick fights with people and just say, if expertise matters in this context, then here is somebody speaking out of their expertise, their training, who has insights into the original Greek, which might be important to consider.
>
> (L. Hurtado, personal communication, March 15, 2013)

Hurtado recognized the prevalence of amateur theologians online, and while he is not worried these alternative voices will replace the influence of credible professional theologians, he does feel his guild is responsible to make their presence known online.

I think it is important for scholars in particular subjects to take it as a responsibility to engage the internet. Because in the absence, if you leave the blogosphere to the students, the nice conscientious students, to the well-meaning or not-so-well-meaning amateurs, then it seems to me that the call of the biblical scholar is to share quality scholarship as a whole, and if we do not share our knowledge online, we are in a sense failing in our responsibilities. I think that scholars as a guild have a collective responsibility to contribute to the informing of a wider public about their subject ... and the internet is the cheapest, quickest, and actually in terms of time and effort probably the least demanding way for scholars to do that (L. Hurtado, personal communication, March 15, 2013).

In July 2019 Larry Hurtado announced online that he was "signing off until further notice" and retiring from blogging, due the resurfacing of an aggressive form of leukemia. He said he hoped his archive of his blog would continue to serve as site of reference for readers interested in New Testament studies (see https://larryhurtado. wordpress.com/2019/07/08/health-issues-and-blogging/). In October he made a surprising reappearance on his blog, when he announced a resurgence in his health and the news that his blog had reached the 2 million + views mark. He remarked, "it was done simply as an experiment, to see how blogging worked. I had no idea how it would take off and continue to be consulted in the years since then" (https:// larryhurtado.wordpress.com/2019/10/15/a-milestone-2million-views/). Professor Hurtado ended being able to make nearly a dozen more blog posts on topics such as New Testament Christology, Exorcism, the role of Paul in the early church and personal reflections on his academic publishing before it was announced on social media of his passing in late November 2019. While his academic and online legacy has come to an end, his writings online remain a testimony to what accessible critical, yet engaging theological communication can look like on the internet.

Many of the theologians and bibliobloggers I interviewed articulated very similar motivations to those of Dr Larry Hurtado. They described their blogging as an attempt to correct uninformed or incorrect theological interpretations of scriptural texts or arguments posted by popular religious bloggers. Blogging becomes a venue for thinking aloud about their biblical scholarship and explaining to Christians the importance of established and scholarly interpretive techniques that are applied in a consistent fashion. They also stress that a clear knowledge of historical context and culture is important to producing an accurate translation of Biblical texts.

Matthew Tan, a theologian based in the Catholic Archdiocese of Sydney and adjunct senior lecturer in Theology at the University of Notre Dame Australia, has been blogging since 2007. For him, blogging is essential to his theological reflection and praxis, forcing him to think about how to apply and explain dense theological concepts to everyday people in the church.

> One of the benefits of blogging is that you are constantly put in a situation that you have to engage theology not as an abstract set of principles, but as contemporary issues. I think the mere act of blogging already puts you at an interface between theology and contemporary issues.
>
> (M. Tan, personal communication, June 28, 2014)

Tan has recently transitioned from his original blog "The Divine Wedgie" to new format called "Awkward Asian Theologian" where he now blogs and also posts longer theological reflections as podcasts. He feels it is important for academic theologians to blog, because it influences not only their own work but also helps address the problematic biblical scholarship he often comes across online.

> In the Australian context, far too many blogs that describe themselves as focused on theology are not really theological blogs, they are just rants. As a result, I see a lot of people's opinions and understanding of faith within the church becoming shaped in problematic ways by these theological blogs. I think that professional theologians have an important part to play in this discursive atmosphere, in providing sound theological reflection, informed by academic study and evidence. Countering the effect that well intentioned, but ill-informed non-professional bloggers can create.
>
> (M. Tan, personal communication, June 28, 2014)

Tan also believes the style of communication and interaction encouraged by blogging practice can encourage theologians to think and write in new ways. He sees the potential for theologians online to move beyond old paradigms of communicating either for fellow scholars or a purely public audience, toward creative forms of theological reflection.

> I think more theologians need to blog, precisely because now it creates the potential to see theology as based on collaboration, which is made possible in viral blog formats. The internet could foster new forms of collaborative knowledge, as theologians learn how to interact together in new ways […] creating new types of collaborative theology.
>
> (M. Tan, personal communication, June 28, 2014)

Blogging becomes a space allowing theologians to step beyond the constraints of their academic disciplines and denominational constraints to address a wider public in a more personal way. Thus, theologians who blog have the opportunity to establish influence outside their specialized fields and the hierarchical structure of the institutions for which they work.

Theologians who blog often hold recognized positions of leadership either within religious educational institutions or specific church contexts. Yet they represent a modified, or hybrid, form of the reformer–critic, in that their traditional scholarly roles and responsibilities often constrain what theological matters they can discuss or how they can discuss them. Online they experience a new level of communicative opportunity and freedom. Many of the theologians who blog interviewed argue their circle of influence has grown to be much wider online than it is in some traditional offline venues.

Online ministers

A third type of digital strategists are those who work for a church and whose main role is to facilitate some form of ministry in the offline context, such as religious education or teaching or care ministry to underserved populations. These RDCs come to recognize that embracing digital technologies can enable them to do their job in more efficient and creative ways. They may even hold a leadership position, such as serving as a priest or pastor, and they choose to use digital media in creative ways to facilitate new forms of engagement with their members. This can lead to the creation of new hybrid positions within some church contexts, where the main tasks they are charged with are quite traditional, such as pastoral care and counseling, but these tasks are done in new ways in mediated, networked spaces.

These types of roles can manifest in multiple ways. One example is the emergence of church-service producers or media directors in church services. It is increasingly common in Protestant evangelical churches to have such roles, where an individual is in charge of overseeing the multiple components of a contemporary service, including directing transitions between music, message, announcements, overseeing the technology team, lighting messages on screens, and ensuring service choreography runs on time. Many services—especially those found in non-denominational, seeker-friendly (focusing their services toward non-Christian guests) type churches—have become increasingly media-driven events. For example, they rely heavily on PowerPoint projection for sharing song lyrics and scripture passages and multiple screens to enable members to see individuals on the stage more clearly. By creating these wired, highly mediated worship events, they create an easy transition, taking their service from embodied to an online experience. Facebook livestreaming, webcasting and video podcasting of services have become common trends for many media-driven churches. The growth and popularity of these worship events has also fueled an increase in the past decade of multisite churches, which are heavily dependent on digital technology. Here, media directors and service producers are often transformed into online ministers or pastors.

Multisite churches began to emerge in the early 1990s in the USA, in many respects as a response to the megachurch movement (defined as churches with over 2,000 individuals attending on a given Sunday). Megachurches were often critiqued for the lack of a sense of community and spiritual accountability for both members and leaders, as their sheer size made it difficult for individuals to build relationships. The multisite church movement sought to address this weakness by creating smaller site congregations and integrating small-group strategies to help people get more connected to one another. Multisite churches typically have a central or parent congregation where the senior or founding pastor is typically based. Then additional sites are planted in different locations, keeping their links with the parent congregation through video feeds during services or by sharing staff, content, and most of all, service structure and liturgy. This creates a network of churches that hold, as it were, to a shared worship experience and ministry brand. When churches move to a multisite model, this often means sending out staff from the main campus to other sites to serve as a campus pastor and including tech-team members to help new sites facilitate the standardized and equivalent worship experience across the sites. Increasingly, multisite churches have also launched online sites as part of their strategies where chatrooms, interactive video channels or Facebook Live have become their own unique campuses within these church networks. Like other campuses, online sites require a campus pastor, but one with a very different set of skills, and tech-team members are often recruited to be these new digital-campus pastors. These digital strategists are like the online pastors described earlier, but in reverse, as their tech expertise elevates them to needed pastoral status. This creates new opportunities and challenges in what it means to be a pastor in these contexts.

One example of this interesting negotiation can be found in the online ministers associated with a multisite church in central Florida. Northland, A Church Distributed began in the 1980s and adopted a multisite model in the late 1990s when it reached over 5,000 members. Northland describes their distributed church model as based on a belief that a church is defined not by its physical building, but by the relationships among its congregants (A History of Northland, A Church Distributed, www.northlandchurch.net/articles/history/). Northland draws its theological support for its church organizational strategy from 1 Corinthians 12, which emphasizes God's distribution of diverse gifts among different believers. Northland is described as a distributed body, with many of its parts connected to the Metro Orlando church hub via technology. "Put simply, it means that church isn't a building … it's people 'being the church,' everywhere, every day. It also means that, in recognition of how God distributes different gifts among different people (1 Corinthians 12:11), we connect with individuals and organizations outside our four walls for long-term support and effectiveness—without blurring distinctions" (Frequently Asked Questions: "What is a Distributed Church?", www.northlandchurch.net/faq/).

Essential to the formation and maintenance of the distributed church vision is Northland's use of technology, which facilitates its church services and has led to the development of various house churches, in which two or more nuclear families gather in a home to worship together. The creation of such house churches, it is claimed, was inspired by evidence gathered from the Book of Acts and the epistles of Paul, which are believed to indicate that early Christians frequently gathered in their own homes to pray together and minister to one another's needs (Lacich, 2008). Technology plays an important role in facilitating Northland's distributed networks of worship sites and thus must be explored in more detail.

This church model has led Northland to plant associated church sites in several locations across the region and even overseas. In the late 2000s they also began to experiment with various online campuses via a webstream internet channel and a Roku channel. These sites are linked to a dedicated chat room that forms the hub of their online campus and is the main area of oversight for online minister Nathan Clark. Clark initially joined Northland's creative and tech teams on their main campus in 2004, and was promoted to Director of Digital Innovation in the mid-2010s. His work expanded to overseeing Northland's web portal and various online vehicles and portals that connect people to the church and services via the internet. By 2014, he was named online campus pastor and began to oversee the chat room on their web portal. A key part of his role is tending to the portion of the congregation that primarily connects to Northland and its worship service through its digital platforms during the five worship services the church's main campus holds each weekend. Besides interacting online with congregants, he often uses phone, email or IM to help individuals with technology needs or pastoral care during the services. The other part of Clark's job focuses on creating resources for the church to support the online congregation, especially designing, implementing and overseeing tools that enable people to worship through digital technologies.

When pushed to answer what kind of skills are needed to be an online minister, Clark quickly responds, "Fast typing! […] Because of the volume of conversations you are going to initiate and respond to during the service" (N. Clark, personal communication, August 11, 2012). Overseeing the online chat room requires an ability to respond quickly to both technical and personal support issues that emerge during the service.

> It is a ministry of response, which makes it a different type of pastoral ministry. Pastors typically are given time to reflect on and respond to personal needs or questions about discipleship. But online our focus is often very practical and immediate, because an online worship service is based on a tech-based system; this creates a different, spontaneous environment. At one moment, you have to deal with a request from someone that they can't log in or their screen froze. And then you can get a comment like, "Gosh my husband hit me last week and should I get divorced? Does that jeopardize my soul?" I'll have probably six or seven private chats going on throughout the service. So you have to be able to respond to both kinds of issues, and quickly.
>
> (N. Clark, personal communication, August 11, 2012)

The online minister's responsibilities include being online before a service starts, ensuring the service live feed is working properly, welcoming online attendees, encouraging them to introduce themselves and helping with any technology issues individuals are having hearing audio or seeing video. During services, online ministers are kept busy overseeing the online discussions, which when observed, look a lot like individuals' passing digital notes commenting on features of service or offering their own interpretation on facets of the sermon or the theology of songs.

> The online minister has the obligation to curate the group conversation to as much a degree as possible, as well as to respond to the need that arises in the chat, and also prepare people for the liturgical experiences of the service. On top of that, we try and cultivate a feeling of community among the attendees so they feel a part of the larger Northland experience.
>
> (N. Clark, personal communication, August 11, 2012)

This involves making sure conversations are appropriate by reminding individuals about online protocols set out in the chat room guidelines and staying focused on service content. It is typical to have to balance troubleshooting tech problems for attendees alongside private conversations with individuals related to personal needs or online congregants' prayer requests. When the service ends, the online minister individually thanks participants for attending, guides congregants to other online resources on the church website, recommends site churches in their area and even connects individuals with pastoral care staff at the main campus as needed.

The context of such an online church experience thus requires the online minister to be able to give both spiritual and technical guidance, sometimes simultaneously. However, when it comes to selecting volunteers to serve as online ministers in the chat room setting, technological skills and expertise typically trump pastoral training as qualifiers for ministry. While Clark minored in Religious Studies for his undergraduate degree, and has a couple years' experience leading youth groups and developing teaching skills, his professional background has primarily been in computers and technology management. He also brags that his formal theological education has been limited to taking only one seminary course in Biblical Studies.

> I have always struggled with the qualifications for a pastoral role being so heavily academic. I understand the basis for it, but it is the reason that I didn't pursue a seminary degree or didn't plan to go to seminary after college, even though I felt like I was called to serve the church.
>
> (N. Clark, personal communication, August 11, 2012)

He took the seminary course when his job at Northland evolved into overseeing the online church services, and he felt this helped him get a sense of what formal pastoral training is like.

Clark now oversees a volunteer team of online ministers who help oversee the service chat room. They come from a variety of backgrounds—e.g., a lawyer, computer professionals and an educator. For example, one volunteer online minister describes the hybrid responsibilities of online ministers as, "serve as part hall monitor, part technology trouble shooter, and part responder to many prayer requests" (online minister 1, personal communication, August 11, 2012). Another volunteer is a thirty-something IT consultant who never went to college, but who has been a part of the Northland church for nearly 20 years. Like Clark and most other online ministers, he has no formal theological or pastoral training, his primary qualification coming instead from his technical expertise.

> I kind of fell into being an online minister. I felt a call to ministry when I was young, I even looked into going to seminary, but did not end up moving in that direction. I have a desire to reach people and engage people in a type of church that is not passive and focused on just consuming. One of my goals is to have people experience church every day of their lives, not confine it to a weekend expression or service. Being part of Northland's online ministry team helps me do this [...] sometimes theology and doctrine can get in the way of someone that is just in pain or hurting or needs a friend. That is not to say that there is not a place for academic theology in the church, it is just not where

> I am called to be. But I find that being plugged into Northland gives me access to relationships and resources that can help those I meet online, should those needs arise.
>
> (online pastor 2, personal communication, August 11, 2012)

One challenge Clark has encountered in building his team is that Northland does not have any established criteria as to what qualifies some to do online work, especially online pastoral work.

He, however, has set down a few traits that he looks for in potential online ministers. These include having a fluency in the culture of Northland, understanding its unique approach to congregational life and having "a heart and mind for God."

> It is important online ministers understand how we execute church and the fact that we want to guide people online on a certain path through our distributed church model, which is on one hand the essence of the Gospel, but on the other hand is a very unique approach. Also, as the online congregation is just one of a number of sites we have, there is a sense we want to create a singular expression of church through multiple sites that needs to be considered.
>
> (N. Clark, personal communication, August 11, 2012)

Yet there is no formal selection process to serve as an online minister. Most online ministers are either recommended to Clark by others on the Northland staff, or individuals in the church he has recruited. The training process is mostly on the job, focused on equipping individuals with skills concentrated on technical protocol for managing the online chat room, as well as making them aware of the staff and resources available through Northland should they encounter counseling situations beyond their knowledge or experience.

Such flexible criteria make the process of building this pastoral team a dynamic and open process, unlike the formal processes other ministries in the Northland church network are subject to. For example, in other church departments, such as pastoral counseling, formal pastoral ordination or credentials are required, and even those wishing to serve on and oversee a church-sanctioned home group need to go through Northland's leadership training course.

So it would appear that the ministry of the online campus is driven by a different ministry logic—the online campus focuses on technical aspects of message delivery and interaction, and so is seen as structural in nature or part of infrastructure. This differs from the work of the main service, which is focused on the liturgy over the user experience, placing it firmly in the traditional pastoral realm of oversight. Because the primary work of the online ministers is driven by technical skills, it is framed as a functional support ministry and is in many ways presented as an extension of the work of the digital media team that oversees instrumental features of church worship such as sound, light, video and digital broadcasting.

Another challenge lies in the fact that it seems Northland leadership still seems to be trying to figure out how they should conceptualize and incorporate this unique, technologically driven ministry into their traditional understanding of church life. This uncertainty is echoed by one of the online ministers, who has no formal pastoral training, but does have previous experience as a volunteer worship leader at Northland's Monday night church service and teaches New Testament at a local bible college.

> When you start to talk about what makes a worship experience legitimate, I think it is hard to say that you have to go to church where there is a thousand people in the room (like the main Northland campus) or it is not a legitimate worship experience […] and that because online worship does not offer that, it is not legitimate. I think that a lot of people who worship online are there because online worship is the only place they feel comfortable. They have been hurt by the church, they have been hurt by their families and friends … there are wounds, and so they especially latch onto whoever is their online minister as a source of support and healing. I have a hard time saying to someone that your connection to God, if it be mediated through this technology or organized around a kitchen table, is inauthentic or ineffective. That judgment requires a knowledge of God's heart that is beyond me, but I think what we try to do online satisfies the demands of what He has called us to be as a church.
>
> (online minister 1, personal communication, August 11, 2012)

This emphasizes the tension this digital expression of church creates, even within Northland's dynamic, distributed understanding of church. Even those churches that value technological innovation, strive to network members across multiple sites, and embrace mediated ministry still struggle with how to conceptually and theologically integrate the new forms of church they help create. Online ministers serve as digital strategists who must actively negotiate between traditional and technological church contexts and forms of ministry while seeking to create new standards of practice in line with the DNA of the religious communities in which they are invested.

The common feature shared by media-driven missionaries, theologians who blog and online ministers, is the fact that they choose to actively embrace and integrate digital media into their religious work. While digital strategists typically are in roles that do not require technology use, they choose to actively engage digital media because they see how such appropriation can enhance both instrumental tasks and missional aspects of their job. This choice can be motivated by a number of factors. Digital media and their creative integration are used by digital strategists to meet a perceived need or add an opportunity, such as providing more accurate information about their religious group or faith online, increasing their community's outreach into digital spaces, or extending traditional religious practices for their members by connecting offline and online religious contexts. Technology thus becomes central to their work by their choice, because they see it as offering new opportunities for creative faith engagement. These religious innovations can also create new dynamics related to issues of authority within their religious communities or groups. These are worth reflection.

Digital strategists' media-making narrative: Missional media negotiators

Digital strategists embrace technology in an effort to augment and enhance their traditional religious roles and ministry practices. Digital media enable them to extend their sphere of influence, create a broader audience for their work and expedite the dissemination of religious messages and agendas. Because they hold recognized religious roles in a specific religious institution, their words and actions are often seen as legitimate by their religious community. Yet because digital innovation becomes central to their work, they also draw the attention and devotion of followers online, both inside and outside their community affiliations.

It is in this spirit that digital strategists emerge. They are individuals who hold recognized positions in their institution or community focused on tasks such as teaching and instruction. Their traditional work tasks primarily involve engagement with textual media, such as the Bible or commentaries, though they may use other media resources to help communicate with their audience in teaching contexts. Digital media offer them not only new ways to communicate these messages but opportunities to creatively reframe and re-present them to their audiences. They can be described as missional media negotiators because their focus is on religious mission. They see themselves as primarily tasked with sharing the faith message of their community, but choose to use new media to aid in accomplishing this goal. Digital media enable them to extend and innovate their traditional tasks focused on informing, educating and advocating their beliefs to others. They serve as negotiators between multiple contexts, especially traditional religious and communicative contexts and new media cultures and settings. As missional media negotiators, they exhibit a number of shared traits.

Traditional practices using new tools

First, digital strategists readily use new media technologies and platforms, but they typically do so to perform very traditional religious practices or tasks associated with their ministry roles. The unique affordances digital media offer them encourage creativity and offer opportunities for them develop new ways of performing their work. Media-driven missionaries use digital tools to enhance and expedite their evangelistic activities. Online ministers use communication opportunities offered by online communication to provide pastoral oversight as well as technological counsel in online church platforms. Theologians who blog are able to teach and educate future church leaders, as well Christians online, about theological debates and issues. Therefore, digital media enable them to create content or tools that allows them to complete important aspects of their traditional roles.

Experimentation with new technologies to perform their work brings with it both opportunities and challenges for digital strategists. Theologians who blog have access to a new teaching forum, a broader public and new ways to collaborate with fellow scholars. However, as one theologian described it, the style of communication required by blogs is much more simplified, succinct and constant than theologians are used to, requiring them to develop a new form of writing that can become a distraction from the slow methodical process of theological study and writing. Media-driven missions have always been about producing communication tools and resources to evangelize, and digital media in many respects make the process of producing and sharing evangelistic material quicker and more efficient. Yet mediated missions mean individuals are further distanced from interacting with actual Christians in the process of evangelism, potentially altering individuals' understanding of community and relationships within the Christian faith. Online ministers are basically trained in technology systems of soundboards and PowerPoints, and that helps contemporary worship services run smoothly. The move to running a service online, however, requires not only technological expertise but forms of pastoral competence they are often not trained to handle. In addition, the move to facilitating church online requires online ministers to alter traditional service structures and even liturgy; online technology subjects service structures to the constraints and rules of technology, which can have theological implications. So while technology integration enables digital strategists to fulfill an established agenda of ministry tasks associated with their position in new and creative ways, it also has the potential to alter these practices in unforeseen ways.

Digital experimentation for extending mission

Second, digital strategists hold ministry roles that do not require technological expertise or knowledge. For example, theologians study ancient languages and engage in systematic study of the Bible in a university PhD program, while future missionaries undertake studies in cross-cultural communication and Bible translation at religious training centers or schools. For most, media literacy and production are not part of their training and technology skills are not part of their job requirements. This means digital strategists acquire their digital competencies and expertise outside their formal ministry training. Most in this study could be described as self-driven digital media hobbyists or those who held jobs requiring some technology skills before they came to church-related work. Digital strategists like to experiment with the internet or develop fluencies with different media tools/skills, and then bring these to bear in their ministry work.

The flexible and dynamic features digital media offer—especially those enabling them to transcend time, geography and cultural constraints—encourage digital strategists to consider how these tools might be leveraged to enhance their ministry work. A main motivation for digital strategists to embrace digital media is the fact that these media are a way to extend their outreach beyond their offline, face-to-face congregation or audience. Media-driven missionaries begin to see the internet as a new mission field, a space they need to go to because it is where the unchurched are found and are easily accessible, extending their reach beyond those with whom they have face-to-face contact in their physical location. Theologians who blog are often motivated to move their writing and scholarship onto digital platforms in order to share their work with a broader audience, making academic theology more accessible and public, which can help break down the perceived elite status of theologians.

The internet also allows members of a church tech team with a heart to serve others and help build Christian community the chance to move beyond the media booth at the back of the church. For digital strategists, embracing and integrating technology into their work is about extending their mission to a larger audience, one used to mediate social interactions.

Blending online and offline ministry and contexts

Third, digital strategists connect their digital and offline work, creating a blended outlook and practice. While their work roles and affiliations are clearly rooted in the traditions and practices of an established offline religious institution, they are technological opportunists. They recognize digital media can be adapted and integrated into their work in ways that extend, but do not fully alter their mission. This means they see that offline and online ministry are complimentary and can be blended together to create a new integrated context for ministry. For online ministers, there is not an online and an offline congregation, but a congregation that is interconnected, situated in different settings. Media-driven missionaries see a single mission field, stretching from online to offline spaces and interactions. Theologians who blog understand that while the internet may represent a very different audience to which their thoughts and teachings are directed, it is still part of the church they are called to speak to and educate. So while digital platforms may represent new spaces for conducting their ministry, informants in this study overwhelmingly conceived of online spaces as simply an extension of the offline, established ones in which they work.

However, the fact that their positions and work are initially rooted in an off-line context does inform the nature of how these two spaces become blended. Digital strategists often describe their digital work as an extension of their off-line institutional affiliation and roles. This means they see themselves as bringing the online setting or aspects of digital culture into an established offline situated locale. In other words, digital strategists integrate digital work and engagement into established ministries in order to create a new blended context. They do this by building on their recognized offline position or authority and adding to it with digital fluency and expertise drawn from their online activities. Their expertise and position in the offline sphere lend credibility to their online activities. I describe this as creating a form of hybrid authority rooted in expertise in online and off-line contexts, a concept explored more in the next section of this chapter. Digital skills coupled with strong organizational recognition and expertise enable them to become digital advocates for their respective institutions.

Digital strategists as missional media negotiators

This chapter presents digital strategists as bridge builders or negotiators who choose to work between two cultures, one based on technological innovations and expertise and another grounded in the traditional institutions they represent. Digital strategists' media use is also motivated by a focused mission. They desire to share religious messages in effective ways that can have broad impact. Digital strategists see that taking their traditional tasks online and modifying them to that environment enables them to accomplish this remit and extend their audience. Rather than being self-appointed, as suggested by Anderson's "reformer-critic" category, the mission of digital strategists is tied to the job or role they hold within an established religious community or institution. While their work is closely associated with specific religious institutions, they do not necessarily look to these institutions for validation and full support for their digital work. That is because their ministry focus trumps the tools they use to carry out that work. Together, this work and the underlying intentions of the RDCs highlighted in this chapter contribute to showing their media-making narrative to be one of missional media negotiators.

This narrative also points to digital strategists having a specific relationship with algorithmic culture. As discussed in Chapter 2, they function in the logic of digital leaders; they understand their work is grounded in the traditional practices of an established institution, which, as they see it, must adapt to a digitally driven culture. They understand their audience lives in an integrated online and offline context and feel they must adapt their work to engage them. They must simultaneously translate traditional practices to a digital culture and moderate the communicative and cultural expectation of digitally mediated culture to their offline institutions. Digital strategists must constantly negotiate between these two arenas and be willing to live in the tension this creates. This chapter explores how digital strategists understand their position as being called to work between the offline, traditionally embodied culture of their religious institution and online, mediated contexts of the digital world they feel called to minister within. This intersection means digital strategists are constantly moving between online and offline conceptual spaces, as they see their work becoming blended and embedded between these contexts. The result is a hybridized reality and notion of authority, explored further in Chapter 7.

How Christian digital creatives understand and perform authority

The stage is now set to discuss the different understandings of authority enacted by each category of religious digital creatives (RDCs) presented in this study. By linking back with discussions from Chapter 1—noting authority can be seen as a role, power, relationship and/or algorithm—I show how digital entrepreneurs, spokespersons and strategists differ in their assumptions about authority. Thus this chapter offers a compelling comparison of how RDC exemplars discussed as case studies in Chapters 4–6 invoke different conceptions of authority and how this informs the way they frame their work and relations with respective Christian communities.

This chapter also lays the foundation for a discussion of the technological apologetics enacted by RDCs, explored in more detail in Chapter 8. Before we can examine the justifications digital entrepreneurs, spokespersons and strategists use to legitimize their work, we must first identify the ways they present that media work they do and how they see this as creating an authoritative platform within their religious institutions. I begin by briefly revisiting each of the RDC media-making narratives outlined in the conclusions of Chapters 4–6. This reminds us of the specific approach to authority each RDC references, in both offline, institutional, and online, digitally driven work contexts.

Digital entrepreneurs performing authority as visionary technology influencers

The digital entrepreneurs, as introduced in Chapter 4, are individuals with expertise and training in digital technology and related fields, who feel a personal sense of calling to use these skills to serve their religious community. They can be "techies for God" who see themselves as tithing their personal time to create digital resources or create initiatives to help spread religious messages and impact. Individuals like Alex Kerr describe themselves as a part of a "huge volunteer army [...] with tech skills and vision" who are waiting for churches to catch their vision (personal communication, February 12, 2013).

Others are theoblogians who create religious content in order to elevate a Christian presence online, such as Jana Riess's description of an online "bloggernacle" giving the Church of Jesus Christ of Latter-day Saints (LDS) members a new space to speak about the future of their church and even challenge traditional structures. Digital entrepreneurs' media-making narrative presents them as visionary technology influencers seeing the new possibilities digital media offer for communication or adapting religious practices, and then making them happen. By leveraging their tech skills combined with a visionary imagination, they see new opportunities for Christian outreach and proclamation through digital-creative work.

Yet as their efforts target a sphere of culture not known for its technological innovation—i.e., religious institutions—and as organizational outsiders, their work is not always understood or appreciated by those they seek to serve. This means their work also involves a great deal of personal promotion and technological advocacy, trying to convince religious structures and leaders of the importance of engaging with digital media and the unique opportunity their innovation can offer these groups. It is in this discourse about their work and their perceived relationship with their religious community we see a distinct understanding of authority presented in their narratives

Digital entrepreneurs draw on authority as power

Digital entrepreneurs' discussion of their work appears to primarily draw on the notions of authority as power, as discussed in Chapter 1, in relation to how they describe and understand the impact of their work within religious contexts. Seeing authority as power based places emphasis on an established social structure's ability to control others. The media-making narrative of digital entrepreneurs engages this notion by describing how they position themselves in relation to the official religious structures and groups they feel called to serve. Descriptions of their digital work emphasize how they seek to navigate between the individually driven media-ministry initiatives they take on and the religious institutions they see this work could most benefit.

As discussed previously, this notion of authority links to the work of Michel Foucault (1977), where authority was presented as based within power, which is a structural condition that shapes human relations and responses toward one another. Power is seen as a power dynamic between not only leaders and followers but as a social force shaping broader relationships within society. Foucault's notion of authority as power requires paying attention to what people say, and the strategies they enact to respond to those power relations they identify within the social contexts they find themselves. This is seen in the media-making narratives of digital entrepreneurs, who recognize the fact that they are institutional outsiders, but perceive their work as done in service of a specific religious culture and its structures. While their digital work may create a unique ministry or network of collaboration, they still describe this work as situated within the broader context of the Christian church and its mission.

The way they frame their work evokes the idea of authority as power based, as digital entrepreneurs acknowledge their work is both independent and dependent.

It is independently motivated and resourced. Digital entrepreneurs see themselves as having a certain level of authority in this way, in that their digital initiatives are making converts to Christianity. Eric Celier of Jesus.net describes his pioneering work as "open-sourced evangelism" empowering individuals to share their faith and creating new global ministry partnerships that should be the new paradigm for evangelistic ministry within Christianity in the twenty-first century. Thus, he situates online evangelism as offering a new structure beyond traditional established church and parachurch evangelistic ministries, enabling more Christians to get involved in such work.

Yet digital entrepreneurs' innovative work is still dependent to a certain extent on social structures of the Christian church, due to their faith affiliations and shared spiritual commitments. As Arjo deVroome emphasizes in his description of his work with Jesus.net, he views the website as a unique online evangelism initiative, but also argues that it does not sit outside the calling of the Christian church to make disciples and coverts. Thus, he sees part of his work is to show other Christian organizations, churches and ministers how online ministry can complement their already established offline religious practices. This independent–dependent, authority-structured context digital entrepreneurs find themselves in can create an uneasy tension related to their technological apologetic, as will be discussed later in this chapter.

So digital entrepreneurs draw on the notion of authority as power, based by situating their work both within the flexible, top-down structures of digital culture and the institutional structures of their religious tradition. This also points to some assumptions about the nature of authority as expressed by Hofstede (2011), described in Chapter 1. As he stated, authority as power based places attention on the strategies individuals use to negotiate their social position and agendas within a given space. He suggested paying close attention to the symbolic actions an individual uses to establish a certain position within their community or the social contexts with which they seek to associate. We see this in Huw Tyler's narrative about his time as director of Share Creative, seeking to model how digital media can be used as part of the organization's designated call. He asserts communication is part of God's and the church's DNA, and each generation of Christians is called to embrace the communication technologies of their day to further their work. Framing themselves as helpmates modeling new ways to accomplish innate goals of the Christian church helps digital entrepreneurs negotiate their internal and external social positions, and the situatedness of the traditional power structures of the church in relation to their work.

Hofstede's discussion of authority highlights the importance of paying close attention to how digital-work narratives draw on perceived and enacted views of authority. RDCs conceive of their work in relation to both digital culture and the established practices of offline religious communities. Their negotiation of this relationship shows how language and actions are used to establish and affirm relational connections and boundaries, even in the midst of doing work that pushes against traditional practices and contexts. Digital entrepreneurs enact the notion of authority as power based by acknowledging the importance of their digital work, yet linking themselves as dependent on established religious structures and social institutions.

Entrepreneurs' algorithmic authority: Privileging technological/online expertise

As argued in Chapter 1, digital entrepreneurs do not only enact an understanding of authority that is grounded in traditional, or what we have referred to in this study as offline-situated notions of institutional authority, but they also perform their work in ways that express certain understandings of algorithmic authority, in which authority is based on their performance online. In this study, digital entrepreneurs emulate media influencers. Media influencers are those who use digital media to broadcast their thoughts and opinions to a broad audience, often through social media. They are characterized by the visibility of their work and the reputation they build from their prominence online. Similarly, many of the digital entrepreneurs' media narratives in this study emphasize their technological expertise and insights into digital culture, which they see as situating their work, and in some cases themselves, in a new technological-social space, outside the realms of offline religious structures described earlier.

As Booth and Matic (2011) claimed, media influencers are often previous unknowns who become "somebodies" online by learning the rules of digital communication and leveraging practices that raise their digital profile. This is illustrated by the work narratives of theobloglians, who without the internet or social media might never be able to achieve such a public viewing of their personal religious reflections. In many respects, it is their knowledge of how to communicate effectively online and their ability to cultivate a broad social network that allowed individuals like Tony Jones to become media influencers within different sectors of the Christian community. Creating online content that speaks consistently into focused topics or a personal agenda over time helped them build prominence online.

Media influencers are criticized, because while they may have a large reach for their message, it can be hard to quantify the actual impact of their messages on their audience. While techies for God and theobloglians can count the number of visitors to their site or profile, it is much harder to quantify their influence. internet evangelists tend to log the number of conversions reported through their digital interactions, but even these numbers can be critiqued as to whether these reports accurately, tangibly report true change among their followers. Reporting engagement with technological structures does not necessarily mean having authority over one's audience. Still, we see that digital entrepreneurs' work narratives privilege digital fluency, engagement and prominent presence as indicators of their authority, or at least of their influence within digital culture, for Christian purposes. This shows digital entrepreneurs situate themselves and their understanding of authority within a dyad linking algorithmic culture and its opportunities with the constraints of offline religious structures and groups.

Digital spokespersons performing authority as identity curators

The media-making narrative presented by digital spokespersons is that of an identity curator. They are employed as media officers and communication directors, tasked with translating the profile, practices and praxis of their religious organizations through digital media content and resources. Their job descriptions focus on a variety of practical communicative tasks, from building websites and app design to monitoring organizational social media accounts or writing and distributing institutional news digitally. They frame these tasks in terms of creating digital performances of their group's official or sanctioned identity. Claus Grue, former communication director of the diocese of Lund for the Church of Sweden, saw his work as focused on keeping up to date with both internet trends and the direction of the Church, in order to advise and implement the best communicative plans for his institution. As a digital spokesperson, he sees his role as helping both church leaders and diocesan structure best use and represent themselves through the internet. Digital spokespersons are in a unique position—they are paid agents representing the agenda and image of an established religious community through online media and monitoring internal communication. David Webster, former webmaster for the Methodist Church in the UK, describes his work as building and maintaining connections between the Church, its members and its website and resources.

However, many digital spokespersons claim the institutions they work for often do not fully understand the digital media culture in which they work. This is a common comment made by both communication directors and webmasters. They also understand the digital resources and content they create can give them a more public profile, both in and outside of their institution. This can move them from their official role as identity curator to being seen as a digital-identity creator. The shift can create an uncomfortable position. In Chapter 2, Catholic webmaster James Abbott described how recognition of his web design work moved him from a behind-the-scenes digital creative to public media figure. Other webmasters and app designers recognize the fact that their digital tools also frame theology and the beliefs of their community, which can elevate them and their work in the eyes of community outsiders to the status of religious interpreter for their community. The situation this can create for digital professionals becomes a space where their work narrative enacts a specific understanding of authority that seeks to mitigate this tension.

Digital spokespersons draw on role-based authority

The media-making narratives of digital spokespersons clearly draw on a role-based notion of authority. As they describe their work, they seek to set a clear boundary around the roles they perform, and their situatedness within a specific Christian institutional structure. Their attempts to frame their work as being for a specific community or group can be closely associated with Max Weber's notion of authority based on the performance of a specific role.

Weber (1947) argued authority is claimed and enacted by those who feel they have the legitimate right to expect members of their community to adhere to their commands in one of three ways: Rational-legal, traditional and charismatic. These three classifications of what Weber saw as forms of "pure legitimate authority" have often been used as analytical tools to describe the character of or classify specific leaders. This is especially true within recent studies of Digital Religion (i.e., Hoover, 2016), which have defined the roles played by certain actors within religious communities online and offline viewed as having authority over others. However, I suggest Weber's intent for these classifications was to highlight the relationships enacted between leaders and their followers in various contexts. Identified leaders derive and establish their role based on the belief their followers have about the mission of the leader in relation to the group.

Weber suggested the authority relationship established between leaders and followers is voluntary and sustained over time, as followers choose to obey because they believe it is in their interest to do so. In many respects, this is true of digital spokespersons and how they frame their work narratives in relation to work affiliations. For example, Arun Arora, former director of communications for the Church of England, describes how he was hired to help the Church adapt its traditional press-office model of communication to the digital era of communication. While he admits this transition was a difficult one both conceptually and practically for church leadership, he describes his role as working within the institution to make change. Rather than seeking to change institutional structures, digital spokespersons choose to work within them, despite the constraints and, at times, resistance to the work they are hired to do. This attitude is linked to an honoring or buying into what the leader represents, which rings true in the discourse narrative of the digital spokespersons in this study, avowing adherence to the mission of their religious institutions.

In this study, Weber's classifications of rational-legal, traditional or charismatic authority resonate with how digital spokespersons describe their roles and frame their relationships to the institutions for which they work. Rational-legal authority is the most common form of authority digital professional's draw on in their work narratives. This form is based on hierarchical relations within a given social structure bounded by accepted rules and structures of that group. This is an acknowledgment of professional authority, as individuals accept the codes and structures established by leaders who create a system of rule that is built on a distinctive rationale about how communities and institutions should be run. Digital professionals like webmaster James Abbott state that they see their job in terms of their responsibilities within their organization, serving the communicative structures of the church and its need to communicate with the public. Webmasters of denominations and denominational tech-team members often use words like *servants* and *supporter* to describe their roles as facilitating the larger mission of the church. Their work narrative describing their relationship to supervisors or church leaders they answer to also emphasizes the professional, hierarchical authority structure of Christian institutions. Instead of challenging them, digital professionals seem to accept their place within the legal structures of their institution, even when those structures challenge their creativity or their vision of what digital tools or strategies could do to improve the position of their organization.

Some digital spokespersons drew on Weber's idea of traditional authority in their narratives. They do this by highlighting rights given to a dominant individual within a group, an individual designated to rule due to established practices and structures. Digital spokespersons who hold positions granted to them by established religious structures, positions designating them a measure of leadership within the field of communications, also note any authority they might have over others comes from the religious tradition and institution simultaneously. For example, Claus Grue former Church of Sweden communication director who had oversight of other media workers in the diocesan office frames his role in terms of traditional authority. While he has often been singled out by media to speak on behalf of the diocese and the bishop he works for, he recognizes the fact that he speaks for the church and not for himself. This is similar to online media ambassadors such as Bishops Nick Baines and Alan Wilson from the Church of England. They under-stand that when they are called upon to step into the role of spokesperson, they step into the area of rational–legal authority. Their words are not their own, they are speaking for the institution, and so are also subject to the legal authority structure it represents. Therefore, while some part of their digital work is done on personal blogs or social media accounts, they recognize the fact that they do this work as institutional representatives. Thus, their autonomy to speak is limited. Similarly, communication directors I spoke to from the Catholic Church spoke about how interacting with secular media places them in the unique position of having to negotiate between their formal role and the temporarily sanctioned one drawn from a different authority relationship.

One thing all digital spokespersons had in common is that they tried to dis-tance themselves from being associated with some form of charismatic authority. Weber described charismatic authority as "resting on devotion to the excep-tional sanctity, heroism or exemplary character of an individual person, and of the normative patterns or order revealed or ordained by him" (Weber, 1947, p. 215). Digital spokespersons understand their digital skills and work give them access to specialized skills or knowledge about technology and digital culture often not possessed by the institutional leaders they work with or for. While such knowledge and expertise have the ability to raise their external profile, most actively resist or shy away from these opportunities. As Navin Motwani, former digital media officer with the Church of England, stated his role is to move the church forward in its digital media use and communication, not to use the space this creates to spread his own agenda for the Church. Digital spokespersons are quick to affirm their allegiance to the established systems of their institutions and describe themselves as simply doing their job to serve the greater good and mission of the church.

Drawing on Weberian notions of authority as performing a distinct role within their religious institution, digital spokespersons seek to establish their place as members, rather than leaders within their respective religious organizations. Therefore, their media-making narrative emphasizes their work-based roles within an established authority system. Even when they express frustration with leaders' views about digital technology, they often seek to affirm the institutional system they might be frustrated with. So digital spokespersons position themselves in relation to authority as a role within a structural relationship of leadership and followership. Drawing on the idea of role-based authority helps these RDCs position themselves within their religious community and characterize themselves as adherent to its constructions and claims.

Spokesperson algorithmic authority: Thought leaders as privileging institutional/offline expertise

This affirmation of religious institutional structures and roles is echoed in the form of algorithmic authority digital spokespersons enact online. They closely align with thought leaders, described in Chapter 1. Thought leaders are similar to media influencers in that they gain prominence online and gather a following due to the content they share. Yet they differ in that thought leaders' primary expertise is in their specialized knowledge, making them a recognized area expert, while media influencers' expertise is primarily in their ability to gain an audience through their communication or technology skills. Digital spokespersons are digital creatives who are more than media savvy innovators; they possess deep knowledge of the religious institutions and the mission they work for. This can make them the go-to person for secular media when an official response to a news event is needed— e.g., communication directors, or individuals who accurately represent the views of their organization via social media are often called upon to act as online media ambassadors.

While thought leaders may be fluent in digital culture and technologies, it is the knowledge they possess that draws an online or external audience to their content. As stressed earlier, digital spokespersons see themselves as identity curators, called on to be skilled at representing their religious institution through digital media. They also recognize the limits of their expertise and official boundaries on their work. For example, Arun Arora recounted opportunity he and his team declined to comment on a prominent news story in the press, choosing instead to let other communication sectors of the Church of England, with previous experience in that area, present the Church's official response. Digital spokespersons focus on information and commentary in line with church teaching and policies rather than on opinion and personal religious interpretation. Just like thought leaders, they privilege established traditional expertise over digital fluency.

As digital spokespersons take on the role of institutional identity curators for their respective religious organizations, this informs their views of authority. Since their digital curation is done within an institutional context, this situates discussions of authority as role based, informed by the structures these RDCs must accept and must submit to. This orientation of work within a religious institution offers them a clear remit for their work. It also requires them to develop institutional knowledge alongside their digital expertise. This expertise is situated in established structures and hierarchy, just as thought leaders' expertise is situated within algorithmic culture. In other words, digital culture and communication must adapt to this context, and not the other way around. Operating within a role-based understanding of authority is not always easy. These creatives know their digital work can position them for public attention when they are required or called upon to serve as voices on behalf of their institutions. Yet digital spokespersons, by choice and by constraint, must perform authority as perceived and enacted within religious institutions in digital culture. This can create frustrations and limitations that will be discussed more when we explore digital spokespersons' technological apologetic.

Digital strategists as missional media negotiators

Digital strategists, as discussed in Chapter 6, act as missional media negotiators. They engage in digital media experimentation in order to see how technology might facilitate new forms of ministry or streamline traditional practices. The term "missional" refers to the fact that they engage the outlook, behaviors or practices of a missionary, in that the ultimate goal of their work is outreach and spreading the Christian faith. They are motivated by personal convictions that digital media afford them unique opportunities to extend ministry opportunities to new peoples and audiences. While the venues or techniques related to their work are new, often what they actually do is not. The everyday ministry work they do is done as part of a religious community or organization closely connected to set tasks their official work roles demand. Take for example Tim Bulkley's description of theologians who blog, as educators who use the internet to share religious teachings and insights. He contends that the accepted practice of biblical interpretation and/or techniques of theological study are not changed by digital media. Instead, the internet simply makes theological writing more public and forces theologians to write in more accessible and conversational ways. Digital strategists often also seek out like-minded strategists doing similar work for encouragement and support, and to share ideas about the new online components of their vocations. This is especially true among "media-driven missionaries" who understand embracing digital tools for communication is essential in the twenty-first century, and benefit from sharing best practices and successful internet-based evangelist strategies with others passionate about similar work.

Digital strategists as missional media negotiators also desire to introduce churches and Christian organizations to digital platforms that help individuals beyond church leadership spread the good news of their conviction to a new generation. They recognize the fact that fewer and fewer young people actually encounter religion through attending an offline church, *ergo*, for many, the online space may be the first and only place they may encounter Christian beliefs and messages. The co-creative nature of the internet encourages these strategists to develop technical and rhetorical resources in order to expand their ministry to meet people where they are at, which is online. Their impulse to engage people in digital spaces and integrate new media tools in their work, while having firms ties to traditional religious institutions, cause them to draw on a distinctive understanding of authority.

Digital strategists draw on relational authority

Digital strategists' work is defined by an institutional remit, which creates certain expectations and boundaries that structure how they are to perform this work. Yet by choosing to engage digital media and experiment with new forms of communication, they can transform or extend those institutional roles. Digital strategists in this study show a strong commitment to developing competencies and expertise in digital media, in order to show how digital media enable them to have a greater missional impact on those outside the church or even inside the church. This living with one foot bound by institutional remits and another planted in digital culture that provides them access to new audiences or forms of religious work places them in a position of constant negotiation. Sister Julie Vieira, introduced in Chapter 2, expressed this balancing act as she speaks about moving between a set religious vocation and the flexibility of digital work. Being committed to the spiritual vocation within the Catholic Church means choosing a life of obedience and structure, which can seem at odds with digital spaces and productions that encourage personal expression, promotion and freedom. In this way, digital strategists must straddle institutional and technological spaces simultaneously and work to integrate their official vocation with what they describe as a digital calling.

I suggest this requires them to see authority in terms of a relationship between two factions, forcing them to find a common ground or space of connection. Authority as relational focuses on social and cultural interdependence between multiple parties, such as between leaders and followers or institutions and their members. It is based on the premise that rather than authority being defined by a concrete role or agreement, it is found within the space of negotiation. Therefore, it is dependent on the negotiation process, where each group has agency and offers reciprocity and respect to the other parties involved. Digital strategists see authority as based on relationship by articulating in their media-making narratives the ways they seek to navigate between their institutional commitments and their ministry calling and actions. As Sister Vieira stressed, her blogging and online work emerged though a process of conversation with her superiors, and from the conviction that it is important to create a bridge between new forms media ministry and the Church.

In this study, digital strategists enact notions of authority similar to those expressed by Lincoln (1994), who stressed authority can be viewed as a relational communication process negotiated and constructed between multiple parties and through communicative interactions. As discussed in Chapter 1, Lincoln described authority as a strategic discourse created by a group leader through shared communication with a set of audience or members. A leader uses language to create and define a relationship with the group, such as a pastor using preaching to frame a relationship with the congregation or a bible teacher using the structure of the classroom to create a certain relationship with their students. A leader is one who presents themselves as having expertise and knowledge a larger group of individual's needs. This establishes a pattern of communication where group members look to the leader for guidance, support and boundaries. In this way, not only can directors or senior staff be seen as leaders within Christian organizations, digital strategists can also act as leaders by highlighting their digital expertise and the impact that is needed to keep their group effective and relevant in contemporary culture. Digital strategists are able to establish authority with certain congregational audiences or within institutional contexts, as seen in the discussions of Turkish media-driven missionaries. Their technological expertise and the impact of their online work is changing traditional notions of Christian evangelization and discipleship within their established organization.

This also creates what Lincoln described as a horizontal distribution of power, where expertise and impact trump position and hierarchy in influencing institutional practices and structure. To be a leader, or in other words to have authority, individuals must make sure their communication remains effective and convincing in order to solidify their position and ensure their relationship as expert within their community of influence. This means authority is more fluid than that presented in the previous models of authority as roles or power. Digital strategists navigate constantly between following institutional structures and being able to transcend them and enact influence through their digital agency. Nathan Clark, director of digital innovation at Northland, illustrates this in describing the online worship services he oversees as situated in a different culture, as a tech-based, interactive system, rather than the viewer-oriented experience members at other church sites encounter. His technical expertise and direct intervention with online attendees enable him to frame the worship experience online in more direct ways than the teaching pastor can influence congregants in the offline services. Lincoln further suggests that when religious leaders seek to make changes to the group culture or relationship, such as integrating new practices and tools like media, this has a direct influence on the communication process already created. Authority comes to the leader through creating a balanced or interdependent relationship. Therefore, leaders must affirm their ability to facilitate such changes in ways that show they are able to maintain a balanced relationship. In this way, online ministers become more than technology troubleshooters or chat-room moderators—they create a technical-spiritual dependency with their online congregational members through both their interactions and advice offered online. This transcends the influence of the offline pastor and senior pastors and can shape established patterns of authority for certain members.

Language becomes a key resource for digital strategists to ratify their work and influence. The strategic use of discourse is clearly seen in this study among theologians who blog, in the way they describe the digital work. They emphasize to their audience the need for traditional religious study, yet advocate the idea that this can and must be done in new contexts to reach the digital generation. Theologians like Larry Hurtado also stress the need for individuals doing theology online to not only understand the opportunities and limits digital media allow them in terms of doing digital theological work. He also advocates making one's language accessible and transparent and says that does not mean changing proved best practices of theological word study and verifying interpretation from ancient texts. Both through advocacy and action, digital strategists seek to model through word and deed how aspects of church tradition should be conducted offline, and the extent to which translation into digitally mediated contexts allows for actual innovation. Digital strategists' work description stresses the need for seeing ministry in the digital age as a blended continuum of offline and online interactions and reflection on how each context should shape the other. While they emphasize technological advocacy in their daily ministry, their relational discourse recognizes the historic traditions and precedence from which their digital work comes.

Strategists' algorithmic authority: Digital leadership as a negotiated hybridization

The described negotiations of digital strategists highlight the fact that their work requires them to navigate their official positions, and frame their work within a relational view of authority. This mirrors how they seek to position themselves within algorithmic culture. They respond to established institutional authority, by situating their digital advocacy and ministry strategies in ways that present them as essential to ministry, and valuable for serving the official discourse and structures they are committed to. They do this as well in relation to algorithmic authority, by taking on the role of a digital leader, which combines and stresses dual expertise in key aspects of digital media and traditional institutional culture.

Digital leaders, as described by Peladue, Herzog and Acker (2017) and noted in Chapter 1, are those whose authority emerges equally from their institutional and skill-based expertise, as well as their digital fluencies in experimentation and networking. Digital leaders establish their authority by demonstrating fluency in both online and offline contexts. They work to articulate and demonstrate their expertise in their religious or institutional roles and in digital media. Digital strategists are similar to digital leaders in that their ability to lead is tied to the emphasis on integrating these dual competencies. Just like digital leaders, they start by first acknowledging the mastered traditional leadership skills coming from their institutional positions or training.

Digital strategists often emphasize certain essential traits needed for ministry in an age of internet, traits which have also been identified as core traits of digital leaders. In line with Peladue, Herzog and Acker's (2017) work identifying the markers of digital leadership, this new generation of digital-creative pastors, theologians and missionaries cite the importance of creativity, experimentation, flexibility, collaboration and networking. They then show how their skills in digital media work and innovation add to and solidify the influence and importance of their position within the community as voices of authority. This is exemplified by the theologian bloggers in this study, who first emphasize their theological training and interpretive proficiencies as giving them essential expertise needed to do true and accurate theological work online. This training is then adapted to the online setting by taking time to learn effective digital-communication tools and social media strategies they can use to share their teachings online. As Matthew Tan stresses, the act of blogging enables theologians to share their expertise with a wider audience and shows how they can move beyond a specialist audience to illustrate ways theology is able to engage important contemporary issues and everyday conversations.

Digital strategists are leaders that must be able to clearly articulate and model the ability to establish referent power, meaning their communication with their audience and co-workers is used to build trust in their knowledge and abilities. The technological expertise of digital leaders extends their offline authority into online or mediated contexts by mapping best practices and stressing digital media integration as essential for the work and life of the community. Northland Church online ministers' media-making narratives stress the fact that their digital expertise was the key qualification that allowed them to serve in a pastoral role online, in ways most could never serve offline. This work also required allegiance to and investment in the church itself, in order to move into this ministry role. They described the hybrid nature of not only their expertise but the work itself; they perform more than a tech-help role, also offering support and healing to online congregants who might never come to an offline service due not only to geographic limitations but perhaps to past hurts experienced in offline churches.

Digital leaders value creativity, collaboration and interactivity between themselves and those they work with and serve. Digital leaders also create support communities that help them innovate and further develop not only their digital work but also the rhetoric that supports their endeavors. Media-driven missionaries in Turkey speak about the essential component of networking in their missions work, not just for sharing resources and best practices but to show broader recognition of this new style of missions activity to their organization and churches. It also creates a support structure for digital strategists, who function in a country hostile to Christian missions work. How digital strategists work as digital leaders is also manifested in the technological apologetic they put forth, described later in this chapter.

Variations in religious digital creatives' approaches to authority

From this analysis, I show each of the three types of RDCs focused on in this study describe their digital media work in ways that draw on very different conceptions of authority (Table 7.1). These media-making narratives show digital entrepreneurs, spokespersons and strategists enact and integrate multiple understandings of authority in how they describe and position themselves. Each category of RDCs draws on a different view of how authority is situated in notions of how authority is traditionally understood relative to established religious institutional and/or chosen community

Table 7.1 Overview of RDCs Approaches to Authority

	Media-Making Narrative	Traditional View of Authority—Drawn on (Institutional/Offline Orientation)	Enacting Algorithmic Authority (Technological/Online Orientation)
Digital entrepreneurs	Visionary technology influencers	Authority as power—Foucault	Social media influencer
Digital spokespersons	Identity Curators	Authority as roles—Weber	Thought leader
Digital strategists	Missional media negotiators	Authority as relational—Lincoln	Digital leader

affiliations. Yet they also understand their digital work takes place in online spaces and social networks that are grounded in an algorithmic culture with different assumptions about what constitutes authority. Thus, their work narratives also highlight how they correlate themselves to ideas of algorithmic authority in the ways they frame and leverage their technological skills and expertise in relation to organizational and religious community boundaries. The differences in their approaches to authority as seen through their media-making narratives are outlined in the chart earlier.

Digital entrepreneurs describe themselves in relation to traditional or religious institutional authority in terms of power, where Foucault's work on power as a social dynamic and Hofstede's idea of power distancing are applied. Here authority is understood as based on RDCs' ability to navigate their social position and agenda within digital and religious spaces, and rhetorically and tangibly establishing their position as a visionary tech influencers in these contexts. They align with the idea of being a media influencer in that they privilege digital expertise and their technical/social impact as giving them religious influence in their media-making narrative, and downplay their lack of institutional authority or position. Thus, they see technology and online prominence as the primary basis for garnering authority. In other words, their ability to enact change and influence religious groups lies in their digital footprint, social network of supporters and media notoriety.

Digital spokespersons' media-making narratives describe authority as primarily role based, and so present a Weberian understanding of authority wherein certain actors have the legitimate right to oversee and govern specific contexts. Here authority is defined in terms of specific roles performed in a set environment, namely leaders being acknowledged as legitimate authorities by their followers or audiences. Digital spokespersons emphasize the fact that the work they perform is commissioned by and in the context of a specific religious institution. This means they see their digital work as bound by organizational accountability structures and protocols. As media professionals working within a religious institution, they see their media work as needing to be officially branded and representing not them-selves but the groups they work for. This means that while their work with digital-media tools and environments elevates them within algorithmic culture, offering new communication opportunities for public influence, they downplay this poten-tial in favor of their role as institutional representatives and identity curators. As thought leaders, they privilege traditional or institutional legitimacy over digital prominence and influence as the basis of their religious impact.

Finally, digital strategists enact a relational understanding of authority in descriptions of their work, where Lincoln becomes a useful discussion partner to explain the relationship negotiation they undertake as part of their digital labor. Here authority is a social and cultural interdependence between RDCs and the religious community members they serve. Digital strategists describe their con-ception of authority in their media-making narratives by emphasizing how they navigate between their allegiance to traditional institutional commitments and the remit of their jobs and the call to and personal conviction of the need to engage media to do this work in the technology-infused world of the twenty-first century. Lincoln emphasized the idea that individuals who are called on to act as authori-tative within a certain sphere of a religious institution do so by constructing dis-tinct discourses used to act out their positions within those institutions. Digital strategists use language to establish their official position as bound up with new social conditions of the time in which they live, in this case the need to engage with digital media to fully live out their missional calling. As missional media negotiators, they recognize the fact that algorithmic culture is in tension with the structures of their institutional affiliation. Rather than privilege digital culture like digital entrepreneurs, or downplay its influence like digital spokespersons, they choose to live and work within this tension between the religious and algorithmic cultures. They understand their work gives them influence in both spheres. They choose to stand as bridge builders between the two cultures, acknowledging both as sources of authority inspiring and informing their work.

While authority is understood and enacted in different ways by these three groups of RDCs, each of them draws on some similar assumptions. First, their understanding of authority is strongly influenced by how and where they see themselves in relation to the traditional religious institutions and communities with which they seek to affiliate or connect in some way. Perceptions of being insti-tutional outsiders, insiders or some hybrid combination shape their assumptions of whether authority resides in their actions or begins within their institutional affiliations. Second, each group of RDCs enacts a distinct positioning of themselves to digital culture and algorithmic authority. This is partially based on the level of sway and importance each gives to digital expertise and fluency, and the social position these allow them to achieve. This points to the need to pay attention to whether RDCs privilege digital expertise over institutional affiliation or vice versa, as this can dictate the amount of credence they give to algorithmic authority in dictating power structures in a digital age. Third, RDCs' understanding of authority can be seen as a performance, a balancing act they undertake between multiple sectors of impact upon religious culture. Goffman's approach to authority, as laid out in this study, draws attention to the fact that RDCs must negotiate their work and investments in digital and religious contexts simultaneously. They must decide how to prioritize and to relate these cultural contexts, and then how to best articulate these intentions. By doing so they map out a distinct prioritization of how they see other religious actors and communities in relation to technology structures and environments. These negotiations are connected to their front-stage and back-stage performance of religious identity as digital creatives, as well. We must pay close attention to RDCs' self-reports about their digital activities—how they link these to religious desires or convictions, then frame them in relation to official religious institutions. Outlining the intentions behind these media-making narratives is only one part of understanding RDCs' negotiations with authority; it forms the basis for a detailed investigation of their rationale and framing of religious community and institutions revealed through the technological apologetic.

Chapter 8

How Christian digital creatives enact a technological apologetic

We finally come to a key part of this book, considering the technological apologetics offered by religious digital creatives (RDCs) in relation to their digital media use and ministries. I argue unpacking the technological apologetic of RDCs is crucial in order to understand not only the motivations behind the tech use but how this serves an key identity narrative helping them frame themselves, as authorities and members, of the specific religious communities and/or institutions they work with. The technological apologetic is a story RDCs tell in order to frame their digital-creative work, perceived authority and religious affiliations in a distinctive light. Unlike media-making stories, which focus on describing the digital work RDCs do and how they engage with digital tools and environments, the technological apologetic focuses on why they do this work. It also reveals how they rationalize this work in relation to their religious institutions or communities.

At the heart of the technological apologetic is a justification narrative, centered on assumption about Christian community and the Church and its relationship with technology. One core assumption they acknowledge is that most religious institutions are seen to be, and often function as if they are, conceptually and/or structurally at odds with digital media. They also recognize that internet culture is often framed as in competition with religion, because the flexible, dynamic and individualistic, user-centered nature of the internet is perceived as challenging institutional authority, structures and leadership. This is articulated in different ways by each group of RDCs. Digital spokespersons in this study frequently evoked this underlying assumption in discussions of their work and took great care in trying to explain how and why their digital media use could be seen as in line with organizational goals and traditional religious practices. Digital entrepreneurs and even digital strategists who stress digital media as a core resource for religious practices and essential for the work of the church in contemporary society, also frequently engaged with these assumptions.

RDCs construct a technological apologetic in order to create a space in which they can justify technology use that shows how one can blend aspects of digital communication and culture with religious institutional practices. They also do this to try and diffuse fears or combat the perception that they do digital work in order to take on an intentional authority role in their community. Therefore, the technological apologetic is a story RDCs tell to justify their digital work and engagement with digital environments for Christian ministry. By focusing on reports of why specific RDCs do the digital work they do and how they interpret the meaning and impact of these activities, we are able to discover the ways RDCs may be perceived to act as authorities within their religious communities and the digital spheres.

At the end of Chapter 3, I laid out a method for identifying RDCs' technological apologetic. First, the core of the justification narrative must be identified and unpacked. However, simply determining RDCs' rationale for their work is not enough. The justification narrative also must address how RDCs' perceive of the implications of their work within their religious community and institution. These two aspects, their motivations and their work's potential impact, are then analyzed though relational dialectics theory. This approach provides an opportunity for reflecting on specific tensions RDCs highlight as existing between themselves and traditional sources of religious authority and algorithmic culture. Reading these justification narratives through the lens of categories of relational dialectic theory (integration vs. separation, expression vs. nonexpression and stability vs. change) helps to identify the central tensions each group of RDCs see being created by their digital work and vision in relation to their specific religious tradition and community. It also helps highlight how RDCs frame and rationalize the relationship between technology and religion. Finally, attention is given to how these tensions are manifested in internal discourses, negotiated in relation to religious affiliations and leaders, and through external discourses, presented as a public negotiation with those outside their faith community. Here one of three rhetorical strategies is highlighted—oppositional views, co-opting of agendas or intermingling of competing views—to show how RDCs frame their religious identity and relationality within their technological apologetic.

Digital entrepreneurs' technological apologetic

Digital entrepreneurs describe themselves as early adopters of the internet, and those fluent in digital communication. As technology professions or skilled communicators keeping a close eye on technology trends, they are often some of the first individuals in their religious communities to use emerging technologies. Their expertise in and advocacy of digital media can give them notoriety as technological advocates and experts both online and offline. The tools and content they create are promoted through personal social networks online, which help raise the public profile of their work. Their focus on technology innovation and their conviction that digital media should play an important role in contemporary Christian church life and work evoke a technological apologetic focused on how new media are essential to the current and future work of the church.

Justification narrative: Digital media use is tied to the successful future of the church

Why?—Digital media are essential for twenty-first-century church

When considering digital entrepreneurs' justification narrative for the digital work they do, attention is first given to the underlying motivation they articulate. This study shows they are driven by an entrepreneurial spirit, desiring to use their technological expertise to develop tools and opportunities to create new forms of outreach for Christian communities. Digital entrepreneurs are guided by a distinctive view that the internet and digital technology are key resources that need to be embraced by the church and related organizations. This is because they see the future of the church depending on technology and the opportunities it affords users to reach a diverse and global audience for the purpose of Christian evangelism. As techie for God, Alex Kerr stated, "The future of what Christian mission and ministry could and should look like" (personal communication, February 12, 2013).

Digital entrepreneurs stress their key motivation for embracing and experimenting with digital media is to expand current ideas of what the Christian church can look like. Digital media, from Twitter to mobile phones, are described as new platforms that transform the reach of religious witnessing and the ways education can be conducted. Internet evangelist Eric Celier noted, "To me in this work, I am keeping the Church aware of what they could be doing, the potential the internet holds for Church outreach" (personal communication, February 7, 2013).

Digital entrepreneurs stress that digital technology is not just a gimmick, but rather should be seen as a core tool for doing Christian work. It is simply the latest in a series of communication technologies that the church has used over its history to spread its message and beliefs. Techie for God Huw Tyler noted:

> In last 2000 years the church has chosen to communicate in very different ways, whether that's been poetry, books, paintings, constructing cathedrals [...] our role now is to show the church how they can use these new communication technologies to do the same thing.
>
> (Personal communication, April 5, 2011)

These RDCs stress using digital media as a resource is in line with the Christian church's call to make disciples in every nation and generation.

Digital entrepreneurs validate the importance of their work by emphasizing the fact that digital technology offers features such as accessibility, pervasiveness and the ability transcend time and space, making it easily adaptable to various kinds of church work. Technology also offers new levels of 24/7 access and engagement. As one theoblogian suggested, "Social media revolution echoes and whispers of where society is going and I think the church needs to follow" (personal communication, November 21, 2012). Digital entrepreneurs insist that missing the communicative potential to reach those outside the church would be a mistake.

Their justification narrative about why they do their work also stresses the idea that, in order for Christian institutions to adapt to these new technological opportunities, they need concrete examples of what digital outreach looks like. Digital entrepreneurs say their work offers such models. Internet evangelist Arjo de Vroome describes this motivation as: "A big part of our work is modeling, activating the church to see the potential for Internet evangelism and that personal spiritual searching is being done online" (personal communication, March 4, 2013). Creating new evangelism tools online, demonstrating bottom-up communication through blogging and showing how social media can be used to create virtual think tanks for Christian work, they show how digital media can display the future of church outreach where individuals as well as organizations are empowered to share the Gospel. Online evangelism illustrates how technology can extend a local church's outreach. "But you know that is the fun thing with the internet. It opens doors into nations and with people who wouldn't have heard the gospel without international connection," says techie for God Marc Van der Woude (personal communication, March 8, 2013). Yet their outspoken advocacy and the tendency to hold themselves up as exemplars of Christian digital work do not simply change how Christian outreach is done, but create cultural change and unintended consequences within religious institutions.

Assumption—Church structures and outreach practices must adapt to digital tools

Second, underlying this justification of why digital entrepreneurs do the work they do is the claim that, as digital media are adopted for Christian purposes, religious culture and structures may need to adapt. While digital entrepreneurs insist engaging digital technology is crucial to the future of the church, these practices are not without implications. Engaging in online outreach allows digital entrepreneurs to bypass traditional institutional gatekeeping systems and accountability structures. As Jana Riess stated, "The internet cuts through the church's controlled authority and its chain of command, for better or for worse" (J. Riess, personal communication, October 12, 2013). This is because digital resources and content produced by individuals in the presumed service of the church cannot be easily monitored or filtered. In this way, individuals are empowered to communicate online with a broad reach and impact in ways only religious institutions were once able to.

Digital entrepreneurs' pro-internet advocacy often speaks to individuals in their religious community. This is especially appealing to networked millennials and the i-generation who see digital media as a tool for religious and social changes. An example of this is the "say yes to women bishops" campaign, as online campaign launched in 2012 by a number of prominent Church of England bloggers and social media users as way to leverage social media to show their support for the ordination of women's bishops. This mentions by several female RDCs and bloggers over the course of my interviews as an example of the power of digital media to transform the church. Up until 2015, only male priests were allowed to be appointed as bishops in the Church of England. The campaign sought to raise support for women being considered for these positions, by using social media to targeting the Church of England senate structure. Known as the "House of Laity," parish representatives, who are seen as speaking for the broader Church membership, are elected or appointed to attend the annual meeting where they vote and advise Church leaders on policy issues.

This online campaign enables supporters within Church of England a chance to not only comment on church policy but to do something about it. The campaign sought to use digital media to change opinions and also the ecclesiastical structure's official position on women bishops. This was done by bloggers and individuals on Twitter driving traffic to a website where people could directly email their general senate representative with their thoughts on this issue. A prewritten, editable response assisted church members in voicing their views and encouraging representatives to vote yes to women bishops. Although the initial efforts to influencing the House of Laity vote in 2012 were unsuccessful, the campaign remained active until 2015, when the House of Bishops and then the House of Laity voted by a slight margin to support this ecclesiastical change. Many credited the work of the "say yes to women bishops" online campaign in helping raise public support for the policy change. It also encouraged many people to see that the internet could be used support church dialogue and enact change in ways that made a tangible difference.

Because digital entrepreneurs are not tied to or regulated by church policies or institutional structures, they have a level of flexibility and freedom these institutions do not have. "Church leaders tend to be resistant to change and the internet. It is the grassroots people that are interested and will listen to this potential for evangelism," comments internet evangelist Tony Whitaker (personal communication, September 23, 2011). Calls made to embrace technology for religious purpose are often more quickly taken up by individual Christians than institutions, especially digital entrepreneurs who see it as a key to the church's future. These same individuals are often early adopters of technology outside of religious contexts, the first to experiment with it for Christian ministry. Techie for God Alex Kerr suggested this in saying,

> I think church ministries need to wake up and see the potential of mobile media and release the unique volunteer possibilities they have within their congregations [...] in our churches' services people are often physically getting on their phones and browsing mobile bible or other apps. Why not capitalize on this trend.
>
> (Personal communication, February 12, 2013)

Digital entrepreneurs are often impatient with church structures that are slow to embrace digital media or see its potential. For them, technological engagement is an essential part of not only doing church work but also of seeing how technology creates new opportunities for experiencing what church is truly meant to be. As techie for God Marc Van der Woude claimed, "Online you can truly be part of a worldwide body of Christ, instead of limiting ourselves to one little club" (personal communication, March 8, 2013). Such framing of technology and the church creates a number of tensions between digital entrepreneurs and the churches they seek to serve.

Relational dialectic: Tensions between expression and nonexpression

Digital entrepreneurs' technological apologetic emphasizes the contention that churches and religious organizations must adapt how they do and understand Christian work in a digital age. This requires not only the adoption of technology but new techniques of outreach. It also says that the forms of digital religious work created will inevitably dictate cultural changes within the church and religious organizations, changes that may be uncomfortable for and push against traditional church structures or patterns of institutional practice. Underlying this apologetic is the claim that digital media use is essential for the future of the church, and its integration necessitates multilevel change that will be uncomfortable for Christian institutions.

As noted in Chapter 3, relational dialectic theory is used to study the discourse that is invoked between communicative partners while seeking to describe and negotiate their relationship. In this study, this theory is applied to the ways RDCs frame motivations for their digital practice and how they choose to relate them to their respective religious affiliations. Investigating RDCs' technological apologetic reveals the challenges RDCs perceive they encounter, or what this theory characterizes as communicative tensions. This is seen in RDCs attempts to negotiate gaps between the intentions of their digital work and the goals and relationships of their faith communities.

In the case of digital entrepreneurs, their technological apologetic draws attention to a tension described as one of expression and nonexpression. Here we see digital entrepreneurs must conceptually navigate and position themselves in relation to the boundaries and protocols of their religious communities and the institutions with which they seek to affiliate. Religious groups often have written and unwritten rules about how community members should behave, rules which are monitored by certain structures and leaders. Negotiations between expression and nonexpression specifically relate to issues around what these religious institutions consider public versus private knowledge and governance. This raises a number of issues about the extent to which digital entrepreneurs' digital work pushes these traditional boundaries. One issue is how they negotiate their position in their community when their digital work moves them from private community member to public digital voice or religious interpreter.

In this study, I have stressed how their digital expertise and creations often elevate these RDCs in unintentional ways to positions of public religious influence. They become "unofficial" religious interpreters representing various sectors of the

Christian community online. This challenges traditional religious leaders who are used to functioning and seeing themselves as the official gatekeepers determining what religious information and resources are accessible to their members, let alone the broader secular public. At the heart of these tensions is the question of who has the right to represent, or who can to speak for, a given religious group in a digital age. This tension between expression and nonexpression and how it is conceptually and practically negotiated between digital entrepreneurs and their religious communities also highlights these RDCs' understanding of authority in terms of roles. Technological expertise allows digital entrepreneurs to transcend traditional knowledge and structural gatekeepers, and this requires them to evoke certain narratives in order to position themselves in relation to their affiliated religious groups.

Framing entrepreneurs' relationship with religious institutions

Relational dialectic theory also draws attention to internally and externally oriented narratives within digital entrepreneurs' technological apologetic. These narratives become spaces to highlight specific tensions raised by their work, then address how they seek to negotiate them. RDCs, in this case digital entrepreneurs, first highlight personal motivations in order to speak to an internal audience and show how their views of technology and innovation complement rather than undermine communal beliefs and patterns of life.

Internally, digital entrepreneurs engage an openness–closedness narrative. They understand that in order to secure and maintain a healthy relationship with their specific Christian groups, they must respect certain traditional boundaries related to the public and private nature of religious community. This means that while they may desire and advocate change in how Christian groups and institutions conduct evangelism, share teaching and do church, they recognize these changes must be accomplished by recognizing the God-given structures and leaders currently in place. As a result, they try their best to frame technological advocacy and church critiques in a way that is respectful of the individuals and organizations they seek to address. While they are very open about their goals and motivations, and have a level of personal freedom because their work stands beyond official institutional constraints, they recognize the same is not true of these institutions. While many RDCs note frustration about the slow-moving nature of Christian institutions, most still recognize their religious cultural importance and the need to be in relationship with them.

Yet this openness–closedness negotiation also creates a tension. Digital entrepreneurs often report their digital work is not acknowledged or valued by the very religious institutions they seek to serve. This is because communication skills and media or technology creation are not recognized as traditional forms of Christian service or spiritual gifting. Thus, religious leaders typically do not acknowledge digital work and creativity as a form of Christian service. This perception makes digital entrepreneurs feel like outsiders to the very groups they seek to serve, even though they see their goals as being similar. Many digital entrepreneurs in this study expressed frustration with church leaders or community members they described as closed off to digital media outreach. They feel most churches do not seem willing to understand their vision of using the internet or support actively engaging digital technology for the church.

This can lead some digital entrepreneurs to feel isolated, or to feel they are treated with suspicion by established religious communities they are or were once part of. They feel their openness of why they do what they do, as well as attempt to work with and stay in relationship with Christian institutions is often not reciprocated or honored. This leads some digital entrepreneurs to create support networks with like-minded innovators outside their church community. Without clear communication and deliberate bridge building on the part of both religious leaders and other RDCs, it appears digital entrepreneurs are easily caught in an inherent misunderstanding that may encourage some to seek validation for their work outside of the local faith community. This leads to a second narrative.

Externally, digital entrepreneurs often engage a revelation-versus-concealment narrative by stressing how digital media can reveal Christian truth to a broader audience. Their justification narrative is driven by a passion to speak to an audience outside the church's traditional structures and even beyond the walls of the church. They believe that by modeling for the Christian community how to embrace digital media for Christian work, they can also show how it can be used to affirm Christian beliefs and identity to broader culture. One of the ways they do this is by trying to emphasize the positives of technology, emphasizing traits like accessibility and global reach over potential problems such as the threat of loss of control of their message.

Digital entrepreneurs also emphasize the suspicion religious institutions often express about media technology and its integration is not mirrored in broader culture. They describe how community outsiders frequently recognize the novelty and importance of their work sooner than other religious community members and leaders. Often, the secular and religious media attention their work receives accounts for why they are described as digital influencers within their community or faith tradition. This online or media attention may be the first time Christian leaders and community members even become aware of their work. This can put digital entrepreneurs in a fraught position. While they may be presented in press accounts or online reports as religious influencers, some fear they are then seen as rebels or boundary pushers within their own faith communities. This leads to further misunderstandings about their work and intentions, as their profile is presented as competitive and outside official oversight and institutional accountability.

Many digital entrepreneurs, while glad for free publicity and validation of their work, are often uncomfortable with being cast in such a competitive position. Being technologists, but branded as media influencer, is a label or role they have not intentionally sought out. Rather it is one they find themselves in as a byproduct of using digital media and creating innovative content. This means digital media use can exalt RDCs, awarding them new authority positions online that create relational tensions for them, as they seek to diffuse or manage tensions that already exist in their technology and change-resistant communities.

Providing concrete examples of digital entrepreneurs' motivations, the strategies they use to try to negotiate these narratives, and the potential tensions these create, helps reveal their distinctive technological apologetic. While their digital work can place them outside traditional institutional boundaries, they often work hard to frame their digital work in relation to their religious affiliations and commitments. This presents a justification narrative that shows these visionary technology influencers' beliefs about the importance of digital media in Christian outreach can challenge Christian organizations and church culture.

Digital spokespersons' technological apologetic

Digital spokespersons emphasize the fact they choose to work within religious institutional structures, even if this limits and delays their technological design or aspirations. They affirm religious institutions as predominant space where the work of their faith community takes place. They also described these institutions as sanctioned by God to accomplish religious purposes in the world today. Digital spokespersons present themselves as commissioned by their organization to create media tools and content to support these institutional contexts. They describe this as their space of religious service, and environments where digital technology is needed. Digital spokespersons choose to function within a realm of bounded creativity while seeking to implement new paths and practices of communication though their digital work. They describe their primary work as using technology to build the religious identity of their respective institutions. Digital spokespersons attempt to underplay any individual notoriety they receive because of their digital work in favor of emphasizing how this work serves the greater mission of their denomination or community. From this, their technological apologetic emerges and draws on digital spokespersons' convictions about the nature of digital media and their influence on religious organizations.

Justification narrative: Stressing technology as key to cultural relevance

Why?—Digital technology is the language of contemporary society

Digital spokespersons' justification narrative is based on serving as internet advocates to the religious institutions they work for. They describe digital technology as an essential tool all religious organizations with communication goals must engage. As former communication director Arun Arora argued,

> The Church can no longer rely on a 1990s model of professional-corporate communication that pushes out information and expect press and media to

pick it up […] The digital era requires us to be proactive, producing material rather than waiting for the phone to ring.

(Personal communication, March 1, 2013)

Digital spokespersons stress the fact that the institutions they work for often do not understand the importance of digital media for doing internal as well as external communication work since these media are the basis of the communicative structure of contemporary society. Therefore, their work involves more than using digital tools to produce content and resources that serve the mission of their institution. Digital spokespersons emphasize they must spend time doing technology trainings, teaching those within their institutions both media skills and how to understand and adapt to this new culture of communication. Former communication director Claus Grue emphasized this in justifying the amount of time he spends on media training in relation to his main remit to facilitate external communication about the work of the church. "It is important that we help our leaders within the church, within the dioceses, to be efficient communicators and to help them do that within the internet," he said (personal communication, June 4, 2013). This training and advocacy work is not only focused on church and institutional leaders; it also involves doing digital media literacy work with constituents and community members.

Digital spokespersons recognize that in an age of digital media, all church members become informal digital spokespersons in their own right, as they go online to share the beliefs and opinions about the church. For these RDCs, internet advocacy and training is about preparing the whole church for this new mode of communication and helping change institutional leaders' understanding of who might be seen as the voice of the church online. Communication director Erika Wipple comments:

Everybody represents the church in some sort of way in an era of internet, so we need to think differently. We need to provide a lot more digital services, because that is where the web is going and what people expect.

(Personal communication, April 17, 2017)

While digital spokespersons curate and are paid to create and moderate the official digital presence of their institution, they recognize the digital footprint of the church goes beyond the content they create and manage.

So digital spokespersons' justification narrative for their work is focused on helping the church understand the institutional importance of using digital technology effectively, and creating resources that help them do this. Their discussion of their work stresses the problem of ignoring the cultural impact the internet is having on religious organizations and modern social structures. As online media ambassador Bishop Nick Baines comments, "The Church is called to engage in the world, where the world is and to get involved, and you can't do that and ignore social media" (personal communication, December 6, 2012). Thus, working with the internet and its tools becomes space where digital spokespersons can either help the church prove itself as media savvy and engaged or show it is out of touch with digital society.

Assumption—Media technology as misunderstood or undervalued by religious institutions

Digital spokespersons' justification narrative emphasizes their conviction of the importance of digital technology not only as a communication tool but also as a force shaping contemporary culture. This reveals an underlying assumption they hold that many individuals with which they work in religious institutions do not understand digital media—the impact they do or can have on them. Digital spokespersons insist that failing to leverage the communicative opportunities digital technology offers is more than just an institutional oversight. It will be their downfall. Former webmaster Navin Motwani argues this, saying, "Other groups with less altruistic aims than the Church are getting involved with digital media, and my worry would be that if the Church doesn't do more in this area in a unified way we will get left behind" (personal communication, February 23, 2012). Many digital spokespersons express a fear that such a failure would make their groups seem even more irrelevant to society and unable to speak into contemporary culture.

Their justification narratives address not only concerns about institutional ignorance about digital technology but concerns that institutions do not see the broader social changes this technology is facilitating. They feel pressured to stay on top of the latest media trends, whether that be fluency in specific technologies, or online discourses that engage the church. As tech-team member Tom Scott explained, "Ideally we want to be people involved online [...] what we see through Worship Central is that the church can be on the frontlines of creativeness and edginess" (personal communication, February 28, 2013). Since technology moves quickly, this means digital spokespersons must continually learn and adapt their communicative strategies and focus. This can be difficult to do within institutions resistant to change and loathe to give quick responses. This resistance can be tied to a lack of recognition of the need for new organizational communication styles to respond to the dynamic, reactive nature of digital media culture—a constant challenge for them. "In a day like today that involves digital media in all of culture, we need to be on the top of our game with that. If we aren't engaged, neither is the church going to be," explains Scott (personal communication, February 28, 2013).

In order to diffuse some of the resistance they often face, digital spokespersons frame their advocacy and training work in terms of collaborating with religious leaders. By presenting themselves as media mentors, they are able to emphasize that their job is to be institutional communication aids. Claus Grue illustrates this when he said, "In helping with Twitter, it provides her (the bishop) with a quick and easy way of responding, to be proactive on social events, but also in a reactive way when other people start debates online" (personal communication, June 4, 2013). By presenting themselves as media mentors, digital spokespersons mitigate the idea they are competitors in their communication. Even when implementing innovative media initiatives or techniques, they stress the idea that they are offering their organization examples of best online communication practices—e.g., online media ambassador Bishop Nick Baines describes how his blogging online is about serving his diocese, rather than about self-promotion. He says,

> It helps me create the illusion of presence. It is important because I can't be in 169 parishes in my region at once, even in a year I can't visit them all. But online I can let people in on what I am doing and where I am and what I am thinking.
>
> (Personal communication, June 4, 2013)

Digital spokespersons emphasize the aim of their work is to fulfill a technical or informational role for their community. Even when their work requires them to serve as information architects, framing their community's identity and presence online, they stress this is done in the service of the institution.

Yet the work of digital spokespersons includes creating communicative structures that represent their institution in digital spaces. Through words, images and design elements, they assemble a digital narrative about the group they work for. So design work and information management can be seen as identity work, framing the character and theological nature of the community, especially on the internet, for a new public. The challenge lies in the fact that digital spokespersons understand that their work sometimes does more than just fulfill a technical or informational role for their community, framing their community in ways they often do not feel qualified or prepared for.

Relational dialectic: Tensions between integration and separation

Digital spokespersons' apologetic stresses the need for religious institutions to adapt to digital culture tools and techniques. They focus on carefully framing their working relationship within their religious organization. They stress they are institutional insiders committed to the goals of the groups they work for. Their justification narratives give attention to describing the purpose of their work to help their respective institutions become effective and relevant communicators able to contribute to and influence contemporary culture. Digital spokespersons focus on how they create a conceptual map of meaning for their work and how they navigate the potential opposition this may create within their institutional relationships and affiliations.

When this justification narrative is examined through the lens of relational dialectics theory, we see digital spokespersons experience a notable tension between connectedness and autonomy. This tension highlights their attempts to achieve balance between their commitment to their community or organization and its mission, and the extent to which this may stifle their creative work or planned media initiatives. They must balance the personal flexibly and freedom offered by digital media with institutional protocols and set media policies. Digital spokespersons often maintain an ideological and emotional connection to an institution that may not fully understand or appreciate their work and its potential cultural impact. This is seen in three ways. First, they affirm their loyalty to their distinctive faith community and the historical and/or theological narratives their institutions reflect. Second, they connect themselves by presenting their media and communication work as religious-identity work, using skills and tools to present the corporate character of their institutions to a broader public. Finally, they present their technological and media expertise as unique ways to not only further the mission of the church but to obey the divine mandate to spread message of Christianity to the entire world, including the world of the internet.

Digital spokespersons downplay the autonomy their digital work offers. Any public visibility their digital media presence creates for them is framed as just doing their job for their organization, and not themselves. While many advocate embracing the opportunities digital technology offers their institutions, and speak openly about enjoying the ability to facilitate new forms of communication through digital tools, they work hard to contextualize these freedoms. First, they downplay their personal identity, especially when their communicative work or roles are featured in digital media. Digital spokespersons carefully contextualize this presence as representative of their organization rather than their personal selves. Second, they stress feelings of uneasiness when they see their work as giving them autonomy and digital prominence. This was especially true of webmasters and tech teams, when supervisors failed to offer them advice or support in these public performances. This tension is managed by stressing their accountability to their respective religious organizations and how they aim to work within those hierarchical structures and echo official communicative protocols.

Framing spokespersons' relationship within their institution

Navigating this tension between connectedness and autonomy requires a distinctive technological apologetic, as digital spokespersons enact distinct internal and external communication strategies to frame and justify their work. Internally, within their organizational or faith community, they employ an integration–separation narrative, highlighting their role as fellow insiders and faithful members of the organization seeking to live within its established culture. Internally, they serve as cultural translators, translating the technology and the features of digital culture to both the digitally hesitant and the enthusiasts they work with. Overall, digital spokespersons seek to identify with their institutions and, for the most part, work to avoid the appearance of separation from its identity and mission.

Externally, digital spokespersons, while interfacing with the media and the online public, present themselves within a dialectic narrative of conventionality and uniqueness. This is a balancing act between adherence to set structures and their commission to work with a form of media that does not follow the same tightly bound patterns of hierarchy and control. Their job requires them to interface with a broad, secular audience directly and indirectly through media content and production. Digital spokespersons acknowledge their desire to express creativity through their digital work to help advance the agenda of the community. Digital media platforms encourage individualization and unquietness, where their work is to cater to the demands of the self-focused i-generation. Yet at the same time these RDCs are asked to portray the organization's religious identity within digital culture, they are pulled toward and asked to replicate communal, historic identity narratives whose character is steeped in tradition. So digital spokespersons are torn between emphasizing the need to embrace technology for the sake of increasing the profile of their religious sect within broader society and not adapting the remix narrative of digital culture.

Overall, the technological apologetic of digital spokespersons focuses on advocating for and implementing technology within an established institution structure. They seek to manage tensions that occur between fixed organizational patterns and hierarchies and the flexible, dynamic nature of digital media, translating between institutions and digital culture. The specific strategy employed by digital spokespersons to navigate these dialectics can be summed up as managing institutional and digital culture tensions by emphasizing their role as identity curators.

The digital spokespersons' apologetic focuses on stressing institutional technology use as key to their religious organization being seen as having cultural relevance. Yet discussions of their work point to an innate challenge within their role. Those frequently serving as digital spokespersons often have very public or institutionally visible positions. They are chosen because of their media experience or technology training, yet their work includes creating communicative structures and representing their institution in digital spaces, and this design work and information management is essentially religious–identity work. They frame the character and theological nature of the community for a new public online. Therefore, internet advocacy can be seen as self-serving if, in the case of online media ambassadors or communicators, they become the online voice of their institutions. The challenge is grounded both in the fact that religious institutions do not fully understand the importance and impact of religious–identity curation online in digital cultures.

Digital strategists' technological apologetic

Digital strategists are convinced of the importance of integrating technology into their often very traditional religious work. Like digital entrepreneurs, they describe their use of digital media as serving as a potential model to those similar religious positions, being an example of what digital communication can do to transform contemporary ministry. They are, however, more pragmatic than entrepreneurs in the ways they frame their efforts and highlight best practices. Also like digital professionals, they advocate seeing digital technology as an essential part of contemporary culture, a technology that needs to be understood and applied in one's religious service. However, instead of focusing on institutional digital media literacy education as a way to address other leaders' fears about digital tools and their impact on religious institutions, they choose to lead by example.

Digital strategists talk openly about both how and why they engage digital media and encourage others in their institution to also experiment with the opportunities these afford. Their media-making narratives primarily spotlight how digital media can enhance traditional forms of Christian work, and by doing so, streamline, yet expand their work and reach to a broader audience. Because their work is often contextual, or locally focused, they stress tailoring digital initiatives to the specific church, country or denominational contexts with which they are affiliated. This is supported by an underlying rationale about how Christians should view digital innovation for religious purposes.

Justification narrative: Digital media expand traditional ministry

Why?—Digital media as central to contemporary Christian ministry

Digital strategists justify their use of digital media by framing it as central part of contemporary ministry. They believe technology integration is essential for those with a missional outlook. Missional in this case means work done in service of the church and focused on religious vocation, biblical teaching and proclamation of religious truth to others. "I feel a certain missionary purpose," said theologian Larry Hurtado,

> … whereby blogging I am basically saying, "This is an attempt to try […] to put out there in the blogosphere and on the internet for those who want it, serious competent information and opinion on a subject by an expert in Biblical Studies."
>
> (Personal communication, March 15, 2013)

Digital strategists' technological apologetic stresses that engaging with media is, in some respects, a required part of contemporary Christian ministry. Christian ministry refers to the responsibilities and tasks those commissioned to serve the church and Christians take on as part of their remit. This digital ministry is more than just using the latest technology in their religious work. It is bringing their ministry to where people are, rather than expecting the digital generation and media users to come to them. One Turkish media-driven missionary emphasized this as, "There is no other means that could have allowed us to do this kind of work or sharing (evangelism). Technology can change the whole idea of discipleship" (missionary 2, personal communication, July 10, 2014). This is echoed by a foreign media-driven missionary in Turkey: "The internet offers us an opportunity we never had to reach Turkey for Christ, and so we want to go for it now because we don't know what tomorrow is going to hold" (male missionary 1, personal communication, July 10, 2014).

While affirming technology as a central part of Christian ministry echoes the rationale of digital entrepreneurs, as noted earlier, strategists' emphasis on digital-media use differs in how they frame technologies' relationship to religious work. Digital strategists see ministry as situated in a broader culture in which the internet is embedded, and which traditional religious practices must be adapted to. Yet they typically do not stress the reformation of the religious institution in which their practice resides; instead, they focus on the innovation of religious rituals themselves. Digital strategists point out how missionaries', theologians' and ministers' communication styles and formats of communication must be modified to meet audience expectations and new cultural communicative styles. Theologian Tim Bulkley described how online media require modification in theological writing. He said,

> Most theological teachers are operating with a kind of head in the sand policy [...] They are trying to pretend that the technology isn't changing culture [...] rather than it being different kind of writing all together and something we in Biblical Studies can't ignore.
>
> (Personal communication, September 19, 2009)

Digital strategists emphasize technology as a helpmate used to modify missional communication techniques, but not the meaning or intent behind these religious practices.

The technological apologetic of digital strategists focuses on how communication-oriented ministries that, in the past, have not been dependent on media use and innovation are in a state of flux. Professional theologians are beginning to recognize that people's popular understanding of dense theological concepts often comes from blogs and Google searches, rather than trickle-down learning from pastor to parishioner. Theologian Matthew Tan asserts,

> I think more theologians need to blog, precisely because it creates the potential to see theology as based on collaboration [...] The internet could foster new forms of collaborative knowledge, as theologians learn how to interact together in new ways [...] creating new types of collaborative theology.
>
> (Personal communication, June 28, 2014)

Many pastors, especially those charged to work in an online environment, acknowledge people living in a busy, mobile world need alternative ways to connect to the church, as expecting weekly attendance from their full congregation is increasingly unrealistic. As online minister Nathan Clark says,

> The online minister has the obligation to curate the group conversation to as much a degree as possible [...] and also prepare people for the liturgical experiences of the service. On top of that, we try and cultivate a feeling of community among the attendees so they feel a part of the larger Northland experience.
>
> (Personal communication, August 11, 2012)

Missionaries understand door-to-door and street evangelism may not be safe or effective in some cultural contexts, and reinventing outreach in the twenty-first century often requires a digital component. "The new media give us great opportunity and open more doors to have a personal relationship with the respondents, and also we can touch their lives through internet access," said one Turkish media-driven missionary (missionary male 2, personal communication, July 11, 2014). Digital strategists advocate the need for creating alternative forms of gathering, teaching, connecting and building Christian community, and their digital work is at the center of these endeavors.

Assumption—Technology should be seen as a strategic helpmate for Christian communication

Digital strategists' justification narrative highlights their conviction that digital media should be seen as a core tool in the toolbox of Christian ministry professionals, even though their official work may not typically be viewed as media oriented, because their job centers on religious communication to a variety of audiences. This contention is also based on a key assumption about technology. Digital strategists believe that in order to communicate and minister to others within contemporary culture, understanding and strategically employing digital media is very important in several ways.

In this study, theologians who blog pointed out that the internet creates a new communicative environment that needs clear and articulate theological presences. As theologian Matthew Tan stated, "I think that professional theologians have an important part to play in this online discursive atmosphere, in providing sound theological reflection, informed by academic study and evidence" (personal communication, June 28, 2014). The general consensus among theologians is that while the blogosphere is making theological thought more accessible to a broader audience, it also lacks the accountability structures of formal theology that help verify information shared as accurate or truthful. Tan and others echo the responsibility theologians now have to move toward "countering the effect that well intentioned, but ill-informed nonprofessional bloggers can create."

While theologians stress that blogging is new and only a small part of their broader job is to educate future church leaders and teachers, it is still of strategic importance. As theologian Larry Hurtado said,

> I don't think it helps things for people to put out inaccurate information or misleadingly presented stuff that is being pumped out daily into the blogosphere. While it is not my job, and I am just not interested in spending all my time policing the internet, I think we have a role to play, to patiently put out accurate information.
>
> (Personal communication, March 15, 2013)

Here blogging is framed as a modification of the theologian's traditional role of religious educator and interpreter, translating their dense work into the contemporary landscape of the internet where much religious teaching and learning now take place for many.

In this study, all digital strategists in one way or another stress technology should be a strategic helpmate to those involved in Christian ministry. Furthermore, they frame their personal digital media use for ministry as providing a model to others for creative technology integration. Online ministers with Northland Church emphasize their reason for serving online is partially motivated by a desire to show others digital media can enhance traditional forms of church. "One of my goals is to have people experience church every day of their lives, not confine it to a weekend expression or service. Being part of Northland's online ministry team helps me do this," online minister 2 said (personal communication, August 11, 2012). Another Northland online minister describes his efforts to integrate technology with ministry as more than just being able to effectively use media or respond to technical issues. It is about learning how to help people spiritually using technology—e.g., addressing an online congregant's personal struggles or prayer need at a moment's notice during an online service. While the internet is a tech-based system, digital ministry is about using media tools to "minister to people, just in a different, spontaneous environment" (online pastor 3, personal communication, August 11, 2012). Online missionaries also emphasize digital media should be seen primarily as a helpmate or partner in ministry. For example, one Turkish missionary described how social media and networking are essential tools for doing twenty-first-century evangelism, enabling them to create a "digital trail that people can actually follow to Christ and link believers all together as a Christian community" (missionary male 2, personal communication, July 11, 2014).

Digital strategists emphasize the fact that they are highly motivated to see how digital media might assist in and advance their pastoral, teaching and evangelistic work to new audiences. Yet this motivation is based on assumption that what is most important is first being missional, focused on serving those inside and outside the church, and then technology is focused. Being a missional media negotiator is about navigating between traditional service responsibilities to others, their community and the dynamic tools and techniques that can be used to address the spiritual needs of those living in digitally mediated cultures.

Relational dialectic: Tensions between stability and change

Digital strategists' technological apologetic focuses on justifying engaging digital media because they are a central tool for contemporary Christian ministry. Digital-media adoption is for the primary purpose of extending tasks seen as a standard part of their vocation. Digital strategists do this by emphasizing the connection between the traditional communication functions of their job and the social practices digital media promote. This technological apologetic is supported by an underlying effort to show that online and offline forms of ministry create a continuum of outreach. Digital strategists contend online and offline tasks differ only in terms of the space in which they take place and the communication techniques they require; the overarching ministry goals guiding their work do not differ at all.

By applying relational dialectics theory to digital strategists' technological apologetic, the primary tension highlighted is that of stability versus change. This focuses on the tension emerging between balancing static, prescribed institutional roles with changes technological integration introduces into their work practice. This tension is seen in the ways digital strategists emphasize the unchanging of focus and aims of their ministry to Christians and those outside the church, even as they use new tools and techniques to accomplish these goals. They also downplay the idea that adopting digital media will bring about unsettling change to established institutional contexts and leadership structures. They employ a rhetorical approach that amplifies the idea that technology merely acts as a tool to extend their work, and their focused use of technology stabilizes the influence the dynamic environment of digital media culture may have. By stressing the unchanging nature of their work, they introduce the idea that technology can be cultured in line with religious values. This helps affirm their claim that technology can enhance institutions rather than destabilize them. Digital strategists do this by framing digital media as enabling them to extend the influence of their work, or to more efficiently carry out expected responsibilities associated with their role.

The language used by digital strategists' points to their strong desire to establish a conceptual bridge, not just between online and offline contexts, but also between their ministry innovations and the established institutions in which they serve. Media-driven missionaries say digital technology allows them to evangelize in contemporary settings, which are volatile and closed to Christianity, "where there is no other means that could be done" (young Turkish volunteer, personal communication, July 10, 2014). Many theologians who blog do so out of a sense of responsibility, because as one said, "If we do not share our knowledge online, we are in a sense failing in our responsibilities" (L. Hurtado, personal communication, March 15, 2013). Both responses suggest the argument that in order for digital strategists to do the work to which they have been called or commissioned in current culture, they must utilize digital media. This frames digital media as more than a complement to their work. Rather it becomes a crucial element of modern ministry, and thus central to both their personal missional goals and those of the organizations they work for.

Framing strategist' relationship with their institution

Seeing authority as relational draws attention to digital strategists' efforts to create a distinct rhetorical relationship with technology based on certain patterns of communication with their audience. These communicative patterns are directed at several groups: Individuals they serve, those they work with and institutional or organizational leaders. For those they serve, they frame technology as a gateway to connect with them where they are in new, more personal ways. To others in their line of work, they highlight how digital media can be seen as a helpmate in ministry, providing unique flexible and dynamic opportunities to users. To those they are accountable to, they emphasize how technology primarily expands, rather than alters their ministry. Each of these different patterns of discourse emphasizes traditional roles or positions digital strategists hold and seeks to affirm their relationship with their audience without undermining established hierarchies of service within their institution.

Digital strategists' technological apologetic emphasizes two secondary tensions or patterns of negotiation they employ when framing their work to the different institutional parties with which they interact. First, they must present an internal justification narrative about their digital work to their faith community members and other institutional leaders. Here they employ a certainty–uncertainty narrative focused on the unchanging nature of the community's values and aims, despite the changing nature of the actual tools and practices associated with their work. When speaking with or about institutional leaders or structures, they stress the constancy of their ministry tasks, despite aspects of these being altered by the integration of technology into established rituals. For members, they also use this certainty– uncertainty narrative to generate excitement about core practices and ministry patterns. They say integrating digital tools into worship and outreach contexts, or transporting religious education opportunities into digital platforms, can help create renewed interest and investment in community members' standardized practices. Overall, the internal narrative of certainty and uncertainty seeks to negotiate between the perceived unpredictable nature of technology and the constancy of a shared vision and importance of the communal relations. This is communicated by digital strategists in order to create a close relationship between the digital strategist and these two groups.

Second, digital strategists often must articulate an external justification narrative aimed at media sources and others external to their community seeking to understand their rationale for digital media integration. This external narrative emphasizes uniqueness over conventionality, or the attempt to balance assumptions about the rigid, static nature of religious communities with the dynamic tools and experimentation of digital strategists. External sources often struggle with the assumption that religious leaders and communities are resistant to modernity, change and innovation. This set identity causes surprise when external sources encounter religious groups openly and enthusiastically embracing digital media. Digital strategists thus seek to explain how digital innovation adds to and extends their group's conventional, established mission. Such discussions require them to illustrate how media enable them to retain their community's unique sense of identity, despite the fact that this appears counterintuitive to institutional outsiders. By its very nature, digital strategists' digital experimentation challenges religious tropes about the conventionality of Christianity and static nature of Christian culture; that can serve as an important public relations strategy for churches seeking to show their ability to adapt to contemporary change.

Overall, digital strategists' technological apologetic aims to offer a map that lays out the relationship between technology engagement and meaning between themselves, institutional leaders and other community members. By addressing assumptions about the instability that digital media introduce to religious institutions and affirming the stability religious groups are seen to desire and function within; they negotiate key conceptual tensions that technology creates. The apologetic of digital strategists focuses on connecting new digital work to their traditional roles. So technology use is presented as motivated by the desire to fulfill their religious calling, intention religious groups and leaders cannot easily critique. By spotlighting how technology creates opportunities to engage new audiences, streamline communication and make proselyting efficient, digital strategists present digital technology and work as a valuable investment. Technology, therefore, extends Christian outreach and accomplishes core religious goals of the tradition.

Summary: Technological apologetics in light of relational dialectic theory

This chapter presents how identifying RDCs' justification narratives reveals their underlying motivation for technology use, presenting a certain technological apologetic. While each technological apologetic centers on similar factors—e.g., seeing digital technology as important for Christian organizations' work—their rationale for it should be engaged and framed drawing on nuanced differences. Digital entrepreneurs use a technological apologetic that states digital media use and experimentation are essential for future of the church. They suggest the church cannot be successful in its work without an openness to technological innovation and adapting to the structural changes digital media create for Christian institutions. Digital spokespersons' technological apologetic stresses understanding and engaging digital technology as key for religious institutions that seek to be seen as culturally relevant. Because digital technology is the basis of contemporary communication, religious groups must seek to understand and learn to use it effectively if they want their beliefs heard in contemporary culture. Digital strategists' technological apologetic states digital media integration in traditional ministry is important for Christian communication. They are driven by the conviction that digital media are central to contemporary Christian ministry because they can serve as a strategic helpmate for missional service to the church.

In this chapter, the technological apologetics of each group of RDCs notes specific challenges each feels their work raises for themselves and their communities. Each apologetic highlighted is closely related to their assumptions about religious authority and how they see their relationship to given religious affiliations. These tensions are investigated by applying relational dialectic theory. Table 8.1 provides a summary of these specific dialectical tensions digital entrepreneurs, spokespersons and strategists see themselves as having to navigate, based on how they position themselves to those inside and outside their faith communities. This provides a

Table 8.1 Overview of RDCs Relational Dialectic Approaches

	Central Tensions within Technological Apologetic	Internal Relational Dialectic (Rationale for Tech Use Offered to Religious Institution)	External Relational Dialectic (Framing Technology to Those Outside Their Faith Community)
Digital entrepreneurs	Expression–Nonexpression	Openness–Closedness	Revelation–Concealment
Digital spokespersons	Integration–Separation	Connection–Autonomy	Inclusion–Seclusion
Digital strategists	Stability–Change	Certainty–Uncertainty	Conventionality–Uniqueness

visual overview of the strategies each group of RDCs relies on to frame their work and relationships.

Digital entrepreneurs draw on oppositional views for framing their relation to a specific religious group. These oppositional rhetorical strategies focus on resisting certain ideas that run counter to their individual core values. This places them in a position of having to justify their ideas and position in the face of the religious groups they seek to connect to, but may differ significantly within terms of priorities about technology use and power structures. Digital entrepreneurs' oppositional rhetoric is clearly seen in their privileging of digital expertise and activities above traditional religious practices and structures. While they may see their work as aligned with the needs of their faith community, and emphasize enabling digital media is simply doing Christian work more effectively in a new-media environment, they come to this conversation as institutional outsiders. This can make RDCs' initiatives appear to religious leaders to be based on individual passion rather than a communal vision, thus setting them up for an inherently oppositional positioning.

Digital spokespersons' discourse highlights the use of co-opting discourse, which relies on adopting certain arguments or beliefs from another's viewpoint to accomplish one's own purposes. In this case, they co-opt institutional rhetoric that identifies their Christian beliefs and community goals and use this language to how their digital work promotes and sustains these. Digital spokespersons rely heavily on their ability to frame themselves as institutional insiders simply curating the identity of the institutions for which they work. This means they must regularly articulate how digital work magnifies official values and positions. While their digital work may appear to be purely focused on providing a technical service or information sharing, they emphasize the idea that, at its heart, it's about identity management and brand promotion for their religious organization. They must translate official, often wordy, complex messages from leaders into succinct, attention-grabbing posts. This requires more than just digital communication skills. It also requires careful interpretive work, co-opting ideas, but translating them into user-/outsider-friendly language. They also stress in their co-opting discourse how they actively seek to work within institutional frameworks, even if this stunts needed technological innovation or limits the creativity of their work.

Finally, digital strategists engage in intermingling discourse strategies to position themselves in relation to their specific religious institution. Intermingling strategies focus on the conscious integration of competing, or what can be seen as contradictory, positions in order to create a new hybrid position or way of looking at things. Digital strategists connect their digital work to the aims of their job, which is in the service of more than a specific religious group. They frame their technology use in terms of a missional focus that echoes the Christian mandate to go and make disciples of all nations. By emphasizing digital communications as a form of ministry, digital strategists seek to build buy-in and investment from their community members, as well as institutional structures. When they talk about technology, they often frame it in instrumental terms, as a tool or a helpmate facilitating their ministerial call to teach, evangelize, provide pastoral care or mentor others in their oversight. They use an intermingling discourse to emphasize how digital technology can easily be integrated into Christian ministry to enhance its reach and impact. This presents digital ministry as important for those in contemporary service. They argue it is not a competitive space or form of ministry, but a hybrid reality that is digitally enhanced and mediated, one the church finds itself in and so must adapt its approach to.

Overall, the mapping of RDCs' technological apologetic enables us to understand in a more nuanced way how these actors frame their digital work in terms of a religious call. They do this by rhetorically framing their digital-creative work as compatible with shared Christian goals and institutional aims. This focuses on negotiating tensions created by mixing the dynamic nature of digital media and its culture with the more static traditional religious institutions.

Conclusion
Rethinking authority through the work of religious digital creatives

Throughout this book, I argue Christian digital creatives are an important, emerging class of actors within religious and digital culture, performing unique media work that is motivated by a personal religious passion and agenda. In many respects, digital creatives represent a unique type of religious prosumers. The term "prosumer" was coined by Alvin Toffler in his book *The Third Wave* (1980) and used to describe an evolving class of consumers who would help create and customize goods within new production processes. Here the once passive consumer of goods and ideas would become an active producer of innovations and content.

Media scholar Henry Jenkins picked up this idea in his book *Convergence Culture* (2006), discussing the role prosumers play in digital media culture. He argued that through digital media, individuals are increasingly able and encouraged to take part in both new media production and consumption process. This is because digital-media tools and platforms are designed in such a way that they lower the barrier to entry for individuals. In other words, instead of requiring individuals to have advanced technological skills and access to expensive, cost-prohibitive media-production equipment, digital media platforms give audiences with access to the internet the ability to produce media channels, content and processes that were once only possible for highly specialized professionals or media corporations to create. This is the space in which religious digital creatives (RDCs) have emerged, a space that encourages individuals and networks of people to take part in creative forms of media appropriation, engagement and production.

The opportunities offered by digital media prosumption cultivate what Jenkins referred to as a participatory culture, one where individuals are encouraged to engage with technology in new ways to interact, share ideas and create media content together. As Jenkins argued, "Our workplaces have become more collaborative; our political process has become more decentered; we are living more and more within interactive knowledge cultures" (Jenkins, 2006, p. 129). Participatory culture gives people new types of freedom to both engage and produce media messages, as well as to create and adopt media forms that enable them to widely share their ideas and circulate their beliefs within digital culture. Jenkins encouraged individuals to recognize this new power they have as both consumers and citizens and embrace the potential to create social and cultural changes by producing new narratives that challenge the status quo. It is in this interactive atmosphere that RDCs become inspired to experiment with how collaborative technologies can enliven and advance religious practices. By embracing the spirit of the prosumer, RDCs are empowered to create change within their religious communities in ways that both support and appear to challenge those religious institutions.

This book showcases the fact that there is a growing population of individuals who feel called to take on digital media work as a form of Christian ministry, as media technologies are increasingly seen as vital resources for serving those inside and outside the church. Christian digital creatives come from many different denominations, cultural contexts and professional backgrounds. They feel led to design distinctive types of media tools, initiatives and content for a variety of religious purposes. Yet they all share a passion for technology and a belief in its ability to tactically build and benefit the work of Christian faith communities.

Carlo Acutis was one such example of this vision. From the age of seven, Carlo showed himself to be a devout Catholic, attending mass on a daily basis and going to weekly confession in his home diocese of Milan, Italy. It was said that he was not afraid to publically voice his faith and spoke openly to friends and family about God and his Catholic commitment. Growing up in the 1990s, he became fascinated at a young age with computers. Despite his youth, he became known as a skilled computer geek, developing expertise in computer programming, web design and film editing in his early teen years. Many described his technical expertise and proficiency as well developed far beyond his years. Also as a teen, he had a vision that he could bring his faith and computer abilities together in an ambitious project.

While his parents themselves were not religious, he convinced them to travel with him to some of the 132 sites around Europe where Eucharistic miracles have occurred and are documented by the Catholic Church. As part of this pilgrimage, he built a website to share with others about his journey, providing historic information and testimonial proof of these miracles, as well as encouraging others through his experiences to also explore the mysteries of the Eucharist. For him, the internet offered the ability to invite others to come to know God more. His website, Miracles of the Eucharist (www.miracolieucaristici.org/en/Liste/list.html), was also recognized by other Catholics and Church leaders as a leading source of historical information and documentation of these miracles. This generated a lot of attention for him and his site. He became known online as a devout Catholic computer geek, and many of his quotes about his faith were circulated around the web—e.g., "To always be close to Jesus, that's my life plan," and, "All of us are born as originals, but many of us die as photocopies" (www.carloacutis.com/en/association/biografia).

His online work and notoriety eventually led to an invitation from Church leaders for him to come to the Vatican as a special consultant in computing, at the age of only 14. In further recognition of his technological gifting and religious passion, religious officials even spoke of grooming him to become a Church scholar or perhaps join a religious order. However, his promising future was cut short. Carlo died of leukemia in 2006, only a few months after he was given the unexpected diagnosis. While it has been more than a decade since his death, the recognition of his digital work and faith commitment continues to grow online.

In 2018, Pope Francis recognized Carlo's unique contribution to the Church and named him a Venerable, a title given to a person posthumously for being "heroic in virtue" in their faith. It also means they are placed under special investigation by the Church for potential canonization as a saint (Catholic News Agency (CNA), 2018, July 8). This led to the creation of an online religious fan club of sorts, the Association and the Cause of Beatification of the Venerable Servant of God Carlo Acutis (www.carloacutis.com/en/association/presentazione). Due to growing online support, a campaign was launched to have his body exhumed to verify accounts of his saintly qualities. In 2019, Carlos was exhumed, and his body was found to be incorruptible, a distinction given when a person's body is identified as not being impacted by normal decomposition processes. This, supporters believe, is a symbol of divine intervention on the person's behalf and a sign of the individual being holy (CNA, 2019, January, 28).

Carlo Acutis represents an interesting example of an RDC, specifically a digital entrepreneur. He was a young computer hobbyist working outside church institutional structures to produce online resources aimed at building the Catholic faith out of sense of personal calling and conviction. Yet his website affected his faith community and garnered the attention of established religious leaders who embraced both him and his work. This shows a very different response and interaction between RDCs and church leaders than those described in the introduction of the book. There, Catholic app designers working on the Confession app generated controversy and condemnation by church officials due to the impact of how their digital work was framed by the mainstream press. I would argue the difference in the response of a religious institution is not based on any noted changes in the past decade in terms of Catholic policies or theology-related digital media or innovation. Rather, these two instances highlight the fact that the way religious institutions respond to RDCs is often largely influenced by the way the public and media outlets frame this work in their public discourse. When digital creatives' work is presented as in some way challenging traditional religious structures by asserting religion and technology are inherently at odds with one another, religious groups may have to offer a reactionary response. Technology being framed as a competitor to religion sets the stage for a struggle over authority between the old and the new. When caught in the midst of this rhetorical struggle, the losers are often RDCs, who are framed as religious mavericks or outsiders. For this reason, and because of this fear, RDCs often are forced to live within this potential fraught narrative, even though this study shows their motivations and intentions for technology use run counter to this perception.

That means RDCs, by their very existence, must engage in a careful negotiation process. This requires them to carefully frame their digital work in distinct ways in relation to their religious communities or institutions. If their work is framed as undermining traditional boundaries or beliefs, even if this is an external framing, they are treated as a threat. If, however, their work can be presented in such a way that it is seen to affirm the core mission or structure of their faith community, their work is more easily accepted, and even applauded. This echoes findings from my previous research and assertions made in Chapter 3 related to the religious social shaping of technology approach. Religious communities are more willing to accept technological innovations that affirm traditional religious beliefs and practices and are seen to be in line with core community or institutional values.

Part of this process of acceptance of technology takes place through communal discourse. This is the fourth stage of the religious social shaping of technology approach. Here religious groups seek to frame media technology in ways that support their religious identity by creating an internal narrative of who they are as faith community and how technology use relates to this. Consideration should be given to a group's communal discourse about technology, which emphasizes the fact that religious groups often stress how members' use and advocacy of technology should visibly display to those outside the community the ways technology use affirms their group's religious identity. When it comes to RDCs, they must carefully engage in a similar strategy; they create discourse that stresses the ways technology is compatible with Christian mission and how it can reflect core religious goals. It is from this narrative their technological apologetic emerges. RDCs have learned that in order to defuse potential fears and stress about technology, they must be able to clearly articulate how their ministry-related technology integration closely coincides with established institutional or community goals.

Religious digital creatives' variation in their technological apologetic

This book has been a journey, introducing three distinct types of RDCs I have encountered in a decade of research on how Christians seek to use their technological skills and expertise to promote their faith and its practices. These categories of digital entrepreneurs, spokespersons and strategists are not meant to be fully exclusive, or the only manifestations of RDCs found within Christian culture or institutions. Indeed, I have tried to emphasize the fact that variations do exist, even within these three categories of digital entrepreneurs, spokespersons and strategists by naming and describing in depth three variations found in these categories. So the book highlights a total of nine different manifestations of RDCs in this study. This diversity of RDCs ranged from internet evangelists who create new evangelistic initiatives and training forums online to denominational webmasters that frame the digital footprint and identity of their religious organization to online ministers who serve in churches as tech experts and pastoral-care workers online while running virtual church campuses. I also suggest the increasing variety of digital media practices emerging in our technologically driven culture, drawing new individuals to experiment with religious–technical strategies, has the potential to give rise to other classes of RDCs. In this study, I argue digital entrepreneurs, spokespersons and strategists represent a common range of digital media workers found in Christian institutions, individuals I have observed doing digital media work in service to various Christian communities and organizations. I further assert that the phenomenon of RDCs is not exclusive to Christian groups. From my previous research studying Jewish and Muslim religious communities and their use of media technology, I see strong correlations between the work and motivations of many individuals in these faith communities and the RDC typologies discussed here (Campbell, 2010, 2015; Campbell & Evolvi, 2019). It is my hope that these categories and the theoretical arguments presented in this book will be of use to other scholars and prove applicable for studying the innovative work and intentions of digital creatives in other faith traditions.

The overall findings of this study, especially as it related to the technological apologetic of RDCs researched here, can be summed up by Table C.1.

Digital entrepreneurs are technology professionals and innovators who see the digital content and resources they create as gifts freely given to their faith community. Their primary expertise lies in digital technology, which they use to create resources that help build their influence and the reputation of the Christian faith within digital culture. They privilege digital knowledge and influence, or the features of algorithmic culture in which they are skilled, to leverage a growing reputation for their work and even their personal profile online. They validate the impact of their work in terms of its visibility or prominence online, which is tied to size of their audience or number of followers as indicators for success. Because most often their work is situated outside religious institutions and leadership, they can feel distanced or alienated by religious structures that do not affirm the good they see their work as doing.

Digital entrepreneurs can be summed up in the example of Eric van den Berg, who was introduced in Chapter 2. Eric owns a digital media company in the Netherlands and is the creator of a leading website on the Dutch Catholic Church, Katholiek.nl. He stressed that he creates his website to fill a need to keep Dutch

Table C.1 Overview of religious digital creatives' categories

	Digital Entrepreneurs	Digital Spokespersons	Digital Strategists
Cultural orientation	Algorithmic culture	Institutional structures	Institutional affiliation & digital influence
Source of influence	Numeric ranking & prominence	Media training & job position	Media work leads to institutional recognition
Basis of expertise	Digital technology	Technical & institutional knowledge	Digital culture & religious knowledge
Work goals	Reputation building for Christian faith	Extending influence of church & institutions	Connecting Christian ministry with digital culture

Catholics informed about news related to the Church and to give them a space where they can interact with one another, as there was no Catholic diocesan website before his. However, over time, as his site has gotten secular and religious media attention, he describes himself as growing into the role of an unintended religious authority, a role he constantly wrestles with. As van den Berg states,

> People look to my site, to me, like I am the official voice of the Church, the diocese of Rotterdam, but I am not. I tell them this. It is because I am really aware of how to use the web and social media, because my site is current with Catholic news. I am not official, but I am authoritative because of this.
> (E. van den Berg, personal interview, March 7, 2013)

Such an experience can lead entrepreneurs to express a sense of alienation or frustration with religious institutions for not valuing the impact of their work or recognizing their need to embrace digital media in their work.

Digital spokespersons are media professionals employed by religious organizations to create digital content or oversee the organization's social media presence. While their primary training is technology or media oriented, they must also build upon and rely on institutional knowledge to help frame and guide their digital work. For example, individuals creating and managing the official social media or Facebook presence for their religious denomination must be well versed in the rules and protocols of the digital platform, as well as in the communicative practices and expectations of their institution. They are commissioned to extend the influence and manage the identity of the Christian institutions they work for. They also face tensions because those they work with and for are suspicious of the impact digital media may have on institutional structures. Therefore, digital spokespersons often take on additional roles as digital media trainers and advocates to mitigate the tensions their work can generate.

This situation was described in Chapter 2 through the example of James Abbott, a webmaster for the Catholic Bishops Conference of England and Wales. Though technical in nature, he sees his work mostly in terms of identity curation and helping the Church "put their best face forward online." Most of the content that comes to him for incorporation into the website has already gone through a multiple-stage vetting process by various committees and bishops. However, incorporating it into the site or social media often requires him to do significant translation work to make the language and ideas accessible to online communication culture.

> Sometimes people get quite presumptuous that their work, their words and format, are very easy to understand, because they are in it all the time. But when we put this online they are not just speaking to the Catholic community, they are speaking to a broader public, even a non-Catholic audience, which they do not fully understand. So I have to repackage it, while still trying to keep its authenticity.
> (J. Abbott, personal communication, May 9, 2011)

So working with information-communication technologies also requires digital spokespersons to be aware of certain established interpretive patterns and practices within their community. This work in online identity curation can be challenging, because it demands certain levels of theological or institutional expertise to accurately portray their organization—areas of expertise that are beyond their technological training.

Finally, digital strategists work as ministry professionals, serving Christian community members in their faith journey or reaching out to those beyond the church, with a heart to bring them in. They see digital media as an essential tool in their contemporary ministry work and seek to integrate it in strategic ways into established religious practices. Thus, they see that religious institutions must embrace the internet and digital culture, as these represent places they cannot ignore, given that the people they are called to minister are embedded within these cultures. They see their religious training as being updated and invigorated through using digital technologies for ministry. While transferring and translating Christian rituals into digital spaces may create nontraditional forms of Christian ministry, they stress the belief that this is important for contemporary outreach. Digital strategists thus seek to live in between two spaces, the church and digital culture. They believe modeling best practices will prove the church and technology can live side by side in harmony, as helpmates, and thus encourage others to engage in similar work.

Sister Julie Vieira who worked on the website and blog "A Nun's Life Ministry," http://anunslife.org/, briefly discussed in Chapter 2, models this strategy. She described her work as being an online advocate for Catholic sisters and using the internet to counter stereotypes about nuns by seeking to show online, through transparent and honest dialogue, what life in a religious vocation is really like. Blogging and podcasting her thoughts and journey became a way for her to help open up to a new generation the possibilities of a religious life.

> Seeing using with the internet as form of religious service is very new in my order. But it has been embraced because it has opened up new avenues for us to show how one can live authentically as a nun and yet engage with contemporary culture. The sisters see the impact it is having and interest that it is creating in religious vocations.
>
> (J. Vieira, personal communication, February 12, 2015)

While Sister Vieira formally stepped away from leading this online ministry in 2017 to pursue other religious vocational goals, the online ministry of A Nun's Life continues under the oversight of other sisters in her order (A Nun's Life, November 10, 2017, https://anunslife.org/sites/www.anunslife.org/files/Press-release-sjvieira. pdf). Her pioneering work laid the groundwork for a unique space that enables people around the world to connect firsthand with Catholic sisters and engage them in conversations about what a religious vocation is really like in the twenty-first century.

By transferring Christian practices into digital spaces, digital strategists show how religious communities can be active contributors to and part of the digital culture where the people they seek to minister to increasingly reside.

This overview of RDCs presents them as individuals who come from different professional backgrounds and training and hold distinctive perceptions of relations to their Christian institutions and/or communities. Yet the chart presented earlier also indicates that the way RDCs map these affiliations points to distinctive understandings of authority.

Christian digital creatives' perspective on the relationship of technology to the church

Throughout this book, I argue RDCs' perceptions of religious authority can be seen in terms of a performance, a conceptual deliberation between ideas of authority tied to those established by traditional institutional frameworks and those emerging from digitally mediated culture or spaces. Digital entrepreneurs, who describe themselves as religious institutional outsiders, draw on notions of authority based on power structures. They seek to situate themselves as drawing on the affordances of algorithmic culture, which privileges digital prominence based on numerical rankings, to justify their work, rather than relying on recognition by institutional and religious social structures. Digital spokespersons, who work to frame themselves as institutional representatives with media expertise, depend on the conception of authority as a specific role performed. They position their work as serving the organizations by which they are employed, privileging institutional positions and knowledge to frame their work and affirm themselves as religious insiders. Digital strategists see themselves as institutional affiliates who perform their work in ways that may move them beyond these boundaries, and so they rely on a relational view of authority. They seek to present digital engagement as essential to their prescribed ministry work, seeking to show how the spheres of institutional and algorithmic authority can be merged in a collaborative and balanced manner. By looking at RDCs' approaches to authority in tandem, we see a key trait emerging. RDCs understand authority as a negotiation.

This study demonstrates the fact that authority in digital culture involving religious actors such as RDCs can be seen as a negotiation between different cultural power structures, institutional roles and the relationships existing between the two. This negotiation also takes place through the ways RDCs frame their work in relation to their perception of how religious institutions think of and respond to digital technology and the culture it creates. In this study and other work, I have described this as a negotiation between conceptions of the online and offline. This refers to how offline-based religious institutions and leaders relate to or understand their relationship with digital or online media and platforms. Over the past decade, I have come to refer to this as the bounding, blending, bridging or blurring of church and digital media contexts. These concepts are illustrated in Figure C.1.

BOUNDED: Online and offline are separate from each other, seen to be in competition.

BRIDGING: Online and offline are distinct, can belinked.

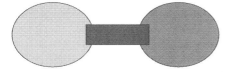

BLENDING: Online and offline are interconnected, allow a flow between contexts.

BLURRING: Online and offline contexts are embedded in another, new context created.

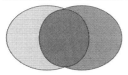

Figure C.1 Mapping range of perceived relationship between religious leaders/institutions and internet

By studying different religious groups' choices and responses to digital media, I have observed religious leaders in particular typically take one of these four stances toward media. Some religious communities see themselves as BOUNDED, in that media technologies represent a culture foreign to their way of life, one from which they seek to distance themselves. They see digital media and online contexts as separate or disconnected from their own offline reality. This is because they perceive online spaces as driven by divergent values or creating patterns that challenge or are in competition with their beliefs. Therefore, they draw strong boundaries between religious, offline and the internet, or online, contexts in attempts to separate themselves from the influence of digital culture. While this perspective was not voiced by any of the RDCs in this study, it is mentioned as one point on a continuum of responses to digital media. This response highlights the fact there are still some religious groups that are strongly resistant to and critical of digital media and seek to distance themselves from them and their influences.

Other religious communities and RDCs see their relationship to digital media as one of BRIDGING. Here the internet and the church are described as distinct contexts, each with its own set of values and priorities. Some of the aspects of technologies and the cultural space their use creates are noted as being contradictory to traditional religious communities' patterns of life, such as the emphasis on the freedom of the individual online over the connections or accountability to the community. Yet other features and affordances of digital media are seen as useful to religious groups' work and aims, such as offering the potential to create global networks of collaboration and share with fellow members. From this perspective, religious leaders and RDCs approach the relationship between religion and technology as one where the potential for bridge-building exists. Individuals look to connect positive online attributes and values with the established, predominately offline institutional culture of the church. This involves building tangible and rhetorical connections between religious and digital cultures to highlight specific purposes and aims they share. The bridging approach is highlighted in the technological apologetic of digital spokespersons. They emphasize the idea that digital media offer religious groups new opportunities for communication, which are critical for them to engage in order for their message to be heard and appear relevant to digitally mediated culture. Digital media are framed as a conduit for relaying religious beliefs in current cultural discourse. Framing digital media as useful for internal and public communication and helping religious organizations maintain a presence in the 24/7 news cycle creates a bridge, thus highlighting the embrace of technology for focused purposes to build the reputation and visibility of the church.

Increasingly, many religious groups are recognizing their dependence on digital media and online platforms to conduct their ministry work and communication. This means that while they may find some aspects of the internet tricky to navigate, they acknowledge the fact that their institutions are interconnected with online culture due to their members' engagement and investment in the internet. Therefore, religious communities and RDCs see online and offline contexts as being BLENDED. They are connected, and each space has the potential to culture or shape the other. This means religious groups must be actively reflective in how they engage with digital media, so that they can culture in line with religious goals. This outlook enables RDCs to develop resources that utilize digital tools and adapt established religious practices to this new communication environment, in order to create a seamless flow of interactions and shared experiences between the two. In this context, religious groups are able to cultivate patterns of use that complement their mission and religious outlook. It is using this logic that allows digital strategists to frame the relationship between digital media and the church as being blended in their technological apologetic. They emphasize digital work as essential to contemporary Christian ministry and stress the fact that technology can be used by religious ministers and teachers to expand their outreach and creatively engage with a broader public. Digital strategists contend the church should see the internet as a helpmate and asset, rather than a competitor or distraction to

Christian mission. This emphasis on seeing technology as blending well with religious instructional aims enables digital strategists to experiment with and model new forms of multisite and digitally integrated ministry.

Finally, some religious groups see their relationship with digital media as hypermediated, a relationship in which religious culture and its structures are increasingly mediated and embedded within the social-technical infrastructure of global society. This I describe as seeing the online and offline contexts as BLURRING into one another. In this way, a hybrid arena is created, informed by traits of traditional religious structures and patterns of life that have become infused and shaped by digital techniques and affordances. This blurred context is not always seen in a positive light. Some church leaders argue the church has been co-opted or seduced by the bells and whistles of digital culture, which is modifying the work and identity of Christianity in significant ways. Others in such groups present this blending as a unique opportunity to experiment and reimagine the life, work and calling of the church as this new context takes shape. Digital entrepreneurs adopt this mindset by emphasizing the idea that social and communication practices in digital culture are, or will lead to, the redefinition of religious institutional structures. For them, blurring of online and offline culture is a given. Digital entrepreneurs urge religious groups to recognize this new social reality and seek to understand and adapt their outreach to it. This pro-internet/technology advocacy can, however, put them in a fraught relationship with religious leaders and structures less enthusiastic about this shift and resistant to change.

From this overview, we see religious organizations and RDCs adopt different outlooks regarding the relationship of religious groups to technology and culture. These range from the religious groups being bounded or separated from technological culture, connected through the bridging or blending of the two, or facing a new hybrid or blurred cultural context creating new responsibilities and forms of interdependence between the church and digital media. The essential perceived relationship between religion and technology surfaces as RDCs' technological apologetic is identified and explored. Highlighting the perspective a particular digital creative adopts helps reveal the potential opportunities and challenges they may encounter with their religious affiliations and suggests how they might best frame their work for greater acceptance.

Rethinking authority in a digital age

The heart of this study has been to unpack the discourses used by RDCs about their digital work, because embedded within the work are their core assumptions about what constitutes religious authority in digital culture. This overview highlights different perspectives RDCs draw on to frame authority in digital culture and provides us with range of theoretical possibilities for discussing the differing conceptions that exist for different categories of RDCs. Figure C.2 provides a visual summary of the arguments presented here.

Table C.2 Overview of religious digital creatives' categories approaches to authority

	Traditional/ Institutional View of Authority (Offline Orientation)	*Algorithmic Approach to Authority (Online Orientation)*	*Negotiating Authority*
Digital entrepreneurs	Authority as power	Media influencers	Blurring online → online authority orientation
Digital spokespersons	Authority as roles	Thought leaders	Bridging offline → offline authority orientation
Digital strategists	Authority as relational	Digital leaders	Blending offline → online hybrid authority, blending offline with online

This study shows that different categories of RDCs draw on different perspectives when describing their understandings of religious authority, whether speaking about institutional authority or authority that emerges within digital contexts, and the relationship between the two. Digital entrepreneurs see authority within religious institutions as rooted in notions of power, where religious leaders seek to maintain control, and which they describe as being threatened by the emergence of digital culture that is shaping the future of the church. They see themselves as gaining authority in broader culture through their online and digital work as media influencers. This enables them to assert influence outside traditional religious structures.

For digital spokespersons, authority is defined and expressed within religious institutional contexts through certain organizational and leadership positions. Though their digital work may lead to online prominence, through their work as spokespersons or thought leaders, they consciously privilege traditional institutional authority. In this way, they consciously underplay their online influence in favor of trying to help solidify the role of their institutions in contemporary culture. Finally, digital strategists approach religious authority as it emerges within religious institutions in terms of relationality. They seek to carefully manage their relationship with the religious organizations they choose to work within, especially because their work as digital leaders means they have dual commitments and spheres of influence. By seeing authority as a relational communication process, digital strategists seek to model a new expression of authority, one that navigates between institutional and media contexts and establishes itself in a new blended space of influence and interaction. While each of these categories of RDCs have varying perspectives about how authority is established and acted out in traditional and digital spheres and the ways these two spheres interact, some commonalities between the two exist.

For RDCs, authority is a balancing act between different roles, relationships and power dynamics that they encounter in their religious communities and digital contexts. They must engage these areas as they are manifested in two very different environments. Their commitment to doing digital work for Christian mission means moving between creating an interrelationship between the two, whether they choose to primarily work outside traditional religious structures like digital entrepreneurs or within them as digital spokespersons do, or choose to try to create a stabilized connection between the two like digital strategists. RDCs are active prosumers, balancing different facets and understandings of authority and trying to create a harmonious practical and conceptual relationship between them.

For RDCs, authority can best be described as performance. They act out their understanding of authority on two unique stages, one formed by technological culture and the other by religious culture. They must somehow act on and connect the two stages by bridging, blending or blurring these contexts and cultures. Only when this engagement is solidified are they able to fully perform their work and fulfill their sense of calling. This means RDCs must be aware of the cultural boundaries set by both traditional religious structures and the rules of algorithmic culture that inform these two spaces, both of which create limits as well as opportunities for interconnection.

RDCs must recognize that they are also in the midst of a balancing act between independence and interdependence. The cultural affordances of digital technology encourage RDCs to experiment with dynamic forms of social engagement and connectivity, stressing individual freedom of choice and self-presentation. The culture of religious institutions, however, is based on values of reciprocity and accountability, where the allegiance to and the building of shared identity encourage responsibility to the community. Therefore, this can be seen as a balancing act between competing outlooks and obligations. Yet it is also important to recognize that religious organizations are not fully constrained. Christian missiology teaches RDCs that church is a cultural institution that historically has had to adapt to new cultures and translate itself for generations that emerge over time. This means adaptation and flexibility are built into the narrative of Christian community. It is also true that the nature of digital media, which suggests they are a space of complete freedom, is not fully accurate. Lev Manovich (2001) described this as the myth of interactivity, which states that technologies are designed as constrained spaces, programmed to fulfill a finite number of tasks based on the constraint language used by the designer. That means religious institutions are not limited by flexible adaptation, and digital spaces are not limitless dynamic spaces.

So what do these factors tell us about how authority is understood and practiced by RDCs? I suggest approaching authority as a negotiation process. For RDCs, authority becomes a cultural and value-based negotiation between religious institutions and digital spaces. It involves engaging varying notions of who or what oversees the social relationships and structures found within religious communities. It also requires digital media literacy and fluency in understanding how authority is derived from within algorithmic cultures. Seeing authority as an arbitration of religious, cultural and technological boundaries and investments frames RDCs as collaborators and helpmates, rather than competitors with religious institutions and leadership. How authority is conceived by RDCs' outlook is ultimately determined by their sense of connection and responsibility to traditional religious institutional structures, as well as their digital work. In summary, authority in a digital age is above all an active negotiation by individuals between multiple cultural contexts, the online and offline, institutional and technological, the traditional and the emerging.

I wish to end this book by highlighting four important observations that can be drawn from this study of RDCs' understanding and enactment of authority. Each is noteworthy and deserves further reflection.

A focused snapshot into a growing trend

As I noted earlier on in this chapter, the goal of this book is to provide a thick and rich description of the work, identity and motivations of different categories of Christian digital creatives seeking to serve various religious communities and organizations with their digital expertise and skills. I recognize that while this research is based on over 120 interviews, it only provides a brief snapshot of the different religious actors engaged as digital creatives. While I have sought to highlight key exemplars in Chapters 4–6, I have only been able to cite a limited sample of voices in this work. We have heard from 11 digital entrepreneurs, 9 digital spokespersons and 10 digital strategists, or about 25% of the individuals interviewed in this study. This means this study is selective and illustrative, rather than representative in its sample. The snowball sampling strategy sought to provide a glimpse of RDCs I have had the privilege to interact with over the past decade within Christian denominations and organizations found mainly within the American and European contexts. Therefore, this book offers a focused rather than an exhaustive profile of the full range of RDCs that may be functioning within Christian institutions and communities.

An established, rather than completely new phenomenon

Since the majority of the interviews took place between 2012 and 2015, many of these interviews are over five years old. This can seem like ancient history to some, as digital culture is characterized by constant social change and techno-logical evolution. However, I argue that being able to follow and engage with a wide range of RDCs over time online, complemented by focused face-to-face interviews with them during a specific timeframe, has enabled me to make several important observations.

First, the rise of RDCs is not a new phenomenon. As stated in Chapter 2, Jon Anderson observed as early as the late 1990s the fact that new religious interpreters and innovators were emerging online within a variety of digital Muslim contexts. Many of the RDCs interviewed here were very early internet adopters and computer users, wedding their technology skills to religious motivations, in some cases to produce decades of ministry work online. Digital entrepreneurs Marc van der Woude and Tony Whittaker, for example, each have two decades of experience using the internet to create religious projects. This means many of these RDCs have been around online for a significant amount of time, doing forms of digital ministry work to accomplish the same goals and mission they described to me during our one-off, face-to-face encounters.

Furthermore, the longevity of their online work and the time invested demonstrated the fact that many of the RDCs I studied have a proven, long-term record of accomplishments and successes. While they may represent peaks of influence or ebbs and flows in their work, most have had a long-term investment of 5+ years online. Just before this book was published, I made sure to connect with each of the RDCs quoted to update their status and affiliations. While a few RDCs who were interviewed have moved on from the digital ministry work spotlighted here and for which they were interviewed during this study, all but four of these individuals have continued in one way or another to do some form of online work and ministry since our conversations. For example, one prominent theoblogian became a social media trainer for pastors and authors. Three techies for God and tech-team members I spoke with have since moved out of their respective religious organizations into jobs as digital or social media consultants. Yet two of the three said they continue doing some limited work with religious groups. This shows that while RDCs may abandon or take a hiatus from digital-ministry initiatives, their investment in using the internet for religious purposes often continues. My aim has been to profile a cross-section of key RDC archetypes and spotlight exemplar actors within Western Christianity, in order to help define their work and motivations. This is done in order to consider what impact digital creatives may be having on understandings of religious and institutional authority within contemporary Christianity.

Are RDCs a gendered class?

One notable observation in this study is that the majority of the RDCs interviewed are white men between their mid-30s to early 50s. This is in part due to the recommendations given me in the snowball sampling strategy used, where RDCs interviewed were asked to identify one to three other individuals fitting the definition of a digital creative they felt would be exemplars of this work. Most men in this study also recommended other men as potential interviewees. The male-dominant nature of the informants also reflects the composition of most religious organizations I visited, as well as the religious technology conferences I attended to identify RDCs. This means only 18 out of 120 RDCs I interviewed were women (or 15% of the total sample), and of 30 individuals quoted in this study, only 4 are women. I do not in any way suggest the gender breakdown in this study accurately reflects a gendered nature of RDCs within Christian organizations. However, it does seem to match some statistics about the male-dominant gender balance found in many religious organizations and leadership structures. Exploring the extent to which digital work is gendered within Christian and religious organizations is an important area for future research. I especially note the need to specifically explore whether categories of digital entrepreneurs are dominated by male creatives. Digital media are framed as space that allows alternative religious actors and voices to emerge, and digital entrepreneurs are presented as those who are freed to work outside religious institutional structures. This situation would suggest such a space could give rise to female digital creatives who offer a unique approach and techno-logical apologetic that would be an interesting area of future investigation.

Authority as negotiated in digital culture

The aim of this book has been to rethink current understandings of what constitutes religious authority in digital culture. Instead of presenting a new definition for authority or a new theoretical approach, this study suggests that understanding authority as enacted through the work of Christian digital creatives presents authority as negotiated. It is a negotiation of different perspectives and positions of privilege. RDCs' negotiation of authority entails deciding whether digital technology must be bridged to religious aims and structures, or if religious institutions must accept the blending or blurring of their practices and mission to the communications and social patterns of digital media. Authority becomes a negotiation whereby RDCs determine whether institutional or algorithmic authority should be given primacy and be seen as shaping the other. It is a negotiation of whether RDCs can or should situate themselves as institutional insiders or outsiders, or straddle the tension of living as both. This negotiation raises a series of relational dialectics from expression–nonexpression and integration–separation to stability and change, which they must rhetorically frame and in which they must situate themselves in relation to the religious groups they feel called to affiliate with. Overall, we end our exploration of RDCs with a range of definitions, perspectives, rhetorical frames and contexts RDCs must navigate and present themselves in relation to. It is not a neat and tidy ending point, but one that offers a repertoire of fruitful possibil-ities for exploring the investments and convictions of digital entrepreneurs, digital spokespersons, digital strategists and other RDCs future research will reveal.

Developments in 2020, related to the COVID-19 global pandemic, further highlight the need to approach religious authority as a negotiated space. At this time religious groups were forced to negotiate between new and established social and cultural conditions resulting from the pandemic. Social distancing policies and community lockdown mandates forced Christian churches to move quickly from face-to-face gatherings to online meetings in mid-March 2020. This tran-sition highlighted the importance of digital literacy for churches, as a pastor's willingness and ability to adapt to technological quickly became a key marker of a congregation's resilience. Religious digital creatives and their technology experience played a key role in helping churches undergo the required digital transition. Church's became dependent on the technical expertise of tech teams, online ministers and media-driven missions experts to navigate both practical and missional shifts required by their churches. The conditions of social distancing also moved many RCDs into temporary, and in some cases even permanent, new leadership positions.

The value of RDCs became further evident as churches realized that technologically-mediated ministry would need to become part of their ministry toolbox for the long run, as uncertainty over the pandemic's long term impact and outcome became evident. The COVID-19 global pandemic thus created an interesting social situation within many churches, by raising the profile and prominence of certain types of RCDs within contemporary Christian ministry. This introduced a potential challenge to established leadership dynamics, as pastors were no longer the holders of all vital knowledge required for church programming. Technological fluency and knowledge became identified as a requirement needed for future pastors and priests. The coronavirus global pandemic thus brought credibility to the work of RDCs and validated the importance they had attributed to themselves in their narratives, which had gone unrecognized in most church contexts.

All this raises interesting questions about what and who is to be considered essential and authoritative in the post-pandemic era of Christian work and mission. How these factors shape the discussion of religious authority and how it should be defined and negotiated within church structures is worthy of deeper reflection and conversation in the days ahead.

Bibliography

Altenhofen, B. (2016). *Sharing the Catholic faith: How priests establish/maintain religious authority on Facebook.* (Unpublished doctoral thesis). Texas A&M University, College Station, TX.

Anderson, J. (1999). The Internet and Islam's new interpreters. In D. F. Eickleman (Ed.), *New media in the Muslim world: The emerging public sphere* (pp. 41–55). Bloomington, IN: Indiana University Press.

A Nun's Life Ministry bids farewell to co-founder Sister Julie Vieira. (2017, November 10). [Press release] A Nun's Life. Retrieved from https://anunslife.org/sites/www.anunslife.org/files/Press-release-sjvieira.pdf.

Barker, E. (2005). Crossing the boundary: New challenges to religious authority and control as a consequence of access to the Internet. In M. Hojsgaard & M. Warburg (Eds.), *Religion and cyberspace* (pp. 67–85). London: Routledge.

Barnes, D. (1978) Charisma and religious leadership: An historical analysis. *Journal for the Scientific Study of Religion, 17*(1), 1–18. Retrieved from: www.jstor.org/stable/1385423.

Barzilai-Nahon, K. & Barzilai, G. (2005). Cultured technology: Internet & religious fundamentalism. *Information Society, 21*(1). Retrieved from www.indiana.edu/~tisj/21/1/ab-barzilai.html.

Baxter, L. A. (2004). A tale of two voices: Relational dialectics theory. *Journal of Family Communication, 4*(3&4), 182–192.

Baxter, L. A. & Montgomery, B. M. (1996). *Relating: Dialogues and dialectics.* New York: Guilford.

Baym, N. K., Zhang, Y. B., & Lin, M.-C. (2004). Social Interactions across media: Interpersonal communication on the Internet, face-to-face, and the telephone. *New Media & Society, 6*(3), 299–318.

Becker, C. (2011). Muslims on the path of the *Salaf Al-Salih.* Ritual dynamics in chat rooms and discussion forums. *Information, Communication & Society, 14*(8), 1181–1203.

Beeching, V. (2018). *Undivided. Coming out, being whole, living free of shame.* New York: HarperCollins.

Berger, H. & Ezzy, D. (2004). The Internet as virtual spiritual community: Teen witches in the United States and Australia. In L. Dawson & D. Cowan (Eds.), *Religion online: Finding faith on the Internet* (pp. 175–188). New York: Routledge.

Body of venerable teen exhumed, too early to declare incorrupt. (2019, January 28). Catholic News Agency Online. Retrieved from https://catholicherald.co.uk/news/2019/01/28/body-of-venerable-teen-exhumed-but-too-early-to-declare-incorrupt/.

Booth, N. & Matic, J. A. (2011). Mapping and leveraging influencers in social media to shape corporate brand perceptions. *Corporate Communications, 16*(3), 184–191. doi:10.1108/13563281111156853.

Brosseau, D. (2014). Ready to be a thought leader? *How to increase your influence, impact, and success*. San Francisco, CA: Jossey-Bass.

Bullingham, L. & Vasconcelos, A. C. (2013). The presentation of self in the online world: Goffman and the study of online identities. *Journal of Information Science, 39*(1), 101–112.

Bunt, G. (2004). Rip. burn. pray: Islamic expression online. In L. Dawson & D. Cowan (Eds.), *Religion online: Finding faith on the Internet* (pp. 123–135). New York: Routledge.

Callon, M. & Latour, B. (1981). Unscrewing the big leviathan: How actors macrostructure reality and how sociologists help them to do so. In K. D. Knorr-Cetina & A. V. Cicourel (Eds.), *Advances in social theory and methodology: Toward an integration of micro- and macro-sociologies* (pp. 227–303). Boston, MA: Routledge and Kegan Paul.

Campbell, H. (2005). *Exploring religious community online*. New York: Peter Lang-Digital Formation Series.

Campbell, H. (2007). Who's got the power? Religious authority and the Internet. *Journal of Computer-Mediated Communication*. Retrieved from: http://jcmc.indiana.edu/vol12/issue3/campbell.html.

Campbell, H. (2010a). Bloggers and religious authority online. *Journal of Computer-Mediated Communication, 15*(2), 251–276.

Campbell, H. (2010b, October 14). *Community identity construction through the technological apologetic*. Unpublished paper presented at Association of Internet Researchers 11.0 Conference. Chalmers University, Gothenburg, Sweden.

Campbell, H. (2010c). *When religion meets new media*. London: Routledge.

Campbell, H. (2011). Religious engagement with the Internet within Israeli Orthodox groups. *Israel Affairs, 17*(3), 364–383.

Campbell, H. (2012a). How religious communities negotiate new media religiously. In C. Ess & P. Cheong (Eds.), *Digital faith and culture: Perspectives, practices and futures* (pp. 81–96). New York: Peter Lang.

Campbell, H. (2012b). Understanding the relationship between religious practice online and offline in a networked society. *Journal of the American Academy of Religion, 80*(1), 64–93.

Campbell, H. (2012c, October 21). *Digital creatives as new cultural authorities*. Paper presented at Association of Internet Researchers 13.0. University of Salford, Manchester, UK.

Campbell, H. (2013). The rise of the study of digital religion. In H. Campbell (Ed.), *Digital religion. Understanding religious practice in new media worlds* (pp. 1–22). London: Routledge.

Campbell, H. (2015). *Digital Judaism: Jewish negotiations with digital media and culture*. New York: Routledge.

Campbell, H. (2017). Surveying theoretical approaches within Digital Religion Studies. *New Media & Society, 19*(1), 15–24.

Campbell, H. & Golan, O. (2011). Creating digital enclaves: Negotiation of the Internet amongst bounded religious communities. *Media, Culture & Society, 33*(5), 709–724.

Campbell, H. & Garner, S. (2016). *Networked theology*: Negotiating faith in digital culture. Grand Rapids, MI: Baker Academic.

Campbell, H. A. & Evolvi, G. (2019). Contextualizing current digital religion research on emerging technologies. *Journal of Human Behavior and Emerging Technologies, 1*(3), 1–13. Retrieved from doi:10.1002/hbe2.149.

Campbell, H. & Lövheim, M. (Eds.). (2011). Religion and the Internet: The online-offline connection [Special issue]. *Information, Communication & Society, 14*(8), Retrieved from URL https://www.tandfonline.com/doi/abs/10.1080/1369118X.2011.597416.

Campbell, H. & Virtullo, A. (2016). Assessing changes in the study of religious communities in Digital Religion Studies. *Church, Communication & Culture, 1(1)*, Retrieved from URL https://doi.org/10.1080/23753234.2016.1181301

Castells, M. (2004). *The network society: A cross-cultural perspective*. Cheltenham, UK: Edward Elgar.

Chavez, M. (1994). Secularization as declining religious authority. *Social Forces, 72*(3), 749–774.

Chavez, M. (2003). Religious authority in the modern world. *Society, 40*(3), 38–40.

Cheong, P. H. & Poon, J. P. H. (2008). 'www.Faith.Org': (Re)structuring communication and social capital building among religious organizations. *Information, Communication and Society, 11*(1), 89–110.

Cheong, P. H., Huang, S. H., & Poon, J. P. H. (2011a). Religious communication and epistemic authority of leaders in wired faith organizations. *Journal of Communication, 61*(5), 938–958.

Cheong, P. H., Huang, S. H., & Poon, J. P. H. (2011b). Cultivating online and offline pathways to enlightenment: Religious authority in wired Buddhist organizations. *Information, Communication & Society, 14*(8), 1160–1180.

Cheong, P. (2013). Authority. In H. Campbell (Ed.), *Digital religion. Understanding religious practice in new media worlds* (pp. 72–87). London: Routledge.

Clark, L.S. (2011). Religion and authority in a remix culture: How a late night TV host became an authority on religion. In G. Lynch & J. Mitchell (Eds.), *Religion, media, and culture: A reader* (pp. 111–119). London: Routledge.

Clark, N. (2009). A quick look back at online worship in 2009. [Northland web log]. Retrieved from www.northlandchurch.net/blogs/a_quick_look_back_at_online_worship_in_2009/.

Dawson, L. (2000). Researching religion in cyberspace: Issues and strategies. In J. Hadden & D. Cowan (Eds.), *Religion on the Internet: Research prospects and promises* (pp. 25–54). New York: JAI Press.

Dawson, L. & Cowan, D. (Eds.). (2004). *Religion online: Finding faith on the Internet*. New York: Routledge.

De Pillis, M. S. (1966). The quest for religious authority and the rise of Mormonism. *Dialogue, 1*(1), 68–88.

Dörr, K. M. & Hollnbuchner, K. (2017). Ethical challenges of algorithmic journalism. *Digital Journalism, 5*(4), 404–419.

Eickelman, D. F. (1992). Mass higher education and the religious imagination in contemporary Arab societies. *American Ethologist, 19*(4), 643–655.

Eickelman, D. F. & Anderson, J. W. (Eds.). (1999). *New media in the Muslim world: The emerging public*. Bloomington: Indiana University Press.

Elliott, I., Thomas, S. D. M., & Ogloff, J. R. P. (2011). Procedural justice in contacts with the police: Testing a relational model of authority in a mixed methods study. *Psychology, Public Policy, and Law, 17*(4), 592–610.

Ess, C. (Ed.). (2004). *Critical thinking and the Bible in the age of new media*. Lanham, MD: University Press of America.

Foucault, M. (1977). *Discipline and punish*. London: Allen Lane.

Foucault, M. (2000). The subject and power. In J. Faubion (Ed.), *Power* (pp. 326–348). New York: New Press.

Geisler, N. (1999). What is apologetics? *Baker encyclopedia of Christian apologetics* (pp. xxx). Grand Rapids, MI: Baker Publishing.

Gibbs, E. & Bolger, R. (2005). *Emerging churches: Creating Christian community in postmodern cultures*. Grand Rapids, MI: Baker Academic.

Gilgoff, D. & Messia, H. (Feb 10, 2011) "Vatican Warns about iPhone Confession App," *CNN. com*. Retrieved from http://www.cnn.com/2011/WORLD/europe/02/10/vatican.confession.app/index.html?eref=rss_latest&utm_source=feedburner&utm_medium=feed&utm_campaign=Feed%3A+rss%2Fcnn_latest+%28RSS%3A+ CNN+-+Most+Recent%29

Goffman, E. (1990). *The presentation of self in everyday life.* London: Penguin.

Goldsmith, B. (2014). Embedded digital creatives. In G. Hearn, R. Bridgstock, B. Goldsmith, & G. Rodgers (Eds.), *Creative work beyond the creative industries: Innovation, employment and production* (pp. 128–143). Cheltenham, UK: Edward Elgar.

Grimes, A.J. (1978). Authority, power, influence and social control: A theoretical synthesis. *Academy of Management Review*, 3(4), 724–735. doi:10.5465/amr.1978.4289263.

Guzek, D. (2015). Discovering the digital authority: Twitter as reporting tool for papal activities. *Online: Heidelberg Journal of Religions on the Internet*, 9(1). Retrieved from http://nbn-resolving.de/urn:nbn:de:bsz:16-rel-262517.

Helland, C. (2007). Diaspora on the electronic frontier: Developing virtual connections with sacred homelands. *Journal of Computer-Mediated Communication*, 12(3). Retrieved from http://jcmc.indiana.edu/vol12/issue3/.

Hennerby, J. & Dawson, L. (1999). New religions and the Internet: Recruiting in a new public sphere. *Journal of Contemporary Religions*, 14(1), 17–39.

Herring, D. (2005). Virtual as contextual: A net news theology. In L. Dawson & D. Cowan (Eds.), *Religion and cyberspace* (pp. 149–165). London: Routledge.

Hofstede, G., Hofstede G. J., & Minkov, M. (2010). *Cultures and organizations: Software of the mind.* New York: McGraw Hill Professional.

Hofstede, G. (2011). Dimensionalizing cultures: The Hofstede model in context. *Online Readings in Psychology and Culture*, 2(1). doi:10.9707/2307-0919.1014.

Hojsgaard M. & Warburg, M. (Eds). (2005). *Religion and cyberspace.* London: Routledge.

Holdren, A. (2011). New confession app is no substitution for the sacrament Vatican says. (February 9). Catholic News Agency Online. Retrieved from www.catholicnewsagency.com/news/new-confession-app-is-no-substitution-for-the-sacrament-vatican-says/.

Hoover, S. & Echchaibi, N. (2014). Third spaces of digital religion (Essay). Retrieved from: https://thirdspacesblog.files.wordpress.com/2014/05/third-spaces-and-media-theory-essay-2-0.pdf.

Hoover, S. (Ed.). (2016). *The media and religious authority.* University Park, PA: Pennsylvania State University.

Horsfield, P. (2016). The media and religious authority from ancient to modern. In S. Hoover (Ed.), *The media and religious authority* (pp. 37–66). University Park, PA: Pennsylvania University Press.

Introvingne, M. (2000). So many evil things: Anti-cult terrorism via the Internet. In J. Hadden & D. Cowan (Eds.), *Religion on the Internet: Research prospects and promises* (pp. 277–306). New York: JAI Press.

Jenkins, H. (2006). *Convergence culture: Where old and new media collide.* New York: New York University Press.

Jenkins, R. (2008). Erving Goffman: A major theorist of power? *Journal of Power*, 1(2), 157–168. doi:10.1080/17540290802227577.

Jensen, T. G. (2006). Religious authority and autonomy intertwined: The case of converts to Islam in Denmark. *Muslim World*, 96, 643–660.

Jones, T. (2001). *Postmodern youth ministry.* Grand Rapids, MI: Zondervan.

Jones, T. (2008). *The new Christians: Dispatches from the emergent frontier.* Thousand Oaks, CA: Jossey-Bass.

Jones, T. (2011). *The church is flat: The relational ecclesiology of the emerging church movement* [Kindle Edition]. Edina, MN: JoPa Group.

Jones, T. (2012). *A better atonement: Beyond the depraved doctrine of original sin* [Kindle Edition]. Edina, MN: JoPa Group.

Kane, G. C. (2018, June 9). Common traits of the best digital leaders. *MIT Sloan Management Review*. Retrieved from https://sloanreview.mit.edu/article/common-traits-of-the-best-digital-leaders/.

Kim, M. C. (2005). Online Buddhist community: An alternative organization in the information age. In M. Hojsgaard & M. Warburg (Eds.), *Religion and cyberspace* (pp. 138–148). London: Routledge.

Kitchin, R. (2017). Thinking critically about and researching algorithms. *Information, Communication & Society, 20*(1), 14–29. doi:10.1080/1369118X.2016.1154087.

Kling, R. (2001). Social informatics. In *Encyclopedia of Lis*. Kluwer. available at www.slis.indiana.edu/SI/si2001.html accessed 24 July 2009 (no longer available online).

Kluver, R. & Cheong, P. H. (2007). Technological modernization, the Internet, and religion in Singapore. *Journal of Computer-Mediated Communication, 12*(3), 1122–1142.

Krogh, M. C. & Pillfant, A. (2004). The house of Netjer: A new religious community online. In L. Dawson & D. Cowan (Eds.), *Religion online: Finding faith on the Internet* (pp. 107–121). New York, NY: Routledge.

Krotz, F. (2018). Media logic and the mediatization approach: A good partnership, a mésalliance, or a misunderstanding?. In C. Thimm, M. Anastasiadis, & J. Einspänner-Pflock (Eds.), *Media logic(s) revisited. Transforming communications—Studies in cross-media research*. London: Palgrave Macmillan.

Kuhel, B. (2017, November 2). Power vs. influence: Knowing the difference could make or break your company. Forbes.com. Retrieved from www.forbes.com/sites/forbescoachescouncil/2017/11/02/power-vs-influence-knowing-the-difference-could-make-or-break-your-company/#558454ca357c.

Lacich, D. (2008, February 19). Starting a Northland house church. [Northland web log]. Retrieved from www.northlandchurch.net/blogs/starting_a_northland_house_church/.

Lake, D,(2009). Relational authority and legitimacy in international relations. *American Behavioral Scientist, 53*(3), 331–353.

Larson, L., Miller, T. & Ribble, M. (2009). 5 considerations for digital age leaders. *Learning and Leading with Technology,* 12–15. Retrieved from, https://files.eric.ed.gov/fulltext/EJ867962.pdf.

Lawrence, B. (2002). Allah on-line: The practice of global Islam in the information age. In S. Hoover & L. Scofield Clark (Eds.), *Practicing religion in the age of media* (pp. 237–253). New York: Columbia University Press.

"Let us go forth," new pope says in first text message. (2005, April 2). Yahoo-Agence France Presse. Retrieved from http://news.yahoo.com/s/afp/20050421/tc_afp/vaticanpopepho netext&printer=1.

Lincoln, B. (1994). *Authority: Construction and corrosion*. Chicago: University of Chicago Press.

Livio, O. & Tenenboim Weinblatt, K. (2007). Discursive legitimation of a controversial technology: Ultra-Orthodox Jewish women in Israel and the Internet. *Communication Review, 10*(1), 29–56.

Lövheim, M. & Linderman, A. G. (2005). Constructing religious identity on the Internet. In M. Hojsgaard & M. Warburg (Eds.), *Religion and cyberspace* (pp. 133–137). London: Routledge.

Lövheim, M. & Campbell, H. (2017). Considering critical methods and theoretical lenses in Digital Religion Studies. *New Media & Society, 19*(1), 5–14.

Lövheim, M. (2019). *Gender, religion & authority in digital media.* Paper presented at workshop on Authority, Internet & religious contexts. Center for Religious Studies (CERES). Ruhr University-Bochum, Germany.

Lustig, C., Pine, K., Nardi, B., Irani, L., Lee, M. K., Nafus, D., & Sandvig, C. (2016). *Algorithmic authority: The ethics, politics, and economics of algorithms that interpret, decide, and manage.* Proceedings of the 2016 CHI Conference Extended Abstracts on Human Factors in Computing Systems, 1057–1062. New York, NY. Retrieved from doi:10.1145/2851581.2886426.

Lustig, K. & Nardi, B. (2015). *Algorithmic authority: The case of bitcoin.* Paper presented at 48th Hawaii International Conference on System Sciences Proceedings. Retrieved from https://artifex.org/~bonnie/lustig_nardi_HICSS_2015.pdf.

MacWilliams, M. (Ed.) (2002). Symposium on religion & Internet. *Religion, 32*(4).

MacWilliams, M. (2004). Virtual pilgrimage to Ireland's Croagh Patrick. In L. L. Dawson & D. E. Cowan (Eds.), *Religion online: Finding faith on the Internet* (pp. 223–238) New York: Routledge.

Manning, P. K. (2008). Goffman on organizations. *Organization Studies, 29*(05), 677–699.

Manovich, L. (2001). *The language of new media.* Cambridge, MA: MIT Press.

McLuhan, M. (1964). *Understanding media.* New York: Signet Books.

Miller, H. (1995). *The presentation of self in electronic life: Goffman on the Internet.* Paper presented at Embodied Knowledge and Virtual Space Conference, Goldsmiths' College, University of London. Retrieved from http://smg.media.mit.edu/library/miller1995.html.

Morley, D. (2003). What's "home" got to do with it? Contradictory dynamics in the domestication of technology and the dislocation of domesticity. *European Journal of Cultural Studies, 6*(4), 435–458.

Owen, R. (2003, January 10). Vatican warning on danger of "online confession." *The Sunday Times Online.* Retrieved from www.timesonline.co.uk/tol/news/world/article810503.ece.

Peladue, P., Herzog, M., & Acker, O. (2017, June 21). The new class of digital leaders. *Strategy+Business, 1*(10). Retrieved from www.the-digital-insurer.com/wp-content/uploads/2017/12/1026-The-New-Class-of-Digital-Leaders.pdf.

Piff, D., & Warburg, M. (2005). Seeking for truth: Plausibility on a Baha'i email list. In M. Hojsgaard & M. Warburg (Eds.), *Religion and cyberspace* (pp. 86–101). Routledge, London.

Pinch, T. (2010). The Invisible technologies of Goffman's sociology from the merry-go-round to the Internet. *Technology and Culture, 51*(2), 409–424. [Johns Hopkins University Press. Retrieved from Project MUSE database.]

Pontifical Council for Social Communications [PCSC]. (1990). *The Christian message in a computer culture.* (Message of the Holy Father for the XXIV World Communications Day). Retrieved from www.vatican.va/holy_father/john_paul_ii/messages/communications/documents/hf_jp-ii_mes_24011990_world-communications-day_en.html.

Pontifical Council for Social Communications [PCSC]. (2002a). *Church and the Internet.* Retrieved from www.vatican.va/roman_curia/pontifical_councils/pccs/documents/rc_pccs_doc_20020228_church-internet_en.html.

Pontifical Council for Social Communications [PCSC)]. (2002b). *Ethics in Internet.* Retrieved from www.vatican.va/roman_curia/pontifical_councils/pccs/documents/rc_pccs_doc_20020228_ethics-internet_en.html.

Pope Benedict XVI. (2009). *New technologies, new relationships. Promoting a culture of respect, dialogue and friendship* (Message of the Holy Father for the XVI World Communications Day). Retrieved from www.vatican.va/holy_father/benedict_xvi/messages/communications/documents/hf_ben-xvi_mes_20090124_43rd-world-communications-day_en.html.

Pope spreads the word by SMS. (2003, January 14). *Ananova*. Retrieved from www.ananova.com/news/story/sm_739682.html.

Prince, R. A. & Rogers, B. (2012, March 16). What is a thought leader?, Forbes.com. Retrieved from www.forbes.com/sites/russprince/2012/03/16/what-is-a-thought-leader/#3d3e0ae97da0.

Raven, B. H. & French, J. (1959). The bases of social power. In D. Cartwright (Ed.), *Studies in social power* (pp. 150–167). Ann Arbor, MI: Institute for Social Research.

Riess, J. (2013). The Twible: All the chapters of the Bible in 140 characters Or Less … Now with 68% more humor [Self-published]. Available through Amazon Digital Services.

Rogers, M. F. (1980). Goffman on power, hierarchy, and status. In J. Ditton (Ed.), *The View from Goffman* (pp. 100–133). London: Palgrave Macmillan.

Shifas, T. (2015). Algorithmic culture. *European Journal of Cultural Studies 2015, 18*(4–5), 395–412.

Shirky, C. A. (2009, November 15). Speculative post on the idea of algorithmic authority. Retrieved from: www.shirky.com/weblog/2009/11/a-speculative-post-on-the-idea-of-algorithmic-authority/.

Silverstone, R., Hirsch, E., & Morley, D. (1992). Information and communication technologies and the moral economy of the household. In R. Silverstone & E. Hirsch (Eds.), *Consuming technologies: Media and information* (pp. 15–29). London: Routledge.

Silverstone, R. H. L. (1996). Design & domestication of ICTs: Technical change and everyday life. In R. Mansel & R. Silverstone (Eds.), *Communicating by design: The politics of information and communication technologies* (pp. 44–74). Oxford: Oxford University Press.

Striphas, T. (2015). Algorithmic culture. *European Journal of Cultural Studies, 18*(4–5): 395–412.

Teusner, P. (2013). Formation of a religious technorati: Negotiations of authority among Australian emerging church. In H. Campbell (Ed.), *Digital religion: Understanding religion in new media worlds* (pp. 182–189). New York: Routledge.

Thumma, S. (2000). Religion and the Internet. *Hartford Institute for Religion Research*. Retrieved from http://hirr.hartsem.edu/bookshelf/thumma_article6.html.

Toffler, A. (1980). *The third wave: The classic study of tomorrow*. New York: Bantam.

Turner, B. S. (2007). Religious authority and the new media. *Theory, Culture & Society, 24*(2), 117–134.

Tyler, T. & Lind, A. (1992). A relational model of authority in groups, *Advances in Experimental Social Psychology, 25*(1), 115–191.

Valentino-DeVries, J. (2011, February 9) New iPhone, iPad app helps you keep track of sins. *Wall Street Journal Online*. Retrieved from http://online.wsj.com/article/AP06a02ad4f29 34ba0beead5745da51d41.html.

Venerable Carlo Acutis: A patron of computer programmers? (2018, July 8). Catholic News Agency Online. Retrieved from www.catholicnewsagency.com/news/venerable-carlo-acutis-a-patron-of-computer-programmers-69517.

Virgin mobile users confess their sin. (2004, December 6). Textually.org. Available from www.textually.org/textually/archives/006286.htm. (No longer available online).

Weber, M. (1947). *Theory of social and economic organization*. (A. A. Henderson & T. Parsons Trans.). New York: Oxford University Press.

Wellman, B. & Haythornwaite, C. (2002). *The Internet in everyday life*. Oxford, UK: Blackwell.

Westerman, G., Tannou, M., Bonnet, D., Ferraris, P., & McAfee, A. (2012). The digital advantage: How digital leaders outperform their peers in every industry. MIT Sloan Management and Capgemini Consulting, MA 2, 2–23.

Wiles, M. F. (1971). Religious authority and divine action. *Religious Studies,* 7, 1–12.

Wilian, P. (2001, June 6). Vatican rules out online confessions. *PC World Online.* Retrieved from: www.pcworld.com/article/51923/vatican_rules_out_online_confessions.html.

Williams, R. & Edge, D. (1996). The social shaping of technology. *Research Policy, 25,* 856–899.

Willan, P. (2001, June 7) Vatican to rule out online confessions. CNN.com. Retrieved from   http://articles.cnn.com/2001-06-07/tech/online.confessions.idg_1_confession-worldwide-web-internet?_s=PM:TECH.

Wilson-Barnao, C. (2017). How algorithmic cultural recommendations influence the marketing of cultural collections. *Consumption Markets & Culture 20*(6), 559–574. doi:10.1080/10253866.2017.1331910

Index